Eyewitnesses to
the Great War

Eyewitnesses to the Great War

American Writers, Reporters, Volunteers and Soldiers in France, 1914–1918

ED KLEKOWSKI *and*
LIBBY KLEKOWSKI

McFarland & Company, Inc., Publishers
Jefferson, North Carolina, and London

LIBRARY OF CONGRESS CATALOGUING-IN-PUBLICATION DATA

Klekowski, Edward J.
　　Eyewitnesses to the Great War : American writers, reporters, volunteers and soldiers in France, 1914–1918 / Ed Klekowski and Libby Klekowski.
　　　　p.　　cm.
　　Includes bibliographical references and index.

　　ISBN 978-0-7864-6348-0
　　softcover : acid free paper ∞

　　1. World War, 1914–1918 — Personal narratives, American. 2. World War, 1914–1918 — France.　 3. World War, 1914–1918 — Participation, American.　 4. Americans — France — Biography.　 5. Idealism, American — France — History — 20th century.　 6. Adventure and adventurers — France — Biography. 7. Authors, American — France — Biography.　 8. Foreign correspondents — France — Biography.　 9. Volunteers — France — Biography.　 10. Soldiers — France — Biography.
　　I. Klekowski, Libby, 1941–　　II. Title.
　　D640.A2K57 2012
　　940.4'8173 — dc23　　　　　　　　　　　　　　2012010086

BRITISH LIBRARY CATALOGUING DATA ARE AVAILABLE

© 2012 Ed Klekowski and Libby Klekowski. All rights reserved

No part of this book may be reproduced or transmitted in any form or by any means, electronic or mechanical, including photocopying or recording, or by any information storage and retrieval system, without permission in writing from the publisher.

Front cover: top — Edmond Genet in the cockpit of a Nieuport 17 (Thénault, *Story* [see Bibliography]; bottom — American volunteers in the Foreign Legion on July 4, 1915, in Paris. Edmond Genet is seated at center. Seated at right is William Dugan. Victor Chapman is standing behind Genet (Genet, *War Letters* [see Bibliography]).

Manufactured in the United States of America

McFarland & Company, Inc., Publishers
　Box 611, Jefferson, North Carolina 28640
　　www.mcfarlandpub.com

To Amanda, Ulrich, Alexandra and Philip,
our companions in exploring what
remains of the Western Front

Table of Contents

Preface 1

Introduction 5

1. Edith and Henry 9
2. Along the Moselle in a Model T 25
3. Verdun Madness 41
4. Motoring Along the Meuse 56
5. Crossing the River, Too Late 68
6. Other Verdun Ambulance Corps 82
7. Americans in the Foreign Legion 95
8. Rendezvous with Death 110
9. Lafayette's Flyers 121
10. Writers and Reporters 137
11. Lafayette, We Are Here! 155
12. *Gott Mit Uns* 172
13. The Fog of Battle 187
14. Attack, Attrition, Pursuit 200
15. Armistice, Peace, War 215

Chapter Notes 227
Bibliography 243
Index 249

Preface

Eyewitnesses to the Great War explores the forgotten history of the United States' first war on European soil. The book views the events of 1914 to 1918 through the eyes of Americans who were there, telling the story of the famous and the not-so-famous who played a part in the Great War.

The book had its genesis several years ago on a cold dreary winter day in the small French city of Verdun. A slight rain was falling as we walked through the city center looking for a place to stay. One hotel was open; its lobby was warm and dry and it had rooms available — after all, who visits Verdun in the winter? We booked a room. The hotel was the Hostellerie du Coq Hardi, a charming pre–First World War establishment restored after the 1916 German bombardment of Verdun. We learned later that "Le Coq" had hosted a very famous American guest during the war, the novelist Edith Wharton. She was there in February 1915, also on a cold dreary winter day, and it was on Coq Hardi letterhead that she wrote her friend Henry James about what she had witnessed of the fighting nearby. Our view of the Meuse River and the grandiose Cercle Militaire (military club) on the opposite bank mirrored what she had seen nearly a century before. This linkage between place and personality made history more alive, more accessible, and that revelation proved to be the "road to Damascus" for us, a journey that led to libraries, museum archives and used book shops. We entered the generally forgotten world of American memoirists of the Great War, men and women who were "over there" from the war's beginning in 1914, even before America formally entered the conflict in 1917.

Understanding what the memoir writers were describing and experiencing turned out not to be so straightforward. They often wrote of obscure places, French villages that even today are difficult to find, and they described happenings that loomed large in their own lives at the time but were often overshadowed as the war went on. Over the next few years, we spent considerable time in France researching material and battlefields for two documentaries about the war we had agreed to produce for public television.* These visits allowed us to search out places described in the old memoirs and to visit the sites to try to see them as they were during the war years. Fortunately many of the places are still very rural and not smothered by modern development, so it was often possible literally to walk in the steps of the Americans who were there before us. By placing the memoirs in the context of the landscape where the events they describe occurred, the Americans of 1914 to 1918 spoke to us with a clearer voice. We learned much of the information recorded in the memoirs was essentially the forgotten history of American participation in the war. *Eyewitnesses to the Great War* is our effort to bring that history back to light.

As we traveled through France in the footsteps of the Americans who were active in the First World War, we experienced firsthand the hospitality and generosity of the following people: Jean Paul De Vries and Brigitte De Vries at the Romagne '14-'18 Museum; Joseph P. Rivers, Meuse-Argonne American Cemetery, Romagne; Jean-Marie Picquart and Michel Jacquot in Pont-à-Mousson; Isabelle Remy, archivist, the Verdun Memorial Museum; Madame Bergeret, Château des Tilleuls, Stenay, for opening her home to us and sharing her photographs of the war; Marian Howard and David Howard for touring us around Stenay and arranging for our visit to the Château des Tilleuls; Amanda Klekowski von Koppenfels and Ulrich von Koppenfels for their generous hospitality in Liny-devant-Dun and for Ulrich's willingness to translate French and German documents and for reading the entire manuscript.

In the United States, we owe special thanks to the University of Massachusetts Amherst Du Bois Library staff, especially those librarians of the 1920s who assembled a remarkable collection of World War I memoirs and books. Of the current librarians, we are especially grateful to Melinda McIntosh, reference librarian, for her untiring pursuit of the esoteric subjects we asked her to research. We would also like to thank the interlibrary loan staff for their help in borrowing materials from other libraries and Rob Cox, head of special collections.

Our thanks also to the people who were willing to share their family papers with us: the Meryman family, especially Charlotte Meryman; the Garland family; Doris Holden and Priscilla L. Pike; Sue Alward for photographs; and Barbe La Pierre for photographs. Thanks also to Brigadier General Len

---

**Model T's to War, American Ambulances on the Western Front, 1914–1918.* WGBY, Springfield, Massachusetts; *Yanks Fight the Kaiser: A National Guard Division in WW I.* WGBY, Springfield, Massachusetts.

Kondratiuk, head of the Massachusetts National Guard Museum; Al Shane for rifle specifics; Meg Clark for artwork; the American Field Service, New York, especially Nicole Milano and Eleanora Golobic, archivists; the Bienecke Collection, Yale University; Tevis Kimball and Kate Boyle, Special Collections, Jones Library, Amherst, MA; Amherst College Special Collections; the Library of Congress; and the U.S. National Archives.

We acknowledge the Watkins/Loomis Agency, New York City, for permission to quote excerpts from Edith Wharton's letters; the Curtis Brown Agency, London, for permission to quote Winston Churchill; and Michael Hoffman, translator, and the Penguin Group (USA, UK) for permission to quote an excerpt from Ernst Jünger's *Storm of Steel*.

Finally, we would like to thank the Biology Department of the University of Massachusetts Amherst for providing post-retirement office space to EK and especially Charlene Coleman, Steve Brewer and Thomas Carpenter for their assistance.

Introduction

The English call it the "Great War"; in French, it is "*la Grand Guerre.*" For Americans the First World War is neither great nor grand, just forgotten.[1]

The path to war began with the assassination of a Hapsburg archduke and his wife on June 28, 1914, by Serbian nationalists in the Balkan city of Sarajevo. This event should have been of no consequence, except of course to the murdered couple, since Hapsburg royalty seemed always to be dying prematurely of some misfortune. Brand Whitlock, the U.S. minister to Belgium in 1914, remembered learning of the nonevent from his house-servant.

> "Excellence, le prince héritier d'Autriche a été assassiné à Sarajevo!"*
>
> Who, and where? By whom? And why? I had never heard of Sarajevo; I had not the least idea where it was in this world, if it was in this world.... And the Crown Prince of Austria was to me a most immaterial person — a kind of wraith wandering there in those nether regions to which have gone so many of the House of Hapsburg which seems to have suffered in itself as much evil as it caused others to suffer in this world. I confess that it seemed a rather unwarranted intrusion that morning.[2]

Minister Whitlock as well as other American and European officials may have been nonplussed by the murders, but that was not so for the Austro-Hungarian Emperor Franz Josef. Although he strongly disliked his nephew, Archduke Franz Ferdinand, and despised the archduke's wife, Sophia, the emperor felt that he must avenge their deaths even though he did not attend the marriage of the detested couple and certainly would miss their funerals. The archduke had been, after all, the heir to the throne since the other Habsburg contenders had been either shot or committed suicide.[3] However, before revenge there must be consultation with the other German-speaking monarch, Kaiser Wilhelm II of Germany. Would the Kaiser back the Austrians if they

---

*"Excellency, the hereditary prince of Austria has been assassinated at Sarajevo!"

undertook military action against Serbia? The bombastic and often impulsive Wilhelm encouraged Franz Josef to act and be severe. And so it began: Austria attacked Serbia; Russia, in Slavic solidarity, came to Serbia's defense; Germany, in support of Austria, went to war with Russia and France, the latter being obliged by treaty to aid Russia should she be attacked. Confronted by the possibility of a two-front war, Germany launched a pre-emptive attack on August 4, 1914, through neutral Belgium with the goal of quickly knocking France out of the war by taking Paris. The German offensive stalled and ultimately failed, but the violation of Belgian neutrality had the unforeseen consequence of bringing in the British on the side of the French.

All parties believed the war would be short, lasting only a few months at most. James W. Gerard, the United States Ambassador to the German Imperial Court that fateful August, remembered the mood in Berlin as hostilities began.

> the Kaiser was implicitly believed when, on the first day of the war, he appeared on the balcony of the palace and told the crowds who were keen for war, that "before the leaves have fallen from the trees you will be back in your homes." ... Someone has since said that the Emperor must have meant pine trees.[4]

Pines, being evergreens, often retain their needles for more than three years. The war lasted more than four years, the shooting finally ceasing at 11:00 A.M. on November 11, 1918. For most of the conflict, the United States was neutral, entering the war on April 6, 1917, and not having troops in the trenches until February 1918. Even when officially neutral, the United States showed a strong bias to one side: American industry sold arms and munitions to the Triple Entente (the defensive alliance of Britain, France and Russia), American farms fed the starving millions in German-occupied France and Belgium, and thousands of American volunteers crossed the Atlantic to help the British and French, serving as aid workers, nurses and doctors, airmen in the Lafayette Flying Corps, ambulance drivers, and soldiers in the Foreign Legion or in the French or British Armies. Most of the American volunteers were in France, and the majority served in Lorraine and parts of Champagne. The one hundred thirty-mile section of the Western Front stretching from the cathedral city of Reims, east to the Argonne Forest, then to Verdun, then to the city of St. Mihiel and on to where the Western Front crossed the Moselle River is the setting for most American war memoirs. The American experience in this linear piece of French real estate is the focus of this book.

Two singular battles occurred within this area. In 1916, the bloodbath known as the Battle of Verdun, although primarily a contest between the French and German Armies, saw the presence of more than a thousand American volunteers as soldiers, pilots or ambulance drivers. In the fall of 1918, the most costly battle ever fought by the American Army took place in the sector stretching from the Argonne Forest to the hills east of the Meuse River. The fighting lasted six weeks, from September 26 to November 11, 1918, and ranged across a heavily fortified landscape of trenches and concrete pillboxes spread over 500 square miles. The Imperial German Army conquered most of the area very early in the war and spent the following four years constructing defenses. Consequently, the cost of the American assault was enormous: 26,277 dead and 95,786 wounded.

The earliest recorded American presence in this part of the front dates to the winter of 1914-1915. An American volunteer in the French Army entered the trenches in Lorraine that winter and was killed in action on March 23, 1915; he may be the first U.S. combat death of the war. The first American to visit Lorraine and survive the experience was the American novelist Edith Wharton who arrived there a month before the idealistic volunteer perished.

1

Edith and Henry

> Like sunlight outside a stained glass window, Mrs. Wharton's absorbing book illuminates for her countrymen the figure of France at war. — "Fighting France," Wharton Book Review,[1] December 1915

In late February 1915, a large Mercedes touring car made its way through the outskirts of Paris and headed east. Inside were three Americans: Charles Cook of Lee, Massachusetts, the chauffer; Walter Berry, a close friend and long-time confidant of Mrs. Wharton; and of course Edith Wharton.[2] The French government had issued Wharton a special travel pass for the war zone. Ostensibly, the trip's purpose was to inspect military hospitals and transport medical supplies; the Mercedes was packed to the gills with bandages, dressings and blankets. Wharton viewed her trip as a mercy mission, but for the French its value was selling the French cause to America. French hopes were fulfilled; the June 1915 issue of *Scribner's Magazine* carried a feature article titled "In Argonne" in which Wharton described the war's human cost and, of course, lauded the French war effort.

As the Mercedes neared the Argonne Forest, the "mercy mission" nearly aborted when French military authorities in the town of Sainte Menehould blocked the Wharton party. Evidently, the special travel pass issued in Paris was invalid in the military district surrounding Verdun. The general commanding the area refused to honor the pass, travel in the area by civilians was out of the question. A junior officer, who happened to know Mrs. Wharton from before the war, consulted further with the general and argued that her case was special. He soon returned with the good news, "Are you the author of 'The House of Mirth'? If you are, the general says you shall have a pass: but for heaven's sake drive as fast as you can, for we don't want any civilians on the road today." With the competent Charles Cook at the wheel, the car speedily departed Sainte Menehould before the general changed his mind.[3]

Upon reaching the Argonne, the first place the Mercedes stopped was

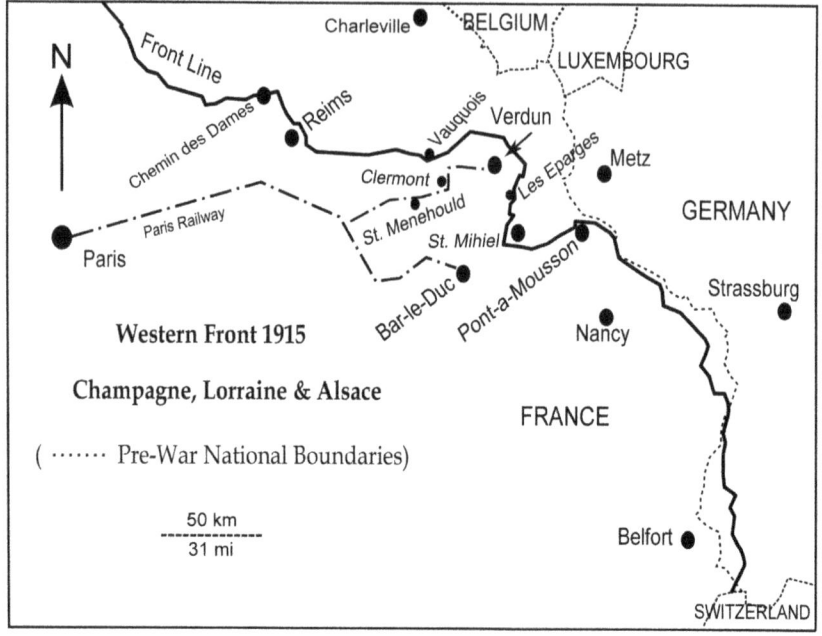

Western Front, 1915.

Clermont-en-Argonne. The Imperial German Army had surged through the village as part of the initial great German attack in August 1914. Then during the night of September 4, for reasons unclear, two German regiments from Württemberg ran amok in occupied Clermont, pillaging and setting fire to buildings before marching south. In late September 1914, the French stopped the Germans not far from Paris in the First Battle of the Marne. This defeat precipitated a pull back by the Imperial Germany Army along the entire front including a retreat through what was left of Clermont. One visit by the German Army had been bad enough, but two visits, and in the same year, turned out to be catastrophic. Clermont was reduced to jagged walls surrounding piles of masonry that marked the sites where houses had once stood. The main street of the village skirted a small ridge upon which the sixteenth century village church, St. Didier, stood. A steep run of stairs cut into the side of the ridge led up to the church. Marauding Württembergers ransacked and partially burned St. Didier. It fared slightly better than the village below; presumably climbing the steep stairs deterred some of the intoxicated soldiers. After the war, German reparation money rebuilt Clermont so that visitors today see a charming village set against a hill overlooked by a late-Gothic style church.

In 1915, the Wharton party found the ruins essentially deserted except for a group of Catholic nuns who ran a hospice for old men. Sister Gabrielle, the mother superior, had so impressed German officers with her pluck they protected the hospice during the occupation. The sisters shared their midday meal with the Americans. While in the garden of the hospice Edith Wharton witnessed her first actual battle. What she saw was a French assault, one of many in the four-year-long contest for the Butte de Vauquois.

The Butte de Vauquois is a small knoll 7.5 miles (12 km) north of Clermont. A flat plain separates Vauquois and Clermont, with the knoll rising approximately 200 feet above the plain, so the knoll stands out. The village of Vauquois was perched atop the knoll. The operative word is "was." In the course of the nearly endless fighting, the village vanished and so did much of the knoll, which is now topped with a couple of large craters, each 65 feet deep, surrounded by minor ones. Today the Butte de Vauquois resembles a volcanic upheaval rather than an old battlefield.

The Germans took the Butte de Vauquois in September of 1914. They immediately recognized its significance; from Vauquois artillery observers could target the main French railroad line connecting Verdun with Paris. If the French held Vauquois, their artillery observers could target positions behind the German lines for miles and miles. For both sides Vauquois was an incredible artillery observation post. The first French assault occurred on October 28, 1914,—the French were slaughtered. On February 28, 1915, Edith Wharton observed the initial phase of the fourth French assault, which lasted until March 4. This time the Frenchmen managed to capture the high ground, but unfortunately, the Germans launched a successful counterattack, and it was back to square one. Five days of fighting had cost the French 3,000 killed or missing. Vauquois was a horror for both sides. A German socialist[4] who later deserted to neutral Holland and then stowed away on a Dutch ship bound for America was a combatant at Vauquois in 1915. His first view of the hill was not reassuring.

> A little farther up on the heights was Vauquois. No houses were to be seen; one could only see a heap of rubbish through the field glasses. Shells kept exploding in that rubbish heap continually, and we felt a cold sweat run down our backs at the thought that the place up there was our destination.[5]

In 1915, French battlefield tactics had not developed much beyond the Napoleonic era; closely packed infantry with bayonets fixed charged German positions. The French high command actually believed that French bravery and Gallic dash could overcome Teutonic technology. However, what worked for Napoleon was considerably less successful against German machine guns. The German socialist (and would-be American) takes up the story.

> The artillery of both sides bombarded the place to such an extent that not a foot of ground could be found that was not torn up by shells. Thousands upon thousands of shells of all sizes were employed. The bombardment from both sides lasted three days and three nights, until not a soldier, neither French nor German, was left in the village. Both sides had been obliged to retreat before the infernal fire of the opponent, for not a man would escape alive out of that inferno. The whole slope and height were veiled in an impenetrable smoke. In the evening of the third day the enemy's bombardment died down a little, and we were ordered to go forward again into the shell torn ruins. It was not yet quite dark when the French advanced in close order.
>
> We were in possession of almost the whole of the village, and had placed one machine-gun next to the other. We could see the projectiles of the artillery burst in great numbers among the reserves of the attackers. Our machine-guns literally mowed down the first ranks.[6]

The German socialist had been a miner in civilian life; he was now in a sapper unit. He was in the right place at the right time, because now the battle would move underground.

In the months and years that followed, the French assaulted Vauquois more than a dozen times, without strategic result. In desperation, they dug long deep tunnels into the heart of the knoll.

> Do not imagine this shaft to be a single straight well into the earth; no, it proceeds "in cascades"; first a drop four yards deep, then a twenty yard tunnel, at the end of which there is another drop eighteen yards deep, and so on. If the hill were split in two, you would see subterranean runways of the sappers take the shape of a gigantic stairway, which sinks into the earth in the direction of the enemy.[7]

Deep within the hill the tunnels became smaller, human burrows usually only three to four feet in diameter; two diggers (sappers) crouched over in the small space, a pick man who scratched at the tunnel face and a shovel man who filled sacks with earth, passing them to men who carried the spoil out of the tunnel. Once under the enemy line a large chamber was excavated, the mine-chamber.

> One can stand up straight here; and smoking candles light up the black walls of the chamber. The sappers are here, clad only in loin-clothes, for the heat is stifling.[8]

The mine-chamber was then filled with tons of explosives; the tunnel leading to the mine-chamber was packed with sandbags for about 20 yards to seal it off and direct the blast upward. The fuse was lit and the explosives in the chamber detonated. If everything went according to plan and the chamber was sited beneath a German trench, rather than under No-Man's Land, the trench would disappear and be replaced by a crater. In response, the Germans also tunneled into the hill. The battle moved underground. Eventually the Vauquois mound, which was only 200 feet high and a mile across at its base, had more than 10.5 miles (16.7 km) of galleries and connecting shafts bored into it. It came to resemble a huge termite mound riddled with passages. It became a mound with its own climate.

> You can either stay near the mouth of the tunnel and endure a fierce draught, or you can content yourself with the heavy, stagnant, vicious air farther in. The latter solution is usually adopted; and that is the reason why, when you look at Vauquois from a distance, you see a kind of mist rising from points here and there. The points are the mouths of the tunnels, and the mist is the vapor from the respiration of the men who live inside the hill.
>
> The Boches are fully aware of this and they are constantly shooting at the points whence the mists arise, hoping to hit soldiers entering or leaving the tunnel.[9]

A total of 519 underground explosions was recorded under Vauquois; the Germans held the record for the largest. They detonated 60 tons of explosive in an excavated chamber beneath the French line, killing 108. The craters grew and coalesced like so many inverted soap bubbles, and still the Germans held on.

> Some of these holes were as much as thirty yards deep, and their steep walls were so difficult to climb, that sometimes Germans who had once got down into a crater could not get out again, because the loose earth gave way under their hands and feet in climbing.[10]

The Butte de Vauquois finally fell on September 26, 1918, during the first day of the American Argonne offensive. By then, the Germans had essentially abandoned it as not worth defending.

After witnessing the explosions and clouds of smoke shrouding Vauquois, the Wharton party continued its journey, ending the day at Verdun about 30 kilometers (18.6 mi) away. That evening on hotel stationary Edith Wharton wrote of her adventures to her very close friend Henry James.[11]

> Grand Hôtel du Coq Hardi
> Verdun
> February 28, 1915
> from a garden we looked across the valley to a height about 5 miles away, where white puffs & scarlet flashes kept springing up all over the dark hillside. It was the hill above Vauquois, where there has been desperate fighting

for two days. The Germans were firing from the top at the French trenches below (hidden from us by an intervening rise of ground); & the French were assaulting, & their puffs & flashes were half way up the hill.

She visited Verdun before the great Battle of Verdun; a battle that began in February 1916 and destroyed much of the city, including Edith Wharton's hotel, the Coq Hardi.

The ruins of the Hôtel Coq Hardi in Verdun; Edith Wharton stayed at the hotel in February 1915. One year later the Germans began to bombard the city as part of their Verdun offensive. The Coq Hardi was (and still is) near the main bridge crossing the Meuse River, an area intensively shelled in an effort to destroy the bridge. The Coq Hardi was rebuilt after the war.

Henry answered her letter that week. The letter was there when she returned to Paris. His first sentence is classic Jamesian.

> 21 Carlyle Mansions
> Cheyne Walk, S.W.
> March 5th, 1915.
> Dearest Edith,
> How can I welcome and applaud enough your splendid thrilling letter — in which though it gives me your whole spectacle and impression as unspeakably portentous, I find you somehow of the very same heroic taille of whatever it was that gave the rest at the monstrous maximum.[12]

Presumably Edith knew what he meant.

Mrs. Wharton and her party were off to Verdun again on March 6, 1915, on another mercy mission. The Mercedes was packed with "bundles of shirts and boxes of eggs and bags of oranges" for delivery to military hospitals. The weather was horrible, lashing bitter rain. The party made its way through Verdun and continued south along the Meuse River. The roads literally fell apart, becoming viscous mud deeply rutted by military vehicles. In some places, the ruts resembled water-filled ditches. Unable to go farther, the Mercedes finally stopped at "a hamlet plunged to the eaves in mud" 4.3 miles (7 km) from the battlefield of Les Eparges. Writing Henry James immediately after returning to Paris, she described the scene.

> 53, rue de Varenne
> 11 March 1915
> Picture this all under a white winter sky, driving great flurries of snow across the mud-&-cinder-coloured landscape, with the steel-cold Meuse winding between beaten poplars — Cook standing with Her* in a knot of mud-coated military motors & artillery horses, soldiers coming and going, cavalrymen riding up with messages, poor bandaged creatures in rag-bag clothes leaning in doorways, & always over & above us, the boom, boom, boom of the guns on the grey heights to the east. It was winter war to the fullest, just in that little insignificant corner of the immense affair![13]

Les Eparges is not a battle that gets much attention in current histories of the First World War, especially if they are in English. In fact, it seldom rates even a sentence, not even a footnote. However, in the spring and summer of 1915, Americans followed the battle almost as a sporting event:

> *New York Times*—Feb. 2, 1915 —"The enemy delivered its seventh counter-attack at Les Eparges."
> *Boston Daily Globe*—Feb. 23, 1915 —"At Les Eparges we won some ground at one point and fell back slightly at another."
> *Boston Daily Globe*—Mar. 21, 1915 —"French carry trenches in Les Eparges section."
> *New York Times*—Apr. 9, 1915 —"At Les Eparges, especially, the last German counter-attack was carried out by a regiment and a half and was completely repulsed."
> *Boston Daily Globe*—Apr. 9, 1915 —"Germans say French attacks were failures."
> *New York Times*—Apr. 11, 1915 —"by mine and counter-mine, our allies stormed the main part of the hill at Les Eparges."

---

*Charles Cook the chauffeur. "Her" refers to the Mercedes.

The hill where the battle took place is between the villages of Les Eparges and Combres, with the former on the French side of the line and the latter on the German side. Thus, the Germans refer to it as the battle of Combres-Höhe (Combres Hill) while the French call it simply Les Eparges. The hill is an elongate ridge or spur about three-quarters of a mile in length, about 300 feet above the Woëvre plain. When the fighting began in January 1915, the Germans held fortified trenches on the hill top while the French trenches clung to slopes on the north and northwest sides. The French would have to fight up hill. Because of the horrible weather that March, Combres-Höhe/Les Eparges was literally a mountain of gelatinous brown mud. Climbing uphill was hard enough as boots were sucked off into the muck, but fighting uphill was insane, rifles were soon clogged with mud, artillery shells often failed to explode, just disappearing with a muddy splash. In places near the crest where the French trenches brushed against the German line, combatants became mobs of mud-covered troglodytes mired knee-deep in muck, stabbing with bayonets and using rifles as clubs. Dead and wounded disappeared into the ooze, trampled down by the fighting. When found, the wounded were skidded down the slope as so many mud-covered logs.

The French finally captured the summit on April 9, but that was all. The Germans immediately established a trench system just below and to the east of the crest, the *Kamm-Stellung*, which the French were never able to breach. In addition to trenches, ferroconcrete dugouts, *Mannschafts-Eisenbeton-Unterstände* or MEBUs, were excavated into the hillside to protect men from shell fire. Typically an MEBU had a yard-thick reinforced-concrete roof slab resting on concrete side walls dug into the slope and a concrete front wall with a cave-like opening that gave passage to the interior. Only a direct hit by a large caliber shell could destroy an MEBU.

That spring another famous author spent time at Les Eparges, only he was an active participant rather than casual visitor. Ernst Jünger was a twenty-year-old soldier in the German Army; after the war he would write *Storm of Steel* (*In Stahlgewittern*), considered the German "Iliad of the First World War." Although in America *All Quiet on the Western Front* (*Im Westen nichts Neues*) by Erich Maria Remarque is better known, in Europe Jünger has probably a wider readership. The two books, although based on experiences of German soldiers, could not be more different. Where Remarque uses the experience to write an essentially pacifist novel of the war's horror and futility, Ernst Jünger only reports, he does not philosophize — at least not too much. His book is akin to a diary of one horrific war experience followed by another, followed by another, and followed by another — in which nearly everyone is killed except Ernst Jünger. Jünger turned out to be the luckiest soldier in the

First World War; despite being wounded 14 times, disregarding "trifles such as ricochets and grazes," he survived the war, dying in 1998 at the incredible age of 102.[14]

Jünger's regiment, named *Les Gibraltars*, originated from the Hanoverian Guards who, with the English, defended Gibraltar against the French and Spanish from 1779 to 1783. After 1714, when the Elector of Hanover became George I of Great Britain and Ireland, the Hanoverians traditionally allied with the British, whether fighting Americans or Napoleon. Actually, the British royal family, being descended from George I and later intermarried with German nobility, is mostly German in heritage. During the First World War, George V changed the family name from Saxe-Coburg-Gotha to the more English-sounding Windsor, deemphasizing the German connection. Therefore, it was natural that the British and Hanoverians should be allies—the First World War was an historical anomaly, in that they were not.[15]

During the last week of April, Ernst Jünger's regiment entered the Les Eparges fray. Under heavy machine gun fire, they fought their way into a wood near the infamous hill. It was Jünger's first big engagement, his baptism of fire. It was not what he had expected.

> Turning round, I took a step back in horror: next to me a figure was crouched against a tree. It still had gleaming French leather harness, and on its back was a fully packed haversack, topped by a round mess-tin. Empty eye-sockets and a few strands of hair on the bluish-black skull indicated that the man was not among the living. There was another sitting down, slumped forward towards his feet, as though he had just collapsed. All around were dozens more, rotted, dried, stiffened to mummies, frozen in the eerie dance of death. The French must have spent months in the proximity of their fallen comrades, without burying them.[16]

French artillery literally cut Jünger's regiment to pieces. Wounded by a shell splinter, he lost his nerve and ran "like a bolting horse" away to safety, collapsing in a grove of trees—an inauspicious start for a soldier who would win Germany's highest award for bravery, the *Pour le Mérite*, in 1918. As he reflected in his diary, the battle was unlike what he had expected; he had never once seen a single living French soldier, there was only the barrage of artillery shells, the storm of steel.

Southeast of Combres-Höhe/Les Eparges is the village of Combres, which served as the German base for the battle. Outside the village, on a hair-pin bend at the base of the hill, is a massive ferroconcrete building, over 50 feet in length with a very thick concrete roof (about 6 feet) and five-foot-thick concrete walls. There is a single wide doorway and three windows. Three substantial buttresses, also of concrete, reinforce the front wall. This is a structure so overbuilt it will probably last a thousand years. Inside the building, opposite the door, a long passage way disappears into Combres-Höhe. Corrugated steel lines the passage way. This building is the mine head, the entrance to the miles of galleries that the Germans tunneled into the hill under the French trenches. When a gallery reached its goal, sappers would pack it with 20 to 30 tons of explosive and detonate it. The effect on the trench above was devastating. An American serving in the French Army not far from Les Eparges described such a mine explosion.

> Then the earth seemed all of a sudden to reel. There was a commotion like the bursting asunder of a volcano. Two hundred yards off, above the trees, a column of huge rocks, lumps of earth, tree trunks, and probably numerous human limbs rose slowly and majestically. The upper fragments as they rose seemed to advance menacingly in our direction as if they must surely hit us when they returned to earth. They seemed suspended in the air for an indefinite space of time, as if there was no hurry at all about their falling back. They seemed to cross and crisscross in all directions, now obscuring half the sky. Gradually the mass assumed the shape of the upper portion of an elm-tree, and then began to subside. Then could be heard the smashing sound of the tree branches, as this mass of rock and earth fell with the crushing force of an avalanche.[17]

On May 11, 1915, Wharton's Mercedes left Paris for its last tour of war time Lorraine.[18] On May 14, from the Grand Hôtel in Nancy, the capital of Lorraine, she wrote her usual letter to Henry James, catching him up on her latest adventures. She got permission to visit Pont-à-Mousson, a besieged French city where the Western Front crossed the Moselle River. The Moselle bisected the city into two districts linked by a multi-arched stone bridge. In 1914, as the Germans approached the city's outskirts, the French blew up a couple of spans, severing the connection. Mrs. Wharton's party entered the city east of the Moselle; thus her visit, because of the destroyed bridge, was restricted to the eastern or right bank. French artillery batteries were sited on nearby Mousson castle hill and German counter fire occurred almost daily. The batteries were high priority targets. Fortunately, Mrs. Wharton's visit coincided with weather inappropriate for artillery duels.

> A little way up the ascent to Mousson we left the motor behind a bit of rising ground. The road is raked by the German lines, and stray pedestrians (unless in a group) are less liable than a motor to have a shell spent on them. We climbed under a driving grey sky which swept gusts of rain across our road. In the lee of the castle we stopped to look down at the valley of the Moselle, the slate roofs of Pont-à-Mousson and the broken bridge which once linked together the two sides of the town. Nothing but the wreck of the bridge showed that we were on

the edge of war. The wind was too high for firing, and we saw no reason for believing that the wood just behind the Hospice roof at our feet was seamed with German trenches and bristling with guns, or that from every slope across the valley the eye of the cannon sleeplessly glared.[19]

The "Hospice" to which Mrs. Wharton refers is the nearby Premonstratensian Monastery, a very large and sprawling monastic complex along the east bank of the Moselle River. It served as a French military hospital and consequently was a target for German artillery. Since Edith Wharton was ostensibly on an inspection tour of French military hospitals near the front, it was the next stop. Inside, just as in the hospice at Clermont-en-Argonne, she met the same "indomitable breed" of Catholic nuns defying the Germans.

> Sister Theresia seems no wise disconcerted by the fact that the shells continually play on her roof. The building is immense and spreading, and when one wing is damaged she picks up her protégés and trots them off, bed and baggage, to another. "Je promène mes malades,"* she said calmly as if boasting of the varied accommodation of an ultra-modern hospital, as she led us through vaulted and stuccoed galleries where caryatid-saints look down in plaster pomp on the rows of brown-blanketed pallets and the long tables at which haggard éclopés† were enjoying their evening soup.[20]

The Premonstratensian Monastery at Pont-à-Mousson functioned as a French military hospital during the war. Edith Wharton visited the monastery in May 1915. The Moselle River backs the monastery and the infamous Bois-le-Prêtre battlefield is on heights across the river.

*"I take my sick ones for a walk."
†Shell-shocked soldiers.

During her visits to Les Eparges and Pont-à-Mousson, Mrs. Wharton saw two sides of the base of the infamous St. Mihiel Salient. The Salient was an outward triangular lobe, 24 miles (38.6 km) wide at its base, bulging more than 19 miles (31 km) into the French battle line; the apex of the salient included the city of St. Mihiel. Bavarian troops pushed into the salient in a series of attacks during September of 1914. Crown Prince Rupprecht, son and heir of King Ludwig III of Bavaria, commanded the Bavarians. The Crown Prince was one of the Kaiser's best field commanders.

As an interesting aside, the Crown Prince was a descendent of the British Royal House of Stuart, a royal line that included Bonnie Prince Charlie, leader of the 1745 Scottish rebellion. Before the war, Scottish Jacobites recognized Rupprecht as Prince Rupert of England, Scotland, France and Ireland. After the war, with the death of his mother, he succeeded to all her British rights and Jacobites recognized him as King Rupert (Robert) of Britain. Ironically the most costly battles fought by the British — the Somme, Arras, Lille and Ypres — were against armies commanded by the Crown Prince. After the war, the Crown Prince, an ardent anti-Nazi, was on Hitler's most wanted list. He escaped death in 1939 by hiding in Italy. When he died in 1955 at the age of 86, the *New York Times* published a laudatory obituary.[21]

The Crown Prince's Bavarians had captured Pont-à-Mousson in mid August 1914. The trench lines were very close to the city, so it was nearly always under bombardment. Mrs. Wharton was very lucky, as she told Henry James, the day of her visit coincided with a lull in German artillery fire. Mrs. Wharton's day-long visit on May 14, 1915, was limited to the city district on the east or right bank of the Moselle. Because of the wrecked Moselle bridge, she was unaware that just across the river a group of 24 young American volunteers, members of an American Ambulance Field Service section, was based in the western district of Pont-à-Mousson, having arrived there three weeks before. The section affiliated with a French Army division whose trench lines were on the slopes of a long forested ridge on the west bank known as the Bois-le-Prêtre. Looking up from the riverside garden of the Premonstratensian Monastery that rainy day, Mrs. Wharton could just see the dark foreboding ridge that was the Bois-le-Prêtre battlefield. She could not realize that another American, a volunteer in the French Army, was buried somewhere on that ridge among the shattered trees and winding trenches. Edith Wharton wrote of her adventures in a magazine article published that fall ("In Lorraine and the Vosges," *Scribner's Magazine*, October 1915). We only know of the American volunteer from letters he wrote to friends in America that were published after his death.[22]

André Chéronnet-Champollion was a naturalized American citizen

1. Edith and Henry

of French descent who in a fit of patriotic passion made the greatest mistake of his short life—he joined the French Army. Chamby, as he was known to his friends, was the great-grandson of Jean François Champollion, the eminent French Egyptologist who had deciphered the Rosetta Stone in 1822. It was probably living up to this heritage that made Chamby do what he did. He was a graduate of Harvard (class of 1902), a painter by profession, and, by all accounts, a man of sensitivity and refinement. When the war broke out in August 1914, he was 34, had a wife, a young son and a home in Newport, New Hampshire. Yet in early October of 1914, he left his family and embarked on what one could only describe as a quixotic adventure. He hoped that because of his Harvard University degree he might be posted as an officer or at least an interpreter; unfortunately, the French only recognized French university degrees. He became a private in the infantry.

Excerpts from his letters from France show his initial euphoria being followed by a realization that he was trapped.[23]

> Oct 14, 1914
> I am still convinced however that I am doing the right thing. If I had remained in America I should certainly have remained under the impression that I was acting in a cowardly manner.
>
> Nov 12, 1914
> Never has America seemed so beautiful. It is horrible to think that I cannot go back there, and that I am a prisoner here in this atmosphere so foreign to my past life, so utterly out of keeping with my tastes and habits.
>
> Nov 24, 1914
> As a private your individuality is absolutely crushed and degraded. You gradually become a nobody.
>
> Jan 17, 1915
> To be sent to the front as a private with a lot of peasants or even worse, holds no attraction to me, and I am damned thankful, and make no bones about it, that I have so far escaped such an ordeal. I never felt that I owed France any sacrifice such as that.
>
> Jan 22, 1915
> I know that it is not soldierly to complain or to kick, but if I said that I had enjoyed myself since getting here, I should be telling the biggest lie of my life.

By March 1915, he was in the trenches at Bois-le-Prêtre. His letters are probably the best description in English of trench life that first winter of the war.

March 1, 1915

We are in a forest in a regular labyrinth of trenches, some entirely underground, and we are plastered with mud from head to foot. It is a life of filth and misery beyond description, but so extraordinarily novel and interesting that, strange as it may seem, I am in good spirits. I have only been here 24 hours.

March 7, 1915

You sleep with the upper part of your body in a hole dug in the wall of the trench and your feet in the trench itself. It is a life of dirt and discomfort indescribable! Over some parts of the trench there are sheet iron coverings, but in others your legs and feet are exposed to the weather all night. You stand or walk in cold mud three or four inches deep all day; your feet are cold all the time. You dare not remove your shoes, in fact you are not allowed to, because of the chances of suddenly being attacked. You therefore spend night and day for an indefinite length of time with wet, cold feet. Your clothes soon get covered with the mud and yellow soil of the trenches; it gets mixed up in your food; your hands are covered with it all the time.

Of course no fires are ever tolerated in the first line trenches. This aggravates the suffering from the cold. All winter long there have been innumerable cases of frozen feet.

Washing is out of the question, as water is extraordinarily rare. We are however kept supplied with wine.

In the Bois-le-Prêtre, the opposing trenches were sometimes only 30 to 35 yards apart and the Germans nearly always held the high ground. Consequently, French trenches were dangerously exposed to sniper fire, and German snipers fired at anything that moved. Where trenches were shallow or particularly exposed, bags of earth in combination with iron shields with rifle loop holes protected the parapets. To be seen was to be a target. Tall men were at a severe disadvantage in trench warfare.

March 7, 1915

Being taller than the average French soldier, I was continually admonished to stoop down and not show the top of my head. This enforced stooping position often resulted in a backache.[24]

On March 23, 1915, the Germans exploded a mine beneath French trenches. Chamby's unit was rushed forward to hold the gap; he was killed defending what was left of the trench line, shot through the forehead. The American lasted less than two months in the trenches. He may be the first American combatant to perish in the First World War. He was buried in a military cemetery near the road to Pont-à-Mousson.

In August 1916, another American visitor was given a tour of Pont-à-

1. Edith and Henry 23

Because of Mrs. W. K. Vanderbilt's financial contributions to the Allied war effort, the French arranged an auto tour of part of the Western Front in 1916. A member of the French nobility, Duc de Clermont-Tonnerre, acted as guide and sometime chauffer. Presumably the French thought she would be impressed, as many Americans would have been. She wasn't. She described the duke's driving as competent but reckless. Mrs. Vanderbilt visited Verdun and Pont-à-Mousson; this photograph was taken in front of Reims cathedral. Mrs. Vanderbilt is sitting in the rear seat. To conceal her identity, she is wearing a nurse's costume as nurses were the only women allowed near the front in 1916. Reims was being shelled by the Germans at the time, thus the sandbag constructions protecting the cathedral's foundation (courtesy the Archives of the American Field Service and AFS Intercultural Programs).

Mousson. Mrs. W. K. Vanderbilt, an ardent Francophile, had funded numerous war charities including the American volunteer ambulance section based in Pont-à-Mousson. The French had arranged for her to see the section in action. She recalled driving into the city,

> we passed by the famous Bois le Prêtre, once a wood, now a wilderness. Here is the grave of André Champollion, an American, killed in the early months of the war, whose great-great-grandfather had been a savant with Napoleon in Egypt. Some of this young man's letters home have been published, they make one of the less known, but, I think, most interesting books of the war. I wanted to get out of the car and put some flowers on his

grave, but was forbidden and told that if we once ventured beyond the screen that hid the road we should be fair targets for the German machine guns in the trenches, which, with a wave of the hand, were always located just over there.[25]

Mrs. Vanderbilt mentions the danger of going "beyond the screen that hid the road." Exposed roads often had poles erected on the enemy side and from rope strung between the poles, cloth (muslin or burlap) was suspended, forming a continuous screen or curtain to hide the road. German gunners targeting the road had to shoot randomly through the screen since they could not see vehicles or troops using the road. The road past Bois-le-Prêtre toward Pont-à-Mousson was very dangerous. As the open touring car began its way down the road, Mrs. Vanderbilt's two traveling companions, a French duke and the head of the ambulance organization, both put on their steel helmets — embarrassingly, they had forgotten to bring one for her. As she wryly remarked, "this occasioned much chaffing." One can only imagine.

A large French military cemetery stands along the road Mrs. Vanderbilt traveled in 1916. André Chéronnet-Champollion is buried in the Nécropole

A screened road behind a Model T ambulance. Where roads were visible to German artillery observers, the French erected cloth screens or curtains to prevent the specific targeting of vehicles or troops. Mrs. Vanderbilt traveled on such roads as she approached the front in 1916 (courtesy the Archives of the American Field Service and AFS Intercultural Programs).

nationale "Le Petant," block 14/18-B, grave number 1477. There is no indication that he was an American citizen.

So why did so many die at Les Eparges and Bois-le-Prêtre in 1915? To answer that question, it is necessary to revisit the St. Mihiel Salient and consider the psychological impact it had on the French. In the autumn of 1914, during the battle of the Marne, the French managed not only to stop the German juggernaut but to push it back. Everywhere in France the Imperial German Army retreated — everywhere except the St. Mihiel Salient. With its point at St. Mihiel, the salient was a huge German thorn piercing the French line. If there was ever a Gallic irritant, an itch that could not be scratched, it was the Salient. Attacks at the apex of the salient had failed, so why not try to sever the thorn at its base. The Salient might be cut off if attacked from two sides simultaneously: on the southeast at Bois-le-Prêtre above Pont-à-Mousson and at Les Eparges on the northwest. Neither attack would be successful in pruning the thorn, but in 1915, no one knew that.

2

Along the Moselle in a Model T

> A small field ambulance with a large red cross on each of its gray canvas sides slips quickly down the curving cobblestone street of a quaint old French frontier town, and turns on to the road leading to the postes de secours [dressing-stations] behind the trenches, which are about two kilometers distant.... A group of little children cry out, "*Américain*," and, with beaming smiles, one of them executes a rigid though not very correct salute as the car goes by.—James R. McConnell,[1] September 1915

Mrs. Vanderbilt's American traveling companion during her visit to Pont-à-Mousson was A. Piatt Andrew, the head of an American volunteer ambulance organization serving with the French Army. It was known as the American Ambulance Field Service (A.A.F.S.), deriving its confusing name from the fact that *ambulance* in war-time French meant military hospital. Thus the A.A.F.S. was actually the field arm of the American Ambulance (American military hospital), a military hospital set up in the Parisian suburb of Neuilly-sur-Seine, established and run by wealthy Americans residing in Paris when the war began.

A. Piatt Andrew was one of those interesting personalities to whom leadership and organization come almost naturally. He had been a member of the Harvard faculty (1900–1909) where he taught economics, Franklin D. Roosevelt had been one of his students; President Taft appointed Andrew director of the U.S. Mint (1909–1910) and then Assistant Secretary of the U.S. Treasury (1910–1912). The latter was an unfortunate appointment for both Andrew and Taft. Andrew did not get along with Taft's Secretary of the Treasury, Franklin MacVeagh, whose erratic behavior, according to Andrew, "would seem inexplicable in a man of normal mind." In other words, the secretary was a bit crazy in Andrew's view. In 1912, the rift between the two came to a head with MacVeagh and Andrew trading accusations in public.[2] Taft supported his secretary and asked for Andrew's resignation. Andrew left Washington and returned to his home in Gloucester, Massachusetts, his professional career at a standstill. He then tried politics, running in the Republican primary for a Massachusetts congressional seat in 1914; he lost. Perhaps on the rebound from this set back, he wrote to Robert Bacon, president of the American military hospital in Paris, about a position with the hospital. Bacon owed Andrew a favor — Andrew had employed Bacon's son as his personal assistant in the Treasury Department. Bacon replied that although he had no management positions open, he had something in the hospital motor pool.[3] Andrew boarded a ship bound for France in December 1914, and would soon be on the Western Front in Belgium driving an ambulance. But first, he had to pass the French driver's exam to get a license. He described the ordeal in a letter to his parents.[4]

> January 7, 1915
> I had to take my driving-license examination yesterday with a fussy and pompous old French official, who made me so anxious with his injunctions and admonitions that I nearly ran over, first a tram-car, and then a flock of sheep, either of which would have been fatal to my hopes, whatever its effect on the car or the sheep. In the end he "passed" me, but it took the greater part of an afternoon of waiting, driving, backing, stopping, turning here and turning there according to his orders.... The old boy would wait until we got to a crowded corner and suddenly scream "A gauche" (to the left), and then, as I had to dodge trams and people crossing the street, he would say, "Ah! too fast! too fast! you are like taxi-drivers, who are assassins!"

After three months of driving an ambulance near Dunkerque, moving British and Belgian wounded from hospital trains to channel ships, a new position was created that might better utilize his talents; he was appointed Inspector-General of the American Ambulance Field Service (A.A.F.S.), a glamorous title with little substance. However, Andrew being Andrew, he set out to make the A.A.F.S. the largest and most significant American volunteer organization in the war.

French authorities initially prohibited American ambulances from operating near the front; America was neutral, and the French feared the possible negative publicity of American casualties. Therefore, American drivers were restricted to jitney duty, usually in the environs of Paris. They found themselves ferrying wounded from one hospital to another or from hospital trains to hospitals — important but not very exciting duty. Andrew changed all that. Realizing that if the A.A.F.S. remained a glorified Parisian taxi service it would have little or no appeal to American volunteers, he set out to get his ambulances to the front. Because of his previous careers in academe and government, Andrew had friends serving at the French General Military Headquarters and through them, he was able to change the rules for American ambulances.

Now they could serve at the front attached to units of the French Army — of course this stretched the concept of American neutrality pretty thin. Needless to say, there were no American ambulances attached to the German Army.

> It was not until April, 1915, however, that we succeeded in persuading the French government to allow our cars, driven by Americans, to go to the front. Quite naturally the government hesitated — although it did not actually object — to give our boys, neutrals, a position almost on the firing line, where they could observe every operation of the armies. There was also some hesitancy about submitting our boys to the risks which such service entailed.[5]

The first section[6] assigned to the front went to the mountainous region of the Alsace. For Andrew the performance of this section was critical, as it would determine whether the French would accept his men in other sectors. Andrew sent his best — and he had chosen well; the tireless drivers and their nearly unstoppable Model T's were so highly regarded by their French field commander that another ambulance section was requested for service at the front. This section was assigned to the French Army fighting near Pont-à-Mousson in Lorraine. Doc Andrew, as he was known to his men, arrived in Pont-à-Mousson with the section in late April 1915. He first sought out the grave of a former student.

> April 28, 1915
> Dear Mother and Father:
> ... and in one of the many improvised cemeteries that dot the hillside we saw where a Harvard man, André Champollion, whom I used to know in Cambridge, and who was killed in the French Army three weeks ago, was buried.
> A. Piatt Andrew[7]

Pont-à-Mousson is a small city on the Moselle River that had a pre-war population of 14,000. As has been previously noted (see Chapter 1), in May 1915, Mrs. Wharton visited the part of the city on the east side of the river and, remarkably, seemed unaware of the A.A.F.S. section west of the Moselle, or at least it is not mentioned in her writings. Pont-à-Mousson is on the southern side of the widest part of the triangle known as the St. Mihiel Salient, about 23 miles (37 km) east of the then German-occupied town of St. Mihiel. The nearby wooded ridge known as the Bois-le-Prêtre (Priest Wood) was a key location in this part of the Western Front. The Germans, as was usual in Lorraine, held the high ground, with their trenches on the crest of the ridge looking down on the French defenses on the slope. If the French could capture and hold the crest of the Bois-le-Prêtre, their artillery could shell the main

The German trenches in the Bois-le-Prêtre; the forest has been literally clear-cut by artillery fire. Because of the intensity of the fighting in this area, the Germans named it *Witwenwald* or Widows' Wood. The soldiers wear pickelhaubes, hardened-leather headgear that offered little protection and had the added disadvantage in that the spike drew the attention of French sharpshooters (*Hamburger Fremdenblatt: Illustrated War Chronic* [Hamburg: Brosckek, 1915]).

German railroad line supplying the St. Mihiel Salient. Thus, the French had an important strategic reason to capture Priest Wood, and the Germans had the same reason to defend it. German soldiers referred to the forest as the *Witwenwald*, Widows' Wood. For the young ambulance drivers, what they witnessed left a deep emotional mark. Here is what one driver remembered of his first tour in the Bois-le-Prêtre.

> As we waited a broken-down horse appeared with a cart-load of what looked like old clothes—"Les Morts." I had never seen a dead body until that moment. It was a horrible awakening—eight stiff, semi-detached, armless, trunkless, headless bodies,—all men like ourselves with people loving them,—somewhere,—all gone this way,—because of—what? I don't know, do you? A grave had been dug two meters deep, large enough to hold sixteen, and then we were asked to group ourselves around the car to be taken "pour souvenir." I managed to do it. I felt like being sick. Then one by one they were lowered into the grave, and when they were all laid out the identification started to take place—the good boots were taken off—and if a coat was not too bloody or torn it was kept—"Surely we must be going," I said. "No, no! not before we have shown you the dead in the fosse there." "Good God," I cried, "I can't do that now"; and I didn't.[8]

Fresh troops were always entering the trenches to replace those lost. It was not difficult to imagine their fate.

> I could tell them that they were going to a place where between their trench and the German trench were hundreds of mangled forms, once their fellow citizens,—arms, legs, heads, scattered disjointedly everywhere; and where all night and all day every fiendish implement of murder falls by the hundred—into their trenches or on to those ghastly forms,—some half rotted, some newly dead, some still warm, some semi-alive, stranded between foe and friend,—and hurls them yards into the air to fall with a splash of dust, as a rock falls into a lake.[9]

The ambulance section spent ten hard months ferrying the wounded out of the *Witwenwald*. The wounded either made their own way if they could walk or were carried on a stretcher to a *poste de secours* behind the trenches for immediate first aid; from there they were picked up by ambulance and taken to hospital in Pont-à-Mousson.

> At this rear post the regimental surgeon cleans the wound, stops the bleeding, and sends for the ambulance, which at the Bois-le-Prêtre, came right into the heart of the trenches by sunken roads that were in reality broad trenches. The man is then taken to the hospital that his condition requires, the slightly wounded to one hospital, and those requiring an operation to another.[10]

The majority of the ambulances used by the A.A.F.S. were Model T Fords. At Pont-à-Mousson, the ambulance section had nineteen in addition to a couple of heavier cars, a Pierce-Arrow and a Hotchkiss. The Fords were very nimble and the preferred ambulances for getting through the rough roads near the front. They were designed in 1908 for roads in America, which at the time were mostly dirt, deeply rutted, and muddy after rain. Model T's had thirty-inch diameter wheels, a high road clearance (ten and a half inches), and wheels that were attached to the chassis by a three point suspension system that allowed the vehicle literally to flex and snake its way through shell-cratered roads. When the craters got too deep, the car could usually go cross-country around them. Besides the suspension system, the springs made for a much softer ride, even though the vehicle was bouncing over rough roads; consequently French wounded (*blessés*) preferred the *petites voitures*, as they called them, to other larger ambulances with less forgiving springs.

Model T's had interchangeable parts; wrecked cars were cannibalized for parts to keep others going; almost nothing was wasted. Because of its simple design, a disabled vehicle could usually be repaired, even near the front under shell fire. Some have said the Model T ambulance was America's most significant technological contribution to the First World War. If there was a disadvantage to the Model T, it was its size. It was a small ambulance with a capacity of only three stretcher cases (*couchés*) or four sitting wounded (*assis*) in the back and three *assis* squeezed in up front, half sitting on the running boards and fenders. In contrast, big heavy ambulances such as Packards, Panhards, Minervas, Hotchkisses or Pierce-Arrows could carry twice as many *couchés* or *assis* per trip. Because of these differences in capacity, large ambulances had a driver and an assistant whereas the Model T ambulances had only a driver. Driving an ambulance alone across a battlefield at night, which was when most of the pick-ups were made, was not for the faint-at-heart.

One of the most effective off-road vehicles of the war; here a Ford Model T ambulance crosses a stream. Note the spare tires on the roof. Sharp objects, *e.g.,* shell splinters, fragments of pointed steel stakes that had once supported wire entanglements, snippets of barbed wire cut free by artillery fire and even broken wine bottles littered battlefield roads. Consequently, tire punctures became nearly everyday events. Ambulances sometimes returned to base running on their rims, the tires having been shredded away (courtesy the Archives of the American Field Service and AFS Intercultural Programs).

The disadvantage of the big cars was that they were restricted to better roads; they did not have the off-road capabilities of the Model T — if a *poste de secours* was near the front and could only be reached via a narrow, muddy, shell-pitted road, the Model T had the best chance of reaching it. Therefore, the Model T was the ambulance of choice near the trenches; over a thousand would eventually be used on the Western Front. The French loved them, the British, did not, probably because the French did. The German Army's views are unknown, but they often targeted them. Cars usually lasted three to four months before a German shell found its mark. Approximately 1,200 Ford Model T chassis were imported into France, and although his company made nearly $60,000,000 profit in 1915[11] Henry Ford gave no discounts.

> From him [Henry Ford] we could obtain not even the favor of wholesale rates in the purchase of cars and parts, and for every Ford car and for every Ford part imported from America, in those difficult days before America came into the war, we were obliged to pay, not the dealer's price, but the full market price charged to ordinary retail buyers.[12]

Because ambulances could operate so close to the trenches, the Americans experienced close calls almost daily when the fighting heated up.

> Wearing the Military Cross for gallant conduct under fire, J. B. Taylor, 22 years old, of 320 West Eighty-third Street, who has been driving an ambulance in France for eight months, returned home yesterday on the liner *Espagne*, Mr. Taylor spent the greater part of his service in the American Ambulance Corps[13] at Pont-à-Mousson, from which place he made daily trips to the rear of the firing lines to bring back the wounded.[14]

Mr. Taylor was loading wounded soldiers into his ambulance when a rifle bullet hit him in the shoulder. Bleeding and in pain, he drove his wounded to the dressing station before having his own wound tended. Not resting from his wound, as he was ordered to by his commander, the next day he was out with his ambulance near the firing lines picking up wounded. On this trip he was fired upon by German artillery, a shell exploded in front of the ambulance, a fragment hit his wounded shoulder and a larger fragment struck the steering gear. The ambulance swerved out of control, crashed, and hurled Taylor through the window of a partly demolished house. Taylor managed to stagger to safety. This time he received a furlough and orders to go home. He told a *New York Times* reporter he intended to return to France in a few weeks, but he was giving up ambulances; he wanted to join the aviation corps of the French Army. The *Times* described Taylor as plucky.

Sometimes thoughts of home intruded at the strangest times. A young

American, James McConnell, remembered a night somewhere near Pont-à-Mousson.

> One very dark night, a few days ago, two of us were waiting at an advanced *poste de secours*. The rifle and artillery fire was constant, illuminating rockets shot into the air, and now and then one could distinguish the dull heavy roar of a mine or torpille[15] detonating in the trenches. War in all its engrossing detail was very close. Suddenly my friend turned to me and, with a sigh, remarked, "Gee! I wish I knew how the Red Sox were making out!"[16]

McConnell's friend missed a great baseball season. The Boston Red Sox won the World Series that year. They also won the next year (1916) and in 1918. McConnell never learned of the 1918 Series win. He switched from driving ambulances to flying fighters, becoming one of the original members of what would become known as the Lafayette Escadrille. On St. Patrick's Day 1917, he was shot down over the Somme and did not survive.

Half way up to the ridge-crest of the Bois-le-Prêtre a ravine broadens into a small shallow valley in which a spring supplies a small fountain. In the early nineteenth century Father Hilarion (Père Hilarion) built a house next to the fountain and lived there in religious seclusion.[17] At the time of the First World War it was a forester's house. For nearly two months, November and December of 1914, a battle raged in that ravine with the Germans entrenched on the uphill side of the house, the French on the downhill side. During the battle the fountain, which lay between the lines, served as a sanctuary where men could fill their canteens, but only at proscribed times — the French had an hour, then the Germans had an hour. After filling canteens, the soldiers returned to their respective trenches and resumed trying to kill each other.

> In several places here the trenches are only fifteen or twenty meters apart and the French and Germans are on quite good terms. They exchange tobacco for wine and paper for cigarettes and then return and shoot at each other quite merrily.[18]

A year later, the trenches had not moved much beyond Father Hilarion's sanctuary. It was in December of 1915 when a young American carefully drove his Model T into the shell-cratered ravine searching for a *poste de secours*.

> I was sent to La Fontaine de Père Ilarion in search of three men — gassed. It is a beautiful name — the Spring of Ilarion. It was a spring in what should have been a sweetly wooded glen. But now it was a spring in what seems like a half-deserted mining camp in the heart of the Bois-le-Prêtre, with open trenches, like ugly, yellow wounds in the earth, ooze of mud, engines of destruction, masses of barbed wire. Over everything hung the horrible sense of impending disaster.

> The ambulances come but seldom here; it is too close to the firing line. The road stops short. As I hunted for the first aid post, the bullets seemed to sing through the air much nearer than they really were. Ten yards away from the machine I saw a dummy put up to draw enemy fire. I moved the car with immoderate haste. But the journey, after all, was fruitless. The men were dead, the three of them. I was glad to leave that gloomy wood, to be out again in what seemed, oddly enough, safety.[19]

Surprisingly, the house of Father Hilarion survived the war, albeit as a shot-up ruin. The fountain is still there. The nearby woods, although furrowed with old trenches, are again a "sweetly wooded glen."

Normally A.A.F.S. ambulances did not enter the Bois-le-Prêtre; men carried the wounded by stretcher down the hill to *postes de secours* sited along the edge of the battlefield. All *postes de secours* were within range of German artillery and frequently shelled. During the worst of the fighting, the Americans moved 75,000 wounded a month from these *postes* to hospitals in Pont-à-Mousson. Four different houses served as *postes de secours* in the ruins of the village of Montauville, about three kilometers from Pont-à-Mousson; another was a couple of kilometers along the same road in a farm house in Clois Bois, described by a driver[20] as "an evil little first-aid post in a horrible wood"; and the most distant was at Auberge St. Pierre. All lay along the road that skirted the battlefield. This was the road Mrs. Vanderbilt traveled during her visit in 1916; she stopped at the auberge.[21]

> The dressing-station is a long, narrow building with a sloping roof that looks like a primitive down-at-the-heel New England farm-house. It has been struck many times by shells or pieces of shells, and the holes have been roughly mended. The ground around it has been torn up by artillery fire, and across the road two telephone poles tilt crazily against each other. The wounded are carried from the trenches on stretchers into the building, where they are given temporary surgical attention before being loaded into an ambulance.[22]

Although today Auberge St. Pierre is a tidy farmhouse, Clois Bois is still a dismal wood, the *poste de secours* site marked by empty graves. Aid stations usually had nearby burying grounds for the wounded who perished. These *ad hoc* cemeteries, out of empathy for the wounded, were usually not visible from where wounded were treated. Burials were quick and graves shallow. After the war, the bodies were exhumed and moved to military cemeteries—thus the "man-sized" depressions in Clois Bois. The village of Montauville was rebuilt; the locations of its *postes de secours* are forgotten. Then there was *poste de secours* X—, its location never identified in drivers' memoirs.

> We go regularly to X — to get our "blessés," and for two of the six kilometers we are exposed to German view and the whole of the way, of course, to shell fire. On my first arrival at this little mountain village I was horrified to see two people lying dead in the road in huge pools of blood. Six German "240's" had been suddenly launched into the village which is full of soldiers, and killed six soldiers and wounded some thirty.[23]

Poste de secours X — is very probably the village of Fey-en-Haye on the southern edge of the Bois-le-Prêtre battlefield. The village was the scene of terrific fighting in 1915, ending up as a heap of ruins. It was never rebuilt.

The headquarters of the A.A.F.S. in Pont-à-Mousson was in the Villa Glycine or Wisteria House. It was here the men ate their meals and waited for calls to pick up wounded. It was where they spent most of their time when not driving. Behind the villa, there was a building for servicing and repairing the cars. Mrs. Vanderbilt had dinner at the villa with the young American drivers during her visit; she purposefully sat between two drivers just returned from a run to pick up wounded and attempted to get them to talk of their experiences. However, they were young, and she was not; she was rich, and they were not; she was famous, and they were not; consequently, her conversational gambits failed. Talk was strained and centered on spark plugs, thick oil and engine knocks. "I gladly did more listening than talking," she wrote; she could have had the same one-sided conversation in an auto repair shop. She described the Glycine as "a big building, gaudy and modern-looking without, and within a riot of color. They say before the war it belonged to a German. It has a large flower and vegetable garden which the boys of the section try to keep."[24]

A young American driver left a less complimentary description of the then modern Villa Glycine — he hated every aspect of it!

> The Glycine — flowerful appellation — was the name, let me add, of the villa in which our section was quartered, unmercifully modern, new, artfully hideous. It was battered and scarred and dreary and debauched, but its roof was still holeless, and some of its broken panes we had replaced with oiled-silk. Entering at the basement through a bulky hedge of sandbags, past the one-time laundry, where were the telephones and the sallow-faced, despondent young French operator, and the villainous flight of stairs, you found the clou of the establishment, salle à manger, salle de lecture, salle de recréation, whichever you liked. It was a high, humorless, vicious room, painted the cheery tone of dried blood. There were a vast, slipshod, oval table, a feeble little stove (labeled misleadingly a salamander), some chairs, portions of a plaster-of-Paris gentleman indelicately attired, a muddy heap of ill-smelling garments — ours — in a corner.[25]

Christmas 1915 at the Glycine: the *salle à manger* was festively decorated, the men sat around the oval table laughing, having just finished a gay meal that ended with a huge plum-pudding, wine bottles littered the table, small gifts had been exchanged, a gramophone sent to the section by a lady from Philadelphia was brought out and the scratchy sounds of the "Roosevelt March" and the "Marche Lorraine" filled the room again and again. More laughter. In the basement the telephone rang, the French operator wearily climbed the stairs and asked someone to come down for a call. They all thought the cars would need to go out that night and pick up wounded. However, the call was not about French wounded; it was about a dead comrade. Richard N. Hall with the ambulance section in the Vosges Mountains in the Alsace had been killed. He had been driving alone on a dark night to the *poste de secours* of Hartmannsweilerkopf. He died alone.

> At midnight Christmas Eve, he left the valley to get his load of wounded for the last time. Alone, ahead of him, two hours of lonely driving up the mountain. Perhaps he was thinking of other Christmas Eves, perhaps of his distant home, and of those who were thinking of him.
>
> Matter,[26] the next American to pass, found him by the roadside halfway up the mountain. His face was calm and his hands still in position to grasp the wheel....
>
> A shell had struck his car and killed him instantly, painlessly. A chance shell in a thousand had struck him at his post, in the morning of his youth.
>
> Up on the mountain fog was hanging over Hartmann's Christmas morning, as if Heaven wished certain things obscured. The trees were sodden with dripping rain. Weather, sight, sound, and smell did their all to sicken mankind, when news was brought to us that Dick Hall had fallen on the Field of Honor. No man said, "Merry Christmas," that day.[27]

The Glycine, now more than a century old, survived the war and has changed very little since 1915, although the street it faces has a new name, Rue Patton. The iron fence separating it from the road is still a trellis for wisteria vines.

For the A.A.F.S. to grow, it needed two things: money and drivers — cash to purchase, ship, and repair its ambulances and recruits to drive them. Both would primarily come from America. The key figure in the campaign to win the hearts and minds and open the pocket books of Americans was Doc Andrew's close friend and Gloucester neighbor, Henry Davis Sleeper. A noted architect and interior designer, Sleeper focused his artistic talents on publicity and fundraising. Ambulance drivers, many of whom were college educated, were encouraged by Sleeper and Andrew to publish their war experiences. One of the first drivers to publish (and unfortunately later to perish) was James McConnell, a driver in the section based in Pont-à-Mousson. His article "With the American Ambulance in France," published in 1915, in the magazine *The Outlook,* gave Americans a first-hand look at the brave young men in their Model T's. McConnell was the first of many "driver-authors"; the men seemed to love to see their names in print. It is because of these accounts that the history of the A.A.F.S. is so well documented.

Sleeper even published letters sent to him without the writer's permission if they helped the cause. In 1915, he published letters sent by his close friend Leslie Buswell. "Buzzy" Buswell came to America in the fall of 1914, after he had failed his British military medical examination. He arrived as part of an

A. Piatt Andrew, head of the American Ambulance Field Service, posing in front of an ambulance purchased by the town of Gloucester, Massachusetts. Wealthy individuals (*e.g.,* the Vanderbilts), towns, clubs, organizations, or colleges donated ambulances. Such ambulances were known by the name of their donor and identified by a donor's plaque. Andrew resided in Gloucester so very much appreciated the seaport's donation (courtesy the Archives of the American Field Service and AFS Intercultural Programs).

English acting troop organized by the then famous English actor Cyril Maude. Buswell, a graduate of Cambridge University, had a supporting role in "Grumpy," a production that played in Boston during November 1914.[28] The young actor became very close friends with Henry Sleeper and Piatt Andrew. In fact, Andrew's magnetism influenced him so much he followed him to France in late May of 1915, joining the nascent A.A.F.S. as a driver. He was assigned to the section in Pont-à-Mousson, where he drove for five months. His letters to his friend Sleeper are extraordinary; Buswell, both a great observer and a wonderful writer, captured the emotions and pathos of what it was like to drive an ambulance on the Western Front in 1915. Sleeper, recognizing the potential of these letters to move donors, published them as a small limited edition book.[29] Copies were sent to Sleeper's and Andrew's "well-heeled" friends, and their friends. Included in the book was an advertising flyer describing the work of the A.A.F.S. and an address where checks could be sent. In 1916, an augmented edition with photographs was published for the general public.[30] Another publicity effort was the memoir book, *Friends of France*.[31] Drivers contributed essays and photographs of their experiences on the battlefields of France. This book also included an advertising flyer requesting donations, but now something new was added — the need for men.

> **Volunteer Ambulance Drivers Wanted**
> New men are also needed from time to time to fill places of those who return to America on leave, or who are unable to re-enlist at the expiration of their six months in the field.
>
> **Requisite Qualifications**
> American Citizenship — Good Health — Ability to drive and repair Automobiles — Sufficient funds to assume Traveling Expenses. (No salary, but living expenses paid)

Applicants were to contact Henry D. Sleeper.

Motion pictures were enlisted to win the hearts, minds and pocket books of Americans. The Triangle Film Corporation was commissioned to produce the hour-long silent movie "Our American Boys in the European War." The documentary film was shot in France in the vicinity of Pont-à-Mousson, probably in 1915 and 1916. It was an immediate hit; Americans were hungry to see the war "in action" and they were especially interested in the young American volunteers. The final few minutes of the film included cameo appearances of American flyers in the Lafayette Escadrille, including former ambulancier James McConnell. The film premiered in Boston in the ballroom of the Hotel Majestic on July 5, 1916, to an audience of enthusiastic Boston notables.[32] It soon was making the rounds at fund raisers in the homes of the wealthy.

NEWPORT, R.I., Aug 6, 1916—"Our American Boys in the European War," a film, in which men well known in Newport's Summer colony appear, will be shown at the residence of Mr. and Mrs. Vincent Astor, the afternoon of Aug. 19, instead of next Saturday, for the benefit of the American Ambulance Field Service on the firing line.[33]

The film was the basis of a "Dog and Pony Show" that Sleeper sent out on a countrywide tour, playing everywhere from western mining camps, small and large towns and cities, to college campuses. An ex-driver accompanied the film for commentary; usually, but not always, it was Leslie Buswell exercising his dramaturgical skills, "touring the Far West like a second Oscar Wilde,"[34] making the pitch for money and volunteers. The drivers filed reports of their experiences with Sleeper.[35]

Cleveland

The films were shown in the ballroom of the Hotel Statler. Such prominence had been given to the event through the continued campaign of publicity that practically all of Cleveland society came together for it.

The Cleveland event resulted in 16 ambulances contributed and raised $87,000. In the Far West, things were not quite so staid.

Butte, Montana

This is essentially a mining town, and with foreigners of every description — some of them whose mother countries were of the Allies, but many whose antecedents were not so. We arrived just before registration day,[36] and as the authorities expected trouble, saloons were closed, the militia in readiness, the crowds freely displaying the red flag. Our meeting was in a large theater, and the place was jammed. I and several of the committeemen, on the stage, were at first hissed. Most of this disapproval seemed to come from the balconies. The authorities had taken every precaution to avoid trouble, and there were plain-clothes men stationed behind the scenery on the stage to protect us. Antagonistic, or at best indifferent, as the audience had proved itself, as the performance went on they became quiet. After the pictures were shown, there was a strong appeal made. The result was surprising. When the committee in charge counted the proceeds, it was found that seven hundred dollars more were given by the miners in the balconies than by the representative citizens in the orchestra.

Campuses were the main source of drivers. Recruiting committees were organized at the larger colleges and universities. Usually headed by an enthusiastic faculty member, the committees funneled applicants to Sleeper. Harvard (325), Yale (187), Princeton (181), Dartmouth (118) and Cornell (105) sent the most men, but large and small colleges from nearly every state were represented. In early 1916, Sleeper intensified his campus recruitment campaign; he needed all the drivers he could get — the French had decided to send the A.A.F.S. to Verdun. Verdun became the defining moment for the Field Service, where more than 36 American ambulance sections served 44 different French Army Divisions during the course of the battle.[37] The battle lasted nearly a year, resulting in 700,000 casualties (378,000 French and 329,000 German) of which 304,000 were dead or missing, the missing mostly blown to bits and never recovered.[38] To understand the Verdun experience for the Field Service, it is necessary to understand the battle itself, where it was fought and the men who directed it.

3

Verdun Madness

> But although Verdun has been a city for longer than anyone quite knows, scarcely one event in her many centuries of history before 1916 was of a sort to endear the place to France or, indeed, to any one.—Clara E. Laughlin[1]

> What can Falkenhayn and his Germans do with Verdun if they get it? They cannot eat it. They can not sell it. They cannot make it into cannon balls. They cannot throw it at their enemies. They cannot even take it home to Germany as trophy. What vital difference does it make to the real war-making capacity of Germany or France whether the French lines are drawn on one side of Verdun or the other?[2]—Winston Spenser Churchill, First Lord of the British Admiralty, 1916

Churchill's question, "Why Verdun?" remained unanswered until after the war when General Falkenhayn published his memoirs. Falkenhayn's idea was that attacking Verdun would be an efficient way for the Imperial German Army to kill lots of Frenchmen. The strategy was not so much to capture Verdun, but rather to bleed the French Army white as they sought to defend it. Verdun was to be the abattoir for the French Army.

> Within our reach behind the French sector of the Western Front there are objectives for the retention of which the French General Staff would be compelled to throw in every man they have. If they do so the forces of France will be bled to death—as there can be no question of a voluntary withdrawal—whether we reach our goal or not.[3]

Just before Christmas 1915, in an audience with the Kaiser, Falkenhayn presented his audacious plan, a plan that would certainly be described today as thinking "outside the box." The Kaiser accepted and endorsed this Christmas gift, a holiday offering that would result in 700,000 dead, wounded or missing in the coming year. Thus, the initial *raison d'être* of the battle of Verdun was simply to cause death—which turned out to be a "Mutually Assisted Suicide Strategy" because death was parceled out pretty equitably to both sides, 162,000 French dead or missing versus 142,000 German dead or missing.⁴ Verdun would be the only battle of the First World War whose stated original strategic goal was not to capture territory—its strategic goal was simply genocide.

Verdun was, and still is, a city ringed with forts. After the debacle of the Franco-Prussian War (19 July 1870–10 May 1871), the French went on a fortress building spree, attempting to block the major invasion routes from Germany. One of those routes passed through Verdun, and it was duly blocked. Eighteen large forts and 40 *ouvrages* (smaller forts) surrounded the town in 1916. The forts stood on the crests of hills within sight of each other, each covering its

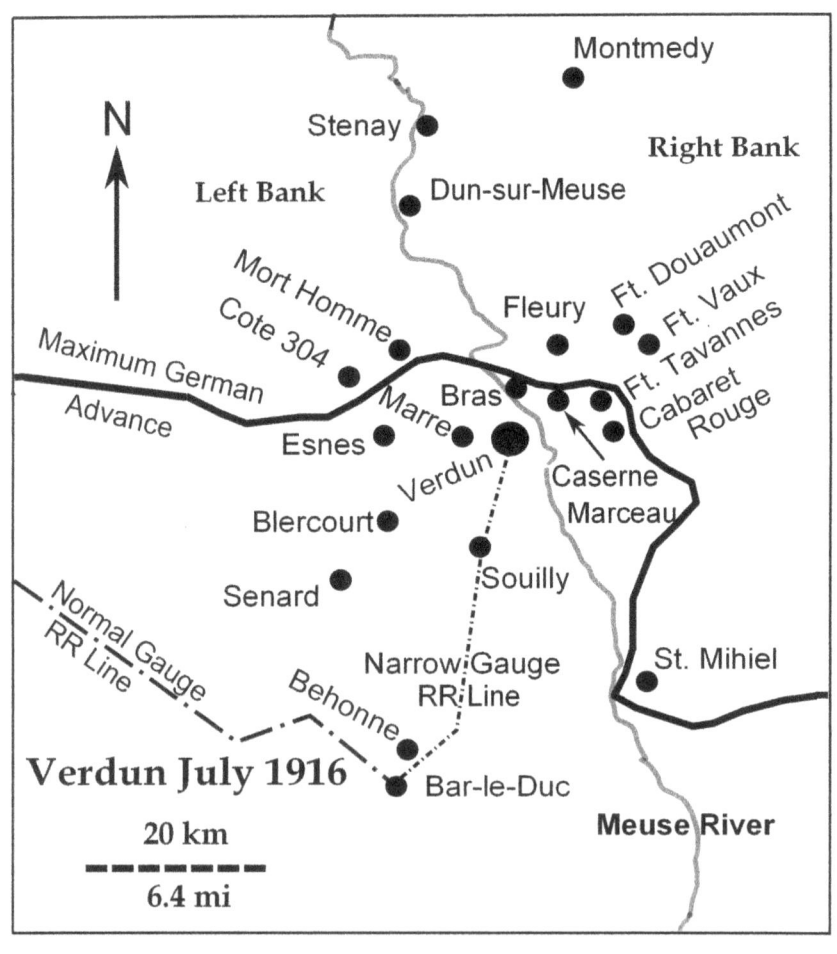

Verdun, July 1916.

neighbors against attacks and defending a perimeter of nearly 40 miles (64 km). However, since these forts were designed and constructed prior to the development of heavy mortars firing armor piercing shells, they were significantly dated in 1916. Efforts were made to rectify these deficiencies prior to the war. For example, Fort Douaumont, a key fort in the Verdun defenses, was rebuilt and improved three times before 1914. The result was a nine-foot-thick mass of reinforced concrete interlaced with layers of shock absorbing sand, all covered with 18 feet of earth. Therefore, between the fort's internal galleries and the outside there was a carapace 27 feet thick, a barrier robust enough to take the impact of nearly anything the enemy could throw at it — the fort could probably survive an atomic bomb. Protruding through the carapace were cupolas in which the fort's guns were mounted. Again, the French tested different designs to find what would best survive hits by large caliber shells. The result was a curved cap-like cupola with a gun port; the cupola's walls were a foot thick, of laminated and specially tempered steel, and virtually indestructible. When not firing, a cupola could retract, thus offering no target to attackers.

The French high command never anticipated an attack on Verdun; why attack a place that was theoretically the most well defended sector of the Western Front? When the battle began, many wondered about the sanity of the German leadership. Kaiser Wilhelm II, as the Supreme War Lord, was ultimately responsible for the attack, even though the plan came from his Chief of the General Staff *(Chef des Grossen Generalstabs)*, General Erich von Falkenhayn. The Kaiser's mental stability was questioned before the war; Verdun helped confirm prejudices.

> The Kaiser is impulsive. He is possessed of great political power. The action which follows his decision is sure to be prompt, decisive, vigorous. It follows that he is sometimes guilty of indiscretions which not only appall his advisers but even cast suspicion upon his sanity.[5]

On February 21, 1916, the German Fifth Army led by Crown Prince Friedrich Wilhelm Victor August Ernst von Hohenzollern or, more simply, Crown Prince Wilhelm (William), attacked Verdun. The Crown Prince was the son and heir to Kaiser Wilhelm II. The British comedians referred to them as Big Willie and Little Willie. Little Willie also was sometimes known as the Clown Prince because of his gangly poor posture and general lack of military bearing. Pictures show him wearing an ill-fitted cinched-in trench coat, a shako of the Death's Head Hussars with a skull and crossed bones monogram, the shako invariably planted on his head at a very unmilitary angle, and an over-sized sword hanging from his belt; he resembled Ichabod Crane in uni-

form. Even after his death in 1951, he was ridiculed, his obituary in the *New York Times* describing him as "waspish and spindle-legged."⁶

Of course, British comedians had to come to grips with the fact that Big Willie was half English, his mother being the daughter of Queen Victoria; therefore the queen was his grandmama. That made Little Willie her great grandson. Both Willies spoke English.

In terms of personality, Big and Little Willie were very different; the Kaiser was straitlaced, disciplined, and monogamous, with a strong sense of family history and honor. The Crown Prince was none of those things. As a young man he was frivolous at best, malicious at worst. His two life-long passions were horses and women. Relations between the Kaiser and his son were often very, very strained. The Crown Prince was one of those offspring whose parent sometimes wonders, "How could it be mine?"

> If ever there was an heir-apparent who understood the fine arts of mischief-making, indiscretion, meddling, and impudent interference in matters beyond his province, Little Willie is the man.⁷

In spite of his difficulties with his father, no one questioned the Crown Prince's personal bravery and daring-do. In the autumn of 1909, Orville Wright was in Potsdam demonstrating his airplane to royal spectators; the Crown Prince volunteered to try the "new contraption." Mr. Wright described the royal flight:

> Although the Crown Prince did not say much more than "fine" when he was up in the air with me I could read all the impressions on his face. I never took up any passenger who looked so pleased. He was absolutely delighted. He smiled when we started, and kept smiling right along. I felt a great responsibility in having the future German Emperor as a passenger; not that I mistrusted my machine, but because I knew how scared the spectators would be if any irregularity occurred, so I kept low at starting. This did not please the Prince, who continually urged me higher. He was not in the least nervous.⁸

The Crown Prince was evidently also very charming. "Among the things which Americans will put to the Crown Prince's credit is his admitted admi-

---

Opposite: On the right is Kaiser Wilhelm II (Big Willie) and on the left his son Crown Prince Wilhelm (Little Willie) speaking with an unidentified officer. The Kaiser had a bit of a clothes fetish, sometimes changing uniforms, including under linen and stockings, three or more times in a single day. Uniforms meant less to the Crown Prince; in the field, he nearly always wore a Death's Head Hussar shako, an oversized trench coat and carried a long saber (just visible in the opposite photograph). The American ambassador to Germany at the time noted that photographs of the Crown Prince did not do credit to the man — one hopes so (*Die Wochenschau* [Berlin: W. Girardet, 1916]).

ration of American girls."⁹ In 1904, the darling of the Berlin Royal Opera was a young American singer, Geraldine Farrar. Stories published in the Berlin newspaper *Welt am Montag* implying Miss Farrar's engagement to the Crown Prince and the enraged Kaiser sternly forbidding the marriage titillated the Berlin public. The editor later recanted the story,¹⁰ but it did not go away. Although vigorously denied over the years, the matter was never put to rest.¹¹

> There were others who had discovered a more congenial life-partner for the Prince in the person of an American member of the Berlin opera, with whom he was said to have fallen violently in love, and to have declared his readiness to forfeit his rights to his father's throne rather than foreswear his devotion to the Yankee beauty.¹²

In 1914, Little Willie was 32 years old; the Kaiser put the Crown Prince in supreme command of the German Fifth Army, more than 300,000 men, perhaps thinking that this might make his son straighten up. The Kaiser appointed Lieutenant-General Schmidt von Knobelsdorf as Chief of the General Staff for the Fifth Army. The Kaiser's instructions to the Crown Prince regarding Knobelsdorf were simple, "Whatever he advises you, You must do!" In 1915, the Prince was taken to task for disobeying the royal instructions; evidently he had been issuing orders to the generals under his command about points of strategy without clearing them with Lieutenant-General Schmidt von Knobelsdorf. To the Prince's embarrassment, his orders were publicly countermanded by both the Kaiser and General von Falkenhayn. Little Willie stormed out of the Kaiser's headquarters complaining that he was being treated like a boy.¹³ But to give the Crown Prince credit, he eventually rated as one of the Kaiser's best field commanders. After the war, Churchill wrote of the Prince, "It may also be said that no group of German armies was more consistently successful than his."¹⁴

Remarkably, the Crown Prince had nearly captured Verdun early in the war. By the first week of September 1914, his Fifth Army had almost encircled Verdun and in another couple of weeks would surely have captured the city. But the Battle of the Marne intervened: the German right wing was too weak to stop the French counter attack, the German armies in the west retreated, and the Crown Prince was ordered to follow suit — the Fifth Army retreated. The Crown Prince's September advance and then retreat resulted in the German Army visiting Clermont-en-Argonne twice in 1914 (see Chapter 1). Finally, a stable front was established along a line from the southern Argonne Forest, east to the Butte de Vauquois, east to the Meuse River, across the river and then skirting the hills surrounding the main Verdun forts. This was roughly the jump-off for the German offensive in 1916 against Verdun.

> My army was and continued to be constantly hampered and weakened by the danger from Verdun. What a gigantic success it would have been could we have captured the bulwark at that time, when it would still have been a comparatively easy undertaking.[15]

For the rest of his life the Crown Prince would lament, what was to him, the unnecessary retreat. Verdun was an easy target in September 1914, but when he attacked it in 1916, it was not. Following the pull back in 1914, the Crown Prince established his headquarters in Stenay, a town on the Meuse about 25 miles (40 km) downstream (north) of Verdun. The German Army's arrival in Stenay followed a pattern that would be repeated again and again whenever a town or village was first occupied that fall: initially the troops were allowed to run amok, pillaging the place and breaking into shops and houses searching for drink; then hostages were taken; finally a heavy indemnity was imposed on the population, which in Stenay comprised about eight hundred women, children and men, the latter either too old or infirm to be in the French Army. After that Teutonic "greeting," order was established, albeit a Prussian order with the military in command and civilians without rights. Stenay suffered "Germanization" with cleanliness and hygiene being the two master-words. The Germans thought the town "grey and rather dirty." Houses were to be repainted and streets cleaned on a daily basis. The traditional manure piles fronting houses were ordered removed and replaced with flower gardens.[16] Public health was a great concern. German doctors cared for civilians, and these efforts earned much praise from the French; a program of compulsory anti-typhoid and anti-cholera vaccinations was established, this was less praised.[17]

The Crown Prince commandeered the Château des Tilleuls on the edge of town from its owner, Madame du Vernier. Château des Tilleuls, a relatively modest building with gracious grounds and nearby stables, was to be his home from September 1914 to February 1918. Nearby, housed in a school house, was Fifth Army headquarters. A correspondent from neutral Sweden who visited Stenay in late 1914 gained entrance. It was from this building that the battle of Verdun was planned and managed.

> The General Staff of the Chief Command of the Army was housed in an École de Garçons, which still contained relics of its former state, such as natural history pictures and maps, and a couple of school benches with the master's desk, above which could still be seen in black and white the golden rules: Ne vous vantez pas,* and Liberté, Égalité, Fraternité. How hollow and foolish did they not seem before the brutal reality now presiding over the world![18]

---

*Do not boast of yourself; Do not praise yourself.

The Kaiser visited Stenay a number of times and there was a constant stream of princes, generals and diplomats who were entertained at the château. Every morning the Crown Prince went riding for exercise and made a great effort to be gracious to the locals, frequently stopping to speak to children and distributing chocolates and coins. He was evidently well liked in Stenay even though the population had to remove their hats when he passed. He lived the life of a rich bachelor, being known as the rake of Stenay. His wife, Crown Princess Cecilie, made only one visit, and nearly did not survive her brief stay.

> In 1915, the Crown Princess paid me a two-days' visit in my headquarters at Stenay. At 4 o'clock in the morning of the second day, there began a French air attack manifestly aimed full at my house which, at the time, had no bomb-proof cellar or dugout. A direct hit would undoubtedly have meant thorough work. The attack lasted two hours. In that time, twenty-four aeroplanes dropped bombs around us and a hundred and sixty bombs were counted. Several of them landed only a few yards from the house and, unfortunately, claimed a number of victims. It was the severest air attack that I had ever experienced.[19]

That was probably the only time the Crown Prince was actually in harm's way during the entire war. In 1916, his vacation in Stenay ended; he now would put many hundreds of thousands in harm's way. He was ordered to attack Verdun.

Verdun 1916 became the Crown Prince's time of infamy; he earned a place in the history books as the butcher of Verdun, *Le Boucher de Verdun*. In truth, the Crown Prince always felt that the 1916 Verdun attack was unwise, and as the butchery grew, he became more opposed to the operation and used his influence in Berlin finally to bring it to a close.[20]

The Germans planned the attack originally to take place on the Kaiser's birthday, January 27. Although a nice family touch, the date turned out to be logistically impossible. The Crown Prince rescheduled the attack for February 12. Thousands of troops secretly came up to the German lines at night and assembled in huge underground shelters (*Stollen*) that had been especially built a couple of hundred yards behind the front line trenches. There they hid, unseen by the French who were unaware that an attack was imminent. Secrecy and surprise were key parts of the German plan. An artillery barrage would precede the troops who would leave the *Stollen* only after French defenses were pulverized. Observers in wicker baskets suspended from hydrogen-gas-filled balloons (*Drachen*) would be lofted near the German lines, allowing artillery observers a view deep into French-held territory. Success depended upon accurate artillery fire and that depended upon the weather,

Captive or tethered balloons functioned as the eyes of the artillery. The picture is of a German *Drachen* balloon with two artillery spotters in the basket who would communicate their observations via telephone to artillery batteries. Balloonists at times suffered from intense air sickness because the basket swung back and forth as the balloon responded to crosswinds (*Die Wochenschau* [Berlin: W. Girardet, 1916]).

Lighter-than-air hydrogen gas, a very flammable gas, gave captive (tethered) balloons their lift. Enemy fighter planes brought down balloons by either firing exploding rockets or incendiary machine gun bullets into the gas bag setting it afire. Harnessed to a primitive parachute stored in a cone-shaped hamper attached to the basket, balloonists had to jump quickly as the burning mass fell from the sky (*Die Wochenschau* [Berlin: W. Girardet, 1916]).

clear weather meant high visibility and accurate targeting. The Verdun attack would be opened by the most massive artillery bombardment of the war to date — everything depended upon accurate targeting.

Early morning February 12, the Crown Prince awakened to a white-out; a snowstorm blinded the artillery. The attack had to be postponed.

Early morning February 13, the snow continued to fall, no attack possible.

Ditto for February 14, 15, 16, 17, 18, 19 and 20. German troops patiently froze in their unheated, underground shelters, and the snow continued to fall.

> The preparations for the attack had quite escaped the notice of the French. The concentration of the artillery had not been interfered with in any way; the attacking infantry had suffered scarcely any losses in the initial assault. Everything had been brilliantly prepared. Then, on the eve of the day originally selected for the attack, storms of rain and snow set in which prevented every possibility of the artillery seeing their objective. From day to day the

attack had to be postponed, so that it actually took place 10 days later than originally planned. The Higher Command of the Fifth Army passed an agonizing time; for, as things stood, every hour lost meant a diminution of our prospects of speedy success. As a matter of fact, in that period of waiting, our purpose was betrayed by two miserable rascals of the Landwehr who deserted to the French.[21]

In spite of the German deserters, the French were caught completely off guard. On February 21, 1916, across a snow-covered landscape, the Germans finally unleashed the attack. More than a thousand artillery pieces erupted fire and steel. The French lines and support areas behind the lines literally disappeared; trench works exploded into open wounds, concrete bunkers were pulverized, *saps* collapsed, men were buried, were blown apart, disappeared; the forested landscape became deforested, tree trunks shattered, stumps blown skyward; the topography was continually remade as crater replaced crater; parts of men, trees, equipment were lofted into the air repeatedly as explosion followed explosion. Thousands and thousands of hot shell splinters, *les éclats*, scythed through the air, impaling trees, sand bags, bodies, ricocheting off concrete, or skidding harmlessly into the torn-up muddy snow, sizzling as they cooled. The bombardment lasted from early morning until four in the afternoon, nine hours, repeatedly plowing, harrowing, and raking the French lines with steel and explosive. The muted roar of explosions could be heard 90 miles (145 km) away in the mountains of the Alsace. At four o'clock, as the sun began to set in the west and shadows lengthened, the first troops emerged from their *Stollen* and probed slowly forward into the smoking battlefield—a battlefield that they rightly assumed to be lifeless. Nothing could have survived the bombardment.

> We ran forward, for to retreat was just as dangerous as to advance. We were caught between two fires: the German artillery firing before us and the French on the site which we had just left. At last we reached the first French trench. We thought we could take it easily, but we were wrong, for the few soldiers who were holding it fought desperately. In several places the wounded kept on fighting before they fell under our blows. Not a section surrendered; such were the orders given the small detachments and even isolated individuals. At last we were in possession of the trench, which had been completely ruined by the heavy German artillery. It was a frightful chaos of human wreckage. One heard groans which seemed to rise from the very bowels of the earth—the cries of unfortunates buried alive in their shelters.[22]

On the opposite side of the line the French, or what was left of the French, emerged from collapsed fortifications to meet the invaders—dazed, shell-shocked, and often suffering from wounds, they took cover with rifles and any still functional machine guns and began firing on the gray forms coming at them. In the Bois des Caures and the Bois le Comte the French were under the command of Lieutenant-Colonel Émile Driant, a man who was known to many Europeans as a writer of science fiction. His books were futuristic fantasies of war and warfare between France and England, or France and Germany; some of his sci-fi epics were translated into German, Turkish, Dutch, Polish and English. He was the Jules Verne of war for early twentieth century readers.

In the summer of 1915, as Driant inspected the French lines he was to command and defend, he realized they were as much a military fiction as his books! The defenses were abysmal: poorly constructed, badly sited, inadequately armed and undermanned. Driant did something unpardonable for a military officer; he wrote a letter outlining these inadequacies to the President of the Chamber of Deputies. Having once served as a Deputy, Driant knew the President. The President passed the letter to the Minister of War, who in turn passed it to Generalissimo Joffre, the French "supreme war lord." Joffre went ballistic at this serious breach of military discipline — an officer should never complain to politicians about things military! Joffre spent more energy on this "breach" than he would to shore up Verdun's defenses. He vowed to see that Driant's military career suffered, but Joffre never got his chance for vengeance; Driant was killed within the first 24 hours of the attack, confirming his letter's assessment of Verdun's defenses.

All along the front, the Germans won success after success. The French were overwhelmed; nothing seemed able to stop the German juggernaut. Even the Germans were surprised.

> That evening [February 24, four days into the attack] we held the whole of the enemy's position! Not only had his defensive system been broken asunder, but his morale had seriously suffered: he had nowhere been able to put up an effective resistance, and all his works, batteries and communications in his back areas as far as Verdun itself lay exposed to the effective and harassing fire of our artillery. We had now to set to work to bring the tottering edifice of his defense crashing to the ground before he could buttress it with the aid of the reserves now being hurried forward by lorry columns from Clermont.[23]

On 25 February, the fifth day into the attack, something even more astounding happened — less than a dozen men captured Fort Douaumont, supposedly the most impregnable fortress on the Western Front.

In one of the great miscalculations of the war, General Joffre, the then supreme commander of the French Army, decided that forts were obsolete and of no value, basing this conclusion on the poor performance of the Belgian forts in 1914. Joffre ordered the forts stripped of any movable guns, thus gutting the French Verdun defenses. The most impregnable of the forts, Douaumont, he manned, or rather undermanned, with the poorest of troops, less than 100 men, mostly old—the normal garrison should have been 500! These old codgers rattled around in the empty corridors of the vast structure totally insulated from the battle raging around them.

> Le stupide abandon de Douaumont, terrible en ses conséquences, demeure la colossale erreur de l'histoire militaire de la guerre de 1914–1918.[24]

Germans captured the fort late in the afternoon of February 25, 1916, without a shot being fired in its defense! Stories of Douaumont's capture have become the stuff of legend, a legend with variations.[25] The following is based on Alistair Horne's classic book on Verdun, *The Price of Glory*.[26] Three German soldiers, Sergeant Kunze and two of his men, squeezed in through an

German aerial photo of Fort Douaumont after its capture; the fort commands the highest point on the Verdun battlefield and fell into German hands four days into the battle. The pentagonal outline composed of counterscarp, dry moat and scarp has a maximum width of 400 meters (433 yds). The interior rectangular structures include barracks and artillery shelters. The zig-zag outline of a trench is visible outside the fort, and the pockmarks are shell craters (*Die Wochenschau* [Berlin: W. Girardet, 1916]).

unmanned gun embrasure and entered a gallery. Two men stayed behind, near the embrasure, intimidated by the cavernous dark gallery leading into the fort's interior. The intrepid Sergeant Kunze pushed on alone. After getting lost, he ran into some Frenchmen, whom he captured and locked up in a room; then discovering some food, and being very hungry, he sat down to eat before proceeding. During his repast, more Germans entered the fort: Lieutenant Radtke and his platoon got inside, then Captain Haupt and his men — they managed to capture the French Sergeant Major in charge of the fort. The next, and last, intruders were Oberleutnant von Brandis and his men. They met the other Germans wandering around in the fort, and Captain Haupt, the ranking officer, sent von Brandis back to report that the fort was in German hands. Von Brandis must have colored the story a bit because only he and Haupt were declared the conquerors of Fort Douaumont; both were awarded the *Pour le Mérite*, Germany's highest award, by the Kaiser. Von Brandis became a soldier celebrity and a good friend of the Crown Prince. Sergeant Kunze survived the war and entered the constabulary, receiving promotion to police inspector for his part in the fort's capture. Lieutenant Radtke, the first German officer to enter the fort, received a signed photograph of the Crown Prince, which he no doubt treasured.

The French response to the loss of the fort was disbelief followed by shock. Over the next 8 months, they would expend 100,000 men in its recapture.

On the day before Douaumont fell, the normally imperturbable Generalissimo Joffre roused sufficiently to realize that something important was happening at Verdun. He moved quickly, for him, having his Chief-of-Staff appoint General Pétain to take charge of Verdun with orders to stop the Germans at all cost. On the evening of February 24, Pétain's Aide-de-Camp Serrigny received a telegram to deliver to Pétain telling of his appointment. However, the general was nowhere to be found. Following a frantic search Serrigny finally traced his general to a room in the Hotel Terminus Nord in Paris. Approaching the door Serrigny noted the general's boots outside the door beside a pair of lady's slippers. Pétain evidently had other plans for the night. Serrigny tentatively knocked; after some time the door opened and a disheveled general stepped into the hall. There followed a hasty discussion and Serrigny was told to find himself a room and return in the morning.[27] Verdun could wait, there were more immediate matters to attend to.

Thus late in the evening on the fourth day of the Verdun attack, General Pétain's response to Joffre's order was to return to the warm bed of his lover, Mlle Eugénie Hardon, a woman 24 years his junior. Pétain, just one month shy of 60 years old, needed all his sleep. The next morning, after meeting Joffre — who believed that things were not going too badly at Verdun!— General Pétain and his Aid-de-Camp Serrigny traveled to Verdun; this was the same day Fort Douaumont fell. For the French, the blackest day in the entire war! Pétain arrived at Verdun very ill, having somehow caught double pneumonia.

Thus the French were off to a good start; an overly optimistic, some would say delusional, Commander-in-Chief, and a medically incapacitated field commander! Fortunately, for them, the German attack began to fizzle on its own. For the Crown Prince the taking of Douaumont was the pinnacle achievement, after that it was all downhill.

> The fatigue of our troops after a huge military performance and the lack of reserves despoiled us of the prize of victory. I bring no accusation; I merely record the fact.
>
> From that day onward, surprises were no longer possible; and the early, impetuous advances by storm gave place to a gigantic wrestle and struggle for every foot of ground. Within a few weeks, I perceived clearly that it would not be feasible to break through the stubborn defense, and that our own losses would ultimately be quite out of proportion to the gains.[28]

Upon arriving in the Verdun fortified zone, General Pétain established his headquarters in a building that housed the school and town hall in Souilly, a small village situated between Verdun and Bar-le-Duc. He had accommodation in a nearby house, and there he climbed into bed and from his sick bed issued orders taking charge of Verdun's defense. General Joffre's second in command, General de Castelnau, had ordered, naturally, that Fort Douaumont be immediately attacked and retaken. The attack occurred, and naturally failed. There was no second attempt. Pétain and his staff now set out to develop a strategic plan to stop the German onslaught and eventually to turn it. Thus, the easy German tactical victories in the first days of their offensive evolved into a brutal slugfest, which would last nearly a year and cost hundreds of thousands of lives, and of which, when it was over, no one could declare a victor. To paraphrase von Falkenhayn, now both the German and French armies would bleed to death. The resulting stalemate was not broken until the American Meuse-Argonne offensive in the fall of 1918.

Writing after the war General Erich Ludendorff recognized the mistake the Germans made in attacking Verdun.

> That offensive should have been broken off immediately it assumed the character of a battle of attrition. The gain no longer justified the losses.[29]

4

Motoring Along the Meuse

> Just before entering the gate of Verdun [Porte St. Paul] we passed a number of ambulances, some driven by the American volunteers. These young Americans have displayed splendid heroism in bringing in the wounded under difficult conditions. Many of them have been mentioned in dispatches, and received from France the *Croix de Guerre*.[1] — Kathleen Burke, 1916, Officier de l'Instruction Publique, France

On the same day the Germans attacked, the Field Service ambulance section based in Pont-à-Mousson started for Verdun. After ten hard months of service at Pont-à-Mousson, the Americans looked forward to a change of scene. On the morning of February 21, 1916, their convoy of 20 battle-scarred Model T's left the city. Because the Germans controlled the St. Mihiel Salient, the convoy detoured around the German lines and the occupied city of St. Mihiel; upstream of St. Mihiel the convoy crossed the Meuse River and headed west toward the city of Bar-le-Duc. Navigating dirt roads and farm lanes, and only cruising at 25 miles per hour on the best stretches of road, the convoy took most of a day to reach Bar-le-Duc where it spent the night before continuing to Verdun.

Bar-le-Duc played a critical role in the French defense of *la Région Fortifiée de Verdun* in 1916. Railroads were very important during the war, as they were the fastest and most effective means of moving troops, equipment, munitions and supplies to the front. Three railroad lines serviced *la Région Fortifiée de Verdun*: two normal gauge, 1.435 meter wide, and one narrow gauge, 1 meter wide. The normal gauge lines allowed larger engines and thus heavier freight loads. One of the normal gauge lines ran from the south along the Meuse River valley; the Germans cut this line when they captured the St. Mihiel Salient in 1914. The other normal gauge line came from the west, passing through Clermont-en-Argonne and then on to Verdun. German artillery observers on the Butte de Vauquois routinely targeted trains on this line, making it an insecure line. The only really secure line was a narrow gauge line from Bar-le-Duc to Verdun. Thus, even though normal gauge lines connected Bar-le-Duc with the rest of France, there remained a narrow gauge forty-mile bottleneck to reach Verdun. To circumvent the bottleneck, the French switched to motor transport. The dirt road connecting Bar-le-Duc and Verdun became the most crucial road in France; in fact, after the war it was named *La Voie Sacrée* to commemorate its importance in 1916. During the war, it was simply *La Route*. The American ambulances from Pont-à-Mousson joined the slow moving procession of trucks driving north toward the battle.

> The picture of the attack that will stay with me always is that of the Grande Route north from Bar-le-Duc, covered with snow and ice of the last days of February. The road was always filled with two columns of trucks, one going north and the other going south. The trucks, loaded with troops, shells, and bread, rolled and bobbed back and forth with the graceless, uncertain strength of baby elephants. It was almost impossible to steer them on the icy roads. Many of them fell by the wayside, overturned, burned up, or were left apparently unnoticed in the ceaseless tide of traffic that never seemed to hurry or to stop.[2]

Immediately recognizing the singular importance of *La Route* in the defense of Verdun, General Pétain established his headquarters in the village of Souilly, a small farming village that straddled the road about 13 miles south of Verdun. There, in the *mairie*, a building that housed the town offices and the village school, his small office was set up on the second floor; from his window he could watch and be reassured by the endless traffic.[3] Pétain and his staff organized a fleet of 3,500 trucks, which every week managed to transport 90,000 men and 50,000 tons of supplies from Bar-le Duc to Verdun. In addition to the trucks, perhaps 11,000 other motorized vehicles were employed for transport, including buses, large touring cars (*voitures de tourisme*), smaller automobiles (*voitures automobiles*) and ambulances, so that on the average one vehicle passed the headquarters at Souilly every 14 seconds, day and night. The endless traffic of heavy trucks soon turned *La Route* into La Swamp, the dirt road literally pulverized into tracks of deep mud-filled ruts. Road crews filled the ruts with gravel from nearby quarries opened for sources of stone; the crews were supplemented with German prisoners of war from a camp at Souilly. One prisoner, who later immigrated to the United States, left an account of life at Souilly in 1916.

> We were sent to the prison camp at Souilly, a former meadow but now a terrain of foot-deep mud, with tents for the prisoners and barracks for the

> guards. It was closed in by a double row of barbed wire, with machine guns
> mounted on high scaffolds.... The rations of bread and canned meat were
> too much for the dying and not enough for the living. This camp was called
> "camp de représailles de Verdun," and a very large poster in the compound,
> signed by the camp commander, stated frankly that this was meant to be a
> reprisal camp.[4]

When a vehicle broke down on *La Route*, it was pushed off the road. Nothing could be allowed to stop the flow. Repair shops positioned at intervals on the road dealt with the crippled vehicles, either fixing them or cannibalizing them for parts. Next to the road endless columns of men marched. There were always more men heading north to Verdun than there were marching south, for many marching north was a "one-way" trip.

> In this "hell of Verdun" even the bravest troops were simply incapable of
> maintaining for any length of time the high morale necessary for a successful
> offensive.... The Mill on the Meuse ground to powder the hearts as well as
> the bodies of the troops.[5]

The "Mill on the Meuse" was voracious, requiring an army of a half million men; an army that had to be fed, supplied with guns, munitions, and supplies, whose casualties had to be replaced, and whose wounded moved to hospitals. It was in the latter that American ambulances would play an important role; by the end of the battle in late summer of 1917, 38 ambulance sections (over 1,500 men) would have served in the Battle of Verdun.

Ambulance sections were usually billeted outside of Verdun because the city itself was too dangerous, with German shells (high explosive and incendiary) arriving at almost any time. When billeted in town, sections stayed at the Cercle Militaire, the Verdun military club. The club was just across the river from the hotel Coq Hardi where Edith Wharton stayed in 1915. However, the Cercle Militaire had changed considerably since Mrs. Wharton had last seen it.

> Our club at Verdun is certainly a snappy place: a big four-story building
> filled with banquet-halls, card rooms, a billiard-room, and a fencing-hall.
> The only trouble with it is that the roof has been blown off, and many of
> the rooms have been wrecked by high explosives. However, the lower floor is
> in pretty good condition and we use the fencing hall.[6]

To understand where these Americans worked and what they achieved, it is necessary to have at least an overview of the geography of the battlefield. Verdun is a small city on the Meuse River. As with many rivers in Europe, *e.g.*, the Seine and Rhine, the Meuse flows from south to north. Verdun is on the west or left bank when one faces north toward the river's mouth. Along the east or right bank, a range of steep hills known as the Heights of the Meuse parallels the river. North of Verdun on the left bank, another range of hills runs west to east, from the Butte de Vauquois to the Meuse River. The Battle of Verdun essentially takes place in the Heights of the Meuse on the right bank and in the west/east hills on the left bank, never actually reaching the city of Verdun, although German long-range artillery shelled the city throughout the conflict. Initially the Germans attacked on February 21, 1916, on the right bank through the Heights of the Meuse. Then, a couple of weeks later (March 6), the Germans extended their attack to the west/east hills of the left bank, spreading the battle to both sides of the river. The first *postes de secours* serviced by the American Ambulance Field Service were on the right bank in the Heights of the Meuse.

To reach the right bank *postes,* the ambulances left Verdun in the darkness of night, passed through a medieval gate known as the Porte Chausée, crossed over the Meuse on a bridge nearly always under German artillery fire but remarkably never hit, and traversed a Verdun suburb on the right bank known as the Faubourg Pavé before the road began its climb into the Heights of the Meuse. In the distance, flashes from artillery batteries silhouetted the hills against the eastern sky; the impacts of in-coming shells sent up billowing

The last days of a Model T ambulance; because Model T's had interchangeable parts, terminally damaged cars were cannibalized to repair those less damaged (courtesy the Archives of the American Field Service and AFS Intercultural Programs).

fountains of dirt and smoke, followed by concussions of explosions; and always in the background, the grind of over-heated motors. Convoys slowly climbed the dirt road to re-supply the battle, traveling at night without lights to evade German gunners.

> We get the car and start off down the road with no lights anywhere, and pray that everything coming our way keeps to its side of the road and goes slowly. There is always something coming the other way — and your way, a steady succession of camions [large trucks] in the centre of the road, and of artillery trains on the side. The camions are mostly very heavy and very powerful, and have no compunction at all about what they run into, as they know it cannot harm them. The ammunition trains consist of batteries of 75's, little framework teams with torpilles [shells] fitted in small compartments like eggs, and other such vehicles in tow of a number of mules, with the driver invariably asleep. The traffic, however, in spite of the pitch darkness, would be endurable if it were not for the mud which often comes up to the hubs. It is a slimy mud, and if spread thinly is extremely slippery. On the roads it is rarely spread thinly, and when one gets out to push he often sinks up to the knee. Then of course there is always the whine of arrivées [in coming shells] and départs [out going shells] passing overhead, and the occasional crump of a German 77 or 150 landing near at hand.[7]

The most dangerous of the *postes de secours* was in the heart of the battlefield in the ruins of an obsolete fort, *Le Fort de Tavannes*, constructed between 1874 and 1880 as part of the ring of forts guarding the hills on the right bank. The outer line of forts, those closest to the German lines in 1914, included Forts Douaumont and Vaux as well as smaller fortifications. Fort Tavannes was part of the second line of defenses and its construction was nowhere near as robust as the concrete forts Douaumant and Vaux. Although originally built of stone blocks, Tavannes added several concrete *abris* (shell-proof bunkers) as reinforcements during the last decade of the nineteenth century. When the battle of Verdun began, Tavannes had only machine guns for defense, no artillery.

After the Germans captured Fort Douaumont on February 25, 1916, their next objective was Fort Vaux, south of Douaumont. In early March, the fighting spread in that direction, but the Germans would not succeed in attaining their objectives until June. For the French it was a fighting retreat; they slowly lost ground, falling back toward their secondary line of fortifications, which included Fort Tavannes. Tavannes now became a very important *poste de secours*. French stretcher bearers, *brancardiers*, brought the wounded here where American *ambulanciers* picked them up for the drive to hospitals near and in Verdun. Naturally Tavannes became a target for German artillery; in the course of the battle approximately 40,000 shells pummeled the fort, including 420 mm monsters fired by Big-Bertha mortars. The fort slowly disintegrated, leaving almost nothing recognizable above ground. The nearly constant shelling made the trip to the fort a perilous journey.

> We mount gradually into the hills toward Fort Tavannes and, reaching a hillcrest, turn from the main northeast road, directly north along a narrow artillery road which runs two or three kilometers through a shell-swept wood to the huge fort. These last two kilometers are the most dangerous....
>
> Words cannot describe the desolation of the woods around Tavannes. The tree trunks are bare and often shattered.... The road itself is little more than a succession of shell holes that are made during the night and filled up with crushed stone during the day while the firing is not so heavy. Dead horses and mules lie and rot by the roadside where they fell. Here and there are wrecks of ambulances and motor cars, torn by shell fragments, sprayed with shrapnel.... The frontline trenches are in earshot over the next valley, and the German artillery is on the next northerly range of hills. The German observation balloons, or *saucisses*, can see our little cars as they climb for the last five hundred metres toward the shelter of the fort, but whether their guns are firing directly and intentionally on us or whether it is all simply the systematic bombardment of the fort and road we will probably never know.
>
> The *poste de secours* is in the subterranean shell-proof caves of the fort, and our cars enter the shelter of one of the tunnels in the fort, remaining in this shelter while they are being loaded.[8]

On June 20, 1916, a German 380 mm mortar sent a high explosive shell onto the fort's entrance tunnel; the explosion collapsed the tunnel, burying wounded and stretcher bearers. Four American drivers were in the fort at the time and only escaped by a miracle. The concussive shock shattered the windows and woodwork of their cars. Fort Tavannes became untenable as a *poste de secours* once the Germans had its range and began shelling it mercilessly. The fort was abandoned as a *poste;* the Americans were relieved not to return. It was not remembered fondly.

> the underground, vaulted tunnels of that fort composed a chamber of horrors which we remember in our dreams. The floors were mud, the ceiling slimy, dripping stone. The light was scant, the wounded were so numerous that we had to step over their prostrate bodies. The stench was terrible.[9]

The French established their new *poste de secours* three kilometers away from Fort Tavannes in a supposedly safer situation, in a ruined house known as the Cabaret Rouge. French artillery batteries surrounded the house. The place became a nightmare with French salvos leaving and German ones arriving almost constantly.

The Cabaret Rouge became our regular *poste de secours*. The picturesque name of the place has a diabolical fitness....

You are asleep in the straw, perhaps dreaming of home. Toward midnight you are awakened by a hand on your shoulder, and a whispered voice says: "We are going to the Cabaret tonight — the Cabaret Rouge."

If hell has its theatres and cabarets, the devil will do well to pattern his entertainments from the spectacle we see nightly at this one. The house is halfway up the slope in a valley. Behind it, in front of it, on all sides of it are the French batteries. The German shells are bursting in the fields around, while our own guns flash and thunder incessantly.... Down from the trenches, along the winding boyous, come the stretcher-bearers with their crimson burdens. They are deposited on the straw, re-bandaged, given a drink of water or cold tea, and loaded into our cars — sometimes groaning, sometimes shrieking, sometimes silent. The wall of the house, with a shell-hole through it big enough for five men to stand in, looms dirty red amid the flashes of artillery. Red Cabaret, red rockets, red fire, red blood.[10]

While at the Cabaret the Germans began shelling the series of batteries which were along the road. Some twenty huge (at least, they seemed huge to us) shells fell around us. This was the heaviest shell-fire I have yet been under, and I sure was glad to have something to do to keep my mind off it. Two men about one hundred yards away were decapitated and there were a number of dead horses about. I can see we are going to have a lively time.[11]

While his men were having a "lively time" in Verdun, A. Piatt Andrew was having a "lively time" fighting bureaucrats at the American Military Hospital in Neuilly outside Paris. The A.A.F.S., with its very successful fundraising efforts, became a financial resource or "cash-cow" for the hospital since the hospital administration controlled all funds raised. In America, because of Andrew's publicity campaign extolling the exploits of his drivers, the organization stole the limelight and became better known than the hospital. The child had essentially gotten bigger than the parent, and, people being people, this resulted in petty jealousy and acrimony. Andrew had particular problems with the hospital's transportation committee (especially with one member, George Washington Loop) regarding funds for the upkeep and repairs of his cars. Mr. Loop was also having a "lively time"; his wife was involved in a series of extramarital affairs that the Paris newspapers reported "in lascivious detail."[12] Then an even more juicy scandal erupted when papers reported that Mr. Loop had beaten not only his wife but also his stepdaughter and, because of his pugilistic proclivities, Mrs. Loop had sued him for divorce. Incidentally, Mrs. Loop's soubriquet was "Lady Nicotine" because of the millions of cigarettes she had imported for the French Army. Her stepdaughter, with head swathed in white bandages, married soon after her beating; her groom was a

A burning Model T ambulance after a lucky hit by a German artillery shell; the ambulances often got too close to the fighting and suffered the consequences (*History of the American Field Service in France* [Boston and New York: Houghton Mifflin, 1920, Volume 1]).

papal knight who ran a motion picture company in California. Perhaps only in war time Paris could such linkages be possible. The American community in Paris was all a twitter with gossip after the "sensational midnight punch-up" and subsequent divorce and marriage, a nice diversion from the war! The hospital removed Loop from the loop and in the ensuing administrative turmoil, Andrew was able to cut the Field Service free. In July 1916, it became an independent organization with its own treasurer, with a new base of operations in Paris and a new name. It became the American Field Service.[13] The A.F.S. would have a long life, being very probably the only American relief organization founded during the First World War still in existence.[14] However, to return to Verdun.

In addition to the *postes de secours* at Fort Tavannes and the Cabaret Rouge in the Heights of the Meuse east of Verdun, A.F.S. ambulances picked up wounded north of the city in the Meuse River village of Bras on the right bank. Mrs. Wharton's party may have visited Bras during her stay in Verdun in 1915, but she identified it only as a village north of Verdun.

> The dreary muddy village was crammed with troops, and the ambulance* had been installed at haphazard in such houses as the military could spare. Arrangements were primitive but clean.[15]

By the summer of 1916, conditions at Bras had deteriorated considerably. Bras is situated about five miles down river from Verdun. The Heights of the Meuse north and east of this forlorn village saw some of the bloodiest fighting that summer. Dazed wounded were carried, walked or literally crawled down the slopes seeking help in what was left of Bras. The very large French military cemetery sited in the village attested that many did not survive.

> Bras is simply a ruined village. At one spot just off the field of battle is a sort of first-aid station to which the stretcher-bearers carry the wounded from the field. If anything can be done to ease temporarily their suffering, they are taken at once down into the cellar and treated. It is there that we are to get our blessés, and from there we are to take them back to Verdun. Every trip from Bras to Verdun has to be made between the hours of 9 P.M. and 2 A.M. No traffic goes over that road in daylight.[16]

The drive to and from Bras was exceedingly dangerous. Nearly every run was a gamble with the Grim Reaper. An anonymous American writing to his uncle back home caught the action and pace of the five-mile drive so graphically, he asked his uncle not to share the letter with his dad, as it would worry him — so his uncle published it!

> Dear Uncle:
> Second night — Most traces of gas gone; heavy firing and lots of blessés. Big detour on account of shelling of grenade factory. Houses and debris burning all along the road from shells. Thunder-storm; impossible to see on account of lightning. Artillery [horse-drawn limbers and caissons] crashing along road at you at full gallop to get by shelling places on the road. Terrible driving. Got to post on second trip; rear wheel completely entangled in barbed wire; tire blown out; no wire cutters; got some from next car; cleared wire (shells going overhead). In act of slipping on new tire; heard a whistle close; slid head and shoulders under car; shell went off right in center of place; my back and legs covered with rocks and stone; corner torn off car; full of shrapnel holes, which I discovered next day. Continuing on tire; another close; French lieutenant made me come into abris; another close; cries of blessés, wounded in my car. Did not know they had been loaded till then. Felt like a cad leaving them, so got out and continued on tire, slipping

*military hospital

under each shell; none awfully close. Could not get blessés to come out and take last place in car, standing 10 feet away between two brancardiers [stretcher bearers]; another close whistle coming, dove under car; shell went off; brancardier dead; other wounded; myself OK except slight scrape on nose from flying rock or shrapnel. Dragged brancardiers into abris, twisting knee a bit in doing this. Waited for next shell, after which dragged blessé into car and got started. Got half down street; time for another shell. Road blocked by three ambulances abreast; drivers sheltered behind doorway. Big shell hole one side; other busted wagon. Put on full speed; smashed glancingly into one; charged my way through; shell went off just then in back of me. Blew out both tires; hit blessé in car, who let out most blood-curdling cries I ever heard; found piece of shrapnel next morning in hair of cushion at my back; had come from rear.

Full speed on rims only; road full of artillery, supply wagons, etc. Back OK.... Car, of course, sensation; looked like a butcher shop inside. All men lived, but floor simply slippery with gore.[17]

In his book *The Vanguard of American Volunteers* Edwin W. Morse solved the mystery of the anonymous American[18]; he is Walter H. Wheeler of the American Field Service, Section 3. In a special preface to the published letter, the editor of *Red Cross Magazine* gushed: "Now for a dash into the black, reeking, maddening, brobdingnagian battle of the ages with this Harvard lad in a shell-battered ambulance and to learn of his reward. You'll be proud of him and of all like him."

Here is Wheeler in action again on the very dangerous run between Verdun and the *poste de secours* at Bras.

Fifth night—Got to post OK. Heavy traffic; firing; road stinking of flesh. On way back heard forlorn cry of Barber. Stopped and found him in arms of Frenchman by side of road. Nerves gone, so he couldn't talk straight. Car been hit; he was wounded; pumping hell out of road ahead where his car was. He had crawled back; was afraid to let him wait. Dragged him back into front alongside of me and made a dash; never drove so fast in my life. Passed his car; whole back shot off and wheels gone. Got to last bridge and found artillery coming across in opposite direction. Crawled across one side on the remains of a railroad track. Grabbed leading horses of a battery by bridle and jammed them over on the side of road, commanding riders to wait; must have thought I was officer, because they did; hurried back and drove across. Got to headquarters OK and got Barber into dressing-room.

William M. Barber, Oberlin undergrad and member of the American Field Service, underwent a couple of operations, one of which removed a small fragment of his Ford's radiator from his back; he survived—his Ford did not!

For what they did during those dreadful nights at Verdun, Section 3 received a French Army citation, Wheeler and three others received the *Croix de Guerre*, Barber the *Croix de Guerre avec Palme* and *Médaille Militaire*.

Ironically, after a night out ferrying wounded, the Americans viewed the actual city of Verdun as a safe haven.

> and then at last I reached Verdun. Poor, shell-riddled Verdun! One comes back to its streets of echoing ruins with a feeling of homecoming, of safety, and of relief inexpressible. As I refilled my boiling radiator and changed a clogged spark plug, three large-caliber shells passed overhead into the upper town, but whether rightly or wrongly one feels protected there — too small in the size of the whole city to be struck.[19]

Often the ambulances that returned to Verdun to refit were "shot full of shrapnel holes." In the First World War shrapnel referred to a specially designed artillery shell that exploded while in the air and released a hail of shrapnel bullets, lead balls about a half inch in diameter. Lieutenant Henry Shrapnel originally invented the shell type in 1784 for the British Army. A German (77 mm) or French (75 mm) shrapnel shell was loaded with approximately 300 lead balls, fired from a normal field gun and timed to detonate over the target. The nose cone blew off and a secondary charge at the base of the shell exploded, firing the lead balls from the mouth of the shell as it flew. Essentially, it was a steel flying shotgun shell about three inches in diameter and a foot long, firing large buckshot at its target. At about 3,500 yards, the cone-shaped hail of lead balls could cover around an acre and a half of battlefield. Shrapnel was very effective against infantry in the open and road traffic behind the lines: horses hauling artillery batteries, mules pulling wagons and, of course, canvas-sided ambulances. At Verdun a young American witnessed just what French 75 mm field guns firing shrapnel could do to a massed attack; the carnage was Napoleonic.

> I shall never be able adequately to describe the sight. Masses of Boches[20] surge forward in counter attack; closer and closer they drew toward the French positions until there was an earth-rending crash and forty sheets of flame from the mouths of cannon beside me.
>
> I was too stupefied to realize what had taken place for a moment, but soon regained control of myself. The guns never stopped a second. Each piece was throwing shrapnel at the rate of twenty-two to twenty-five shots a minute into the oncoming ranks. We could observe quite clearly the shells landing among them and over them, and with each explosion could see gaps torn in their lines and men mowed down like so many weeds. Finally they faltered, and the next instant fell back in disorder to the positions they had left. The ground was literally strewn with their dead when the cannon ceased.[21]

Shrapnel was useless against fortified positions, ruins of stone houses or trenches; for those kinds of targets high explosive shells were used, creating craters and blowing apart ambulances.

> The difference between shrapnel and high explosive is the difference between a shot-gun and an elephant rifle. The high-explosive shell, which is considerably stronger than shrapnel, contains no bullets but a charge of high explosive. The effect of the high explosive is more concentrated than that of shrapnel, covering only one-fifteenth of the area affected by the latter. Though shrapnel has practically no effect on barbed-wire entanglements or on concrete, and very little on earthworks, high-explosive shells of the same caliber destroy everything in the vicinity, concrete, wire entanglements, steel shields, guns, and even the trenches themselves disappearing. The men holding the trenches are driven into their dugouts, and may be reached even there by high-explosive shells fired from high-angle howitzers.[22]

It was not just the blast effects of high-explosive shells that killed; the resulting *les éclats* or shell fragments could be even more deadly. When a shell exploded, the thick steel case ripped apart into sharp hot fragments that were flung into the air. A storm of steel became airborne surrounding the point of the shell's impact, and depending upon the shell's caliber, the fragments ranged from razor-blade-sized to double-bitted axe heads or even larger. These deadly fragments punctured flesh and cleaved bone. The fragments (*éclats*) lofted 360 degrees around the shell's point of explosion and could strike men or vehicles hundreds of feet away.

> I saw three shells burst within seventy-five meters of the road, one piece of éclat passing through the car body.[23]

High explosive shells landing either in front of or behind could still kill or wound. This was in contrast to shrapnel, which was unidirectional; the target had to be within the cone of fired bullets to be hit, therefore hiding in the lee of a stone wall meant safety. Troops were often cavalier about seeking protection from shrapnel shells, but this was not the case for high-explosive shells, which were greatly feared. *Les éclats* are thought to have resulted in more casualties than machine gun fire in the First World War.

> As I went out to bring in my car a vague procession appeared up the side lane, a score or so dim figures in gray each pushing a two-wheeled canvas cradle, and I stopped close to ask if they had the wounded.
>
> *Non, ceux sont les morts* (No, these are the dead) answered one. Poor, broken, swaying things in their huddle of bloody rags, how far they seemed from the thrill of martial music![24]

5

Crossing the River, Too Late

> In the presence of the Chief of Staff of the Field Armies we once again took up the question of assuming the offensive on the western bank. This of course seemed to us all the more necessary, on account of the extremely serious affect of the flanking fire from the Marre ridge against our troops on the eastern bank. — Crown Prince William[1]

The initial German attack on February 21 occurred only on the right bank of the Meuse. The Crown Prince agitated during the attack's planning for his army to assault the left bank simultaneously. However, Berlin, through the Kaiser's appointed tutor/controller, Lieutenant-General Schmidt von Knobelsdorf, said *nein*. This denial turned out to be a colossal mistake, a mistake that probably cost the Germans their victory at Verdun. Within days of the February 21 attack, the French under Pétain established artillery batteries on hills on the left bank, just across the Meuse from where the Germans were attacking on the right bank. One of the hills, aptly named *Le Mort Homme,* commanded the German right bank positions. From here, French gunners rained shells down on the hapless Germans; it was a turkey shoot. Realizing their blunder, the powers in Berlin changed the order, *nein* became *ja* — the delayed left bank attack commenced March 6, but, as the Crown Prince lamented, in a heavy, driving snowstorm. Now the Germans no longer had the element of surprise.

The left bank/right bank battles of Verdun can be a bit confusing, so it is perhaps best to repeat some Verdun geography: the Meuse has a north-south orientation with its waters ultimately debouching into the North Sea. Thus if one faces toward the river's mouth, the Meuse right bank is the east bank and the left bank is the west bank. A year before Verdun, in the beginning of 1915, the Germans had already established their trench lines on the left bank, but they were north of *Le Mort Homme*, north of the hills from which French gunners were enfilading German positions on the right bank in 1916.

A German attack on Mort Homme; note the absence of rifles. The men throw hand grenades with a flame thrower in support as they charge the French lines (*Die Wochenschau* [Berlin: W. Girardet, 1916]).

The goal of the German left bank attack was to capture *Le Mort Homme* and its neighboring hills; the attacks came, and there were many, from left bank German trench lines. The path from those trenches to *Le Mort Homme* would become a German *Via Dolorosa*, a path of sorrows, but it was a path traversed only by following the rules of the children's game of umbrella steps — for every two steps forward you had to take one backward.

The following pattern characterized the fighting for months: first German artillery pummeled French trenches, then the Germans would rush up to occupy the destroyed trenches driving the French out, then the French artillery would pulverize what was left of the trenches and their German occupants, then French troops would drive out the Germans and now occupy shell holes where the trenches had been. In a few days, the cycle repeated. American newspapers of the time recorded these seemingly endless cycles of loss and capture in this very small sector of the Western Front. Press reports from Paris never mentioned the French losses, stressing only how the Germans were being driven back; those from Berlin also omitted losses, and, as you would expect, praised the heroic German gains. An American reporter witnessed the Red Cross trains arriving in Potsdam, southwest of Berlin, in the bloody summer of 1916.

> One of the trains had just stopped. The square was blocked with vehicles of every description. I was surprised to find the great German furniture vans, which by comparison with those used in England and the United States look almost like houses on wheels, were drawn up in rows with military precision. As if these were not enough, the whole of the wheeled traffic of Potsdam seemed to be commandeered by the military for the lightly wounded — cabs, tradesmen's wagons, private carriages — everything on wheels except, of course, motor-cars, which are non-existent owing to the rubber shortage. Endless tiers of stretchers lay along the low embankment sloping up to the line. Doctors, nurses, and bearers were waiting in quiet readiness.[2]
>
> Of the great crush of wounded at Potsdam I doubt whether any appreciable portion of the serious cases will return to anything except permanent invalidism. They are suffering from shell wounds, not shrapnel, for the most part, I gather.[3]

The reporter soon learned the purpose of the mammoth furniture vans; they were to hide the seriously wounded.

> Then it was, I realized that these vans are part of Germany's plans by which her wounded are carried — I will not say secretly, but as unobtrusively as possible. In some of the mammoths were put twelve, into others fourteen; others held as many as twenty.[4]

Germany, of course, was not the only country hiding her seriously wounded, minimizing the human cost of war — they all were, and still do.

Most American newspapers really could not say who was winning the blood bath, although they usually favored the French. In spite of all the "to and fro" movements, the Germans did more "to" than "fro" and consequently, but at great human cost, they slowly advanced. The Germans were winning. But first they had to detour. Where the French artillery on *Le Mort Homme* had played havoc on the Germans attacking on the right bank, the French artillery on a nearby left bank hill known as Côte 304 was doing the same to the German attacks on the slopes of *Le Mort Homme*. Thus the infinite regress of the First World War, seemingly anywhere you attacked, there was nearly always a position from which the enemy could direct enfilading fire. To attack the right bank successfully, you had to attack *Le Mort Homme* but to attack *Le Mort Homme* successfully, you had to attack Côte 304.

Côte 304 is a hill on the left bank just to the west of the *Le Mort Homme*. The nomenclature of French hills around Verdun follows two patterns: if a hill has no name it is referred to by its height, thus Côte 304 takes its name from the fact that it is 304 meters above sea level; if a high point has a name, it is used, thus *Le Mort Homme*, a name that predates the war. *Le Mort Homme* also appeared on maps as Côte 295 — at least on some maps.

During the war, there was considerable confusion over what hill was where. A *New York Times* article ominously titled "Mystery of the Dead Man" (May 26, 1916) tried to sort out the mess for its readers. When the German command first announced it had captured *Le Mort Homme* on March 16, which the French vigorously denied, they had actually captured Côte 265, a hill labeled on German maps as *Le Mort Homme,* but not on French maps. A couple of months later, May 24, 1916, the Germans captured Côte 295, a hill labeled *Le Mort Homme* on French maps but not on theirs! Therefore, for the French *Le Mort Homme* finally fell on May 24 but for the Germans it first fell around two months earlier.

Wherever the fighting occurred and whatever its name, the French established two main *postes de secours* in villages south of the disputed hills; it was these aid stations French and even German wounded struggled to reach, either walking if they could or carried on a stretcher, to be picked up by ambulances. The villages, or rather their shell-shattered ruins, were Esnes and Marre. The wounded from Côte 304 went to Esnes and those from Mort Homme, to Marre. The American Field Service ambulances made runs to both *postes.*

> Esnes itself was absolutely in ruins, with débris littered about every where. The remains of the church were especially impressive on moonlight nights, and from it led a sort of broken road to the ruins of what had once been a château, in whose cellar was the *poste de secours.*[5]

Behind the Esnes château, there was a battery of 90 mm howitzers firing upon German positions on Côte 304. German counter-battery fire, trying for the howitzers, first set fire to the château and then methodically blasted apart its walls. As the walls slowly collapsed inward, the ever-growing thickness of fallen masonry gave more and more safety to the *poste de secours* in the cellar. Of course, ambulances sometimes had to run a gauntlet of shell fire before reaching that safety.

The Marre *poste de secours* was much more dangerous than Esnes, being very exposed and only 600 yards from the German first line in the ruins of a railroad station. In addition to regular artillery bombardment, the Germans often raked it with volleys of machine gun and rifle fire. Reaching Marre was best done under the cover of darkness. The Field Service suffered its first Verdun death at Marre. It was ten o'clock in the evening of September 23, 1916; a stray artillery shell exploded near a Model T as it slowly made its way into the village. Red hot shell fragments (*éclats*) ripped through the front of the car. One American, Roswell Sanders, the driver, was hit; two fragments cut his neck and cheek and a third entered his mouth, breaking teeth, and lodged in his skull. Remarkably, trepanned twice and after many months in hospital,

Edward Kelley behind the wheel of a Model T ambulance; Kelley perished on his first run to a *poste de secours* near Mort Homme on the evening of September 23, 1916, when a German artillery shell exploded near his car (courtesy the Archives of the American Field Service and AFS Intercultural Programs).

he lived, although disfigured. The other American, Edward Kelley, was less fortunate; he was killed. He had only recently joined the section and this trip was to show him the roads. He was so new that most men in his section did not know his first name. After the war, Sanders wrote of that fateful day.

> On the night of September 23, 1916, I took Edward E. Kelley, of Philadelphia, to show him the road to the village of Marre. We had dinner at about six o'clock, and it was just getting dusk as we left the village of Ippécourt, which was then our base. Kelley asked me what he should take, and I told him his gas-mask and steel helmet. In his hand he had a bottle of jam which we were to share with the brancardiers when we arrived in the village of Marre. Arriving at Fromeréville, we talked with the officers until it was dark enough for us to go to the front. Coming out, I decided to go slowly so as to give Kelley a good idea of the road. As we neared the village of Marre, two shells landed about 150 or 200 yards away from us, and I turned to Kelley and said, "As these are the first shells you have seen, they sound pretty good, don't they?" and he answered, "Yes, if they don't come too close." Not more than twenty minutes later, when we were in the village, a shell landed directly in front of the car — not more than three feet away. My first thought was, as I regained consciousness, to ask myself if Kelley was alive. I put my arm around him and tried to speak, but was unable to make any sound. Perceiving that Kelley was still unconscious, and knowing that if I should make

any noise the Germans would play the machine gun on us, I stepped over Kelley, got out of my car — both my eyes were closed — and started to crawl.[6]

Sanders crawled away from the ambulance, blind, into a barbed-wire entanglement. He called out, a German machine gun answered. After a few minutes, two Frenchmen dragged him, his strength ebbing, into the safety of the *poste de secours*. Later he was taken to the American military hospital at Neuilly.

Kelly's funeral was in the village church of Blercourt, not far from Marre, with American drivers and high French officers in attendance. The mood was very somber; Andrew was seen to be crying. Kelly was buried on a hillside overlooking the village.

> Then each of us tossed some earth onto the coffin in its resting-place and turned away, eyes dry, throats queerly tight — turned away, back to the scurrying tasks of the day's service.[7]

The funeral was not the first time the Blercourt church had distinguished American visitors. Edith Wharton's party stopped there in 1915. They were driving from Clerrmont-en-Argonne to Verdun delivering medical supplies when a Red Cross flag over a house caught their attention.

> The house was little more than a hovel, the village — Blercourt it was called — a mere hamlet of scattered cottages and cow-stables: a place so easily overlooked that it seemed our supplies might be needed there.[8]

Wharton was invited to see the church, which was then serving as a ward. Rows of wooden cots filled the nave, in each a seriously wounded soldier covered with a brown blanket. She attended Catholic vespers that afternoon.

> It was a sunless afternoon, and the picture was all in monastic shades of black and white and ashen grey: the sick under their earth-coloured blankets, their livid faces against the pillows, the black dresses of the women (they all seemed to be in mourning) and the silver haze floating out from the little acolyte's censer.[9]

She was struck that throughout the service the soldiers never moved.

> but the bodies in the cots never stirred, and more and more, as the day faded, the church looked like a quiet grave-yard in a battle-field.[10]

In the fall of 1916, an A.F.S. ambulance section was ordered from Verdun to the Argonne Forest to move wounded from *postes de secours* in that sector. On a free day, a driver visited a nearby village, Clermont-en-Argonne. Thus, the A.F.S. again crossed paths, so to speak, with Mrs. Wharton's earlier Lorraine tour. The village Mrs. Wharton visited in 1915 was already very much changed.

> October 1, 1916. Clermont en Argonne is beautiful in its desolation and nature is already busy covering the ruins with ivy and other creepers. Now the ruins are toned down and the autumn foliage is very beautiful. By the time the ubiquitous American tourist comes camera-snapping and souvenir-hunting, however, nature will have hidden much of the harsh starkness still to be seen. The handsome church on the top of the hill, reached by a long flight of some hundred or more wide stone steps, is completely gutted; and the fine stucco work and stained-glass windows litter the floor. From there we could easily see the lines five miles away and the shells still bursting.[11]

On October 24, 1916, the French recaptured Fort Douaumont. The fort that they earlier believed not worth defending was won back at a horrific cost — 100,000 casualties.[12] A French officer described the still smoking ruins:

> All approaches are badly battered and comprise a series of holes of various dimensions. One can clearly make out the site of ditches whose sides and bottom are in shocking condition; the masonry has almost entirely collapsed, the slopes are destroyed, and the grating of the escarp no longer exist. The wire network is demolished. Some blocks of concrete are still to be found, with fragments of iron stakes, these having formed part of the battlements. The premises of the entrance to the fort have been destroyed.... The facade of the concreted rooms, which were in ordinary masonry of 2.5 feet in thickness, has been very severely damaged.
> All the basement rooms are in perfect condition, except the last one to the east, in which was a store of bombs that has been blown up. Possibly this explosion dates back to the early days of the German occupation; all the prisoners state that the explosion of a store of bombs in the interior of the fort claimed numerous victims.[13]

On May 8, 1916, an enormous explosion roared through this part of the fort, killing 700 German soldiers. The fort had been crowded that day with men seeking refuge from the fighting around it; someone heating coffee or food ignited flame thrower fuel near where hand grenades and artillery shells were stored. The resulting explosions, confined in galleries packed with men, burned many beyond recognition. The Germans decided to wall up that part of the fort and leave the dead where they died. No longer viewed as a safe refuge, Douaumont became a mausoleum. The interior reeked of death; cadaverine seemed to have permeated into the stone. Visitors were always conscious of a sickly smell.

The Germans had made improvements to Fort Douaumont during their eight-month tenure: they had installed electric lights, replacing the French oil lamps; put in new radio and telephone communications, which were still functional; and they left the French a small surprise, a German cat.

> What was once the German headquarters, a fine room lighted by several electric globes, now houses the garrison commandant. On his writing-desk, a fat grey tom-cat is sleeping.
> "He is German," says the Major, "but we have naturalized him." And indeed he wears a tricolor ribbon around his neck.[14]

By the end of 1916, what was known as the Battle of Verdun was formally concluded; although fighting in the sector continued throughout 1917, reaching a peak with the French right bank attacks that summer, much of the left bank territory captured by the Germans in 1916 would only be recovered during the American Meuse-Argonne battle in 1918.

The American Field Service recruited heavily in 1917, with new volunteers boarding ships for France throughout the spring and early summer. Enlistment surged after America entered the war on April 6, 1917.[15] Many of these idealistic Americans would see action in Verdun. They evidently all kept diaries, or at least started to.

> I only kept a diary for a few days. I found that everyone was keeping a diary. One day on deck I heard a man reading a page of his to an acquaintance and I heard him remark with a show of pride that the other fellows in his stateroom were keeping their diaries by copying his. I heard him read: "Arose at seven o'clock, took a bath at seven-fifteen; had breakfast at eight, on deck at eight thirty, sea choppy." And I thought to myself as I moved about the deck: "What an inspiring document to leave to one's descendants."[16]

Philip Rice boarded the French liner *Chicago* in New York on May 19, 1917, bound for France. On board, he valiantly, but unsuccessfully, attempted to strike up an acquaintance with a certain Miss Katherine G____, who had caught his eye. But alas, she was being courted by two dashing aviators.[17] He tried his luck with another mademoiselle, with similar result.

> At another table was a young French girl surrounded by admiring men. She was vivacious, possessed of a high color and beautiful teeth — even if she did smoke cigarettes.[18]

What is known of him suggests a man with a droll sense of humor. After the war, he was asked to fill out a biographical questionnaire by his alma mater (presumptive class of 1901) describing his academic and war activities; the form instructed alumni not to be modest.[19] Rice began his essay, "Flunked out of Princeton at end of first term. It served me right. I am glad I went to Princeton. I went to work. I did not like it. Went to war, I am glad I went.

An American Field Service poster sure to catch the attention of young men on college campuses; a fetching maiden draped in a diaphanous American flag keeps death at bay while saving the wounded (Library of Congress).

I liked France, but did not like the war." After his very brief academic career, Rice tried to enlist in the U.S. Army in 1898 during the Spanish American War but failed the physical because of a bad heart. He worked at the job he did not like until 1917 when he joined the A.F.S. He was 40 years old at the time, a bit pudgy and certainly mentally and physically unprepared for the chaos he would soon be entering. It would nearly break him.

After checking in at A.F.S. headquarters when he reached Paris, Rice made the usual rounds of places visited by American volunteers in the city of light: at the Café de la Paix he met the two aviators from the *Chicago,* who had gotten nowhere with the elusive Miss G_____. In all probability he also visited the Folies Bergères since it was a favorite haunt for Americans.[20] Rice joined Section 1, the most veteran of the A.F.S. sections, and was assigned car #13. He states, "but as I am not particularly superstitious this did not make me nervous." The section was first assigned to Epernay in Champagne, not far from the cathedral city of Reims. As all new men were, he was anxious to experience what war was actually like.

> That night we were billeted in the second story of a dilapidated barnlike building from which the windows were all gone, and lying in my cot I could see the stars through the roof. That night a rat ran across my face. At last I was getting into the war.[21]

He made friends with Frederick Norton, another new man in the section. The two men became very close and developed the habit of shaking hands, followed by "good luck and have an interesting trip" whenever one or the other went out on a mission.

> On the afternoon of July 12 I saw Fredrick Norton starting for the front, and, following our custom, I went over to his car, shook hands with him and wished him "good luck."[22]

It was the last time he would see his friend Norton alive. German planes on a bombing run targeted the house where Norton was seeking refuge; the resulting explosion and flying bomb fragments cut his throat and pierced his heart.

> The following night I walked beside my friend Fredrick Norton for the last time. He was not laid to rest until after dusk because his burial place was on the side of the hill in view of the enemy — in view of the towers of the desecrated cathedral at Rheims — as fine a place as any for a volunteer who had earned an honorable rest.[23]

Philip Rice had finally gotten into the war and found it was more than a rat scurrying across your face.

In August 1917, his section arrived at Verdun. The French had captured Fort Douaumont the previous fall and were using it as a *poste de secours* for the fighting going on around them. A field hospital established in the ruins of a barracks complex a couple of miles away at Caserne Marceau served as a base for Philip Rice's section. The road between the caserne and the fort was memorable even when the Germans were not shelling it.

> Working out around Douaumont the roads are frightful. Dead horses lie around for days and also bits of human beings — for when a shell lands near some one the pieces are never all gathered. The only signs of life one sees are flies, rats, and ravens. Passing along that road the other day to get one of our men out of a ditch, I saw a boot lying on the way. I picked it up to throw it out of the road and found a rotten leg still in it.[24]

The Caserne Marceau was a large complex of barracks and administrative buildings located at the edge of the Verdun battlefield. The barracks were four stories in height, robustly constructed of stone and masonry and surrounded an open drill ground. Because of the prominence of the buildings, the caserne was an easy target for German gunners who shelled the buildings remorselessly for two years, 1916 and 1917. Fires had gutted the buildings and high explosive shells had punctured the thick stone walls in many places.

> This caserne — now demolished by shell fire — had topped the crest of a considerable hill which rose to the northwest of Verdun, and about two kilometers beyond. It was an exposed spot ... swept by almost continual shell fire.[25]

In 1916, the caserne was close to the extreme advance of the German attack; thousands of wounded passed through this *poste de secours*. Rice was based there a year later in 1917. The active front line had shifted toward Forts Douaumont and Vaux, about four miles (6.4 km) to the north and east. *Brancardiers* carried the wounded on stretchers to *postes de secours* in the forts where they waited for ambulances to carry them first to Caserne Marceau, and later to hospitals near Verdun.

> My first call to go from here to a front line poste came before sunset. The poste was near Fort Vaux. An officer rode with me to observe whether the road could be covered by car. It was a road that no sane person would undertake in peace times under any consideration. Down a ravine between two hills, in a country laid absolutely barren by continual shell fire, the sides of the hills were pock-marked with shell holes; and where at one time, three years before, there had been a beautiful forest, there was not now a tree stump, a bush or a patch of grass. We drove along the road very slowly indeed, for there was danger of breaking springs and axels in passing, as we drove close to the artillery as they were firing. I was later glad for the oppor-

> tunity of seeing the road before sunset, for I sometimes covered it afterward in the darkness without lights.
>
> We reached the *poste de secours*, picked up three wounded artillerymen and returned with added caution to Cassiarne [sic] Marceau. It was very trying when we wanted to drive fast, in order to get back as quickly as possible to a place of comparative safety, that we were obliged to drive most slowly to save our wounded and our cars.[26]

Since the Germans constantly bombarded the caserne, the only safe place lay deep underground in an operating room set up in a shell-proof bunker. Rice slept in this room on an empty stretcher, usually with a blood stained blanket pulled over his head trying to block out the groans of the wounded. As the battle heated up, there was little sleep to be had; the men were sometimes on the road driving to and from *postes de secours* for thirty hours before they could put their heads down...

> Sometimes we were on duty thirty hours at a stretch, though perhaps in that time we could snatch a little sleep; sometimes there was no sleep at all. The days were bad, the nights were worse, and day and night, either on or off duty, we were always under fire. Almost every time a man came back from post he had an experience to tell — it seemed that on our runs we escaped by a matter of seconds; shells were always hitting just behind us, in front of us and around us. We saw bloodshed all the time.[27]

All through August, the fighting went on and on, the French seeming bent upon paying the Germans back for their deeds of 1916. Casualties were in the thousands. Wagons brought in the dead, bodies stacked like cordwood, the smell so bad that the drivers always wore gas masks. The ambulance sections had been under fire for six weeks without let up.

> The men and the cars are sights — plastered with mud from top to bottom. No fenders or side boxes left; nearly every car full of holes from "éclats" of shells, and two of them with their entire sides blown out. We use these for the gassed men as much as possible, as they need all the air they can get.[28]

Philip Rice was rapidly undergoing a nervous breakdown. He was losing the ability to relax and recuperate when off duty; sleep came with much difficulty, if at all, regardless of how tired he was. He was plagued with premonitions; all the near misses he had survived were becoming realities that were waiting for him in the future — only this time he would not survive. He became afraid of himself, afraid he would be a coward. His road to Damascus occurred on the road from Fort Douaumont where, although tempted, he did not quit.

The wounded were coming in fast at Douaumont, both French and German, and all of our cars were on duty — at least all that were able to run. It was just about noon when I started, and the sun was shining cheerfully enough overhead but it was hell on earth. A short distance out I passed one of the English cars[29] coming out and the driver shouted to me to have my gas mask ready. I confess I had a feeling of fear. I had seen the victims of poison gas and had a greater dread of that than I had of shells, if such a thing were possible, and besides a couple of nights before during a period that I had been on constant duty for thirty hours in which time I had punctured six tires, had had a slight touch of gas and had felt rather ragged ever since. About four miles out, I passed one of our cars and the driver called to me something about big shells and gas. I stopped to call back for more particulars, but he was too far back to hear me. I was wavering but I drove on. A little further and I could see the shells coming in. I could see the gas clouds. I stopped my car — I got out and then I had the hardest argument I have ever had with myself. First I argued: "It is suicide to go on, I am justified in turning back and reporting the road is impassable." Then I argued with myself, "But if I do go and am hit, the agony will be over in a few minutes, but if I turn back, the agony will be with me the rest of my life." So I put on my gas mask and drove on.[30]

Just six days after this trip, on September 6, 1917, Phil Rice had his breakdown, going to pieces at dinner time. Fortunately, a week later, the section left Verdun and Rice was on his way to a doctor in Paris. His section chief, William Stevenson, told him, "Take a month off or as long as you need, but I want you to come back." On September 29, he returned to the section, which by that time was out of harm's way in the Alsace.

The French decorated Mr. Rice with the *Croix de Guerre* for bravery and a Divisional Citation: "Philip S. Rice, driver, has always set the example of the greatest courage and devotion in the most trying circumstances during the evacuations of the wounded, in the attacks of August and September, 1917 before Verdun."

Philip Rice died of a heart attack in 1927; he was only 49 years old. The closing line, written in blunt pencil, on his Princeton class questionnaire is perhaps a decent epitaph: "Am writing a comedy. I like comedy and hate work. Maybe that had something to do with flunking out of Princeton."

Philip Sidney Rice's war memoir, *An American Crusader at Verdun*, is probably the most introspective memoir written by an American ambulancier in the Great War. Whereas others catalog and describe events, Rice includes his feelings, whether they be noble or fearful, and where possible he remembers the comedy of the events he passed through.

In addition to Philip Rice, hundreds of other A.F.S. volunteers arrived in France during the spring of 1917. The Sleeper/Andrew publicity machine was almost too effective. There were more ambulance drivers than the French could use. The French had another idea, what they really needed in 1917 was not ambulance drivers but truck drivers. The French logistical effort depended on truck (*camion*) convoys to move men, food, munitions, artillery, tanks and even airplanes to the front. Could the American volunteers supply their need for hundreds of drivers? For Andrew this request raised a delicate publicity problem — could he convince men volunteering to drive ambulances at the front, with all the associated glory that he and Sleeper had drummed up, to drive trucks behind the lines, a task certainly less romantic. Driving an ambulance seemed somehow nobler than driving a truck. Andrew tried to jazz up the idea by saying they were ammunition trucks, but he still caught the wrath of irate parents writing to ask why their sons were switched from ambulances to trucks. One could say with pride at a cocktail party, "My son is driving an ambulance in France." It was a bit more prosaic to announce he was a mere truck driver, even if it was an ammunition truck. Andrew's view was a volunteer should do what needed to be done. And Andrew being Andrew, he persisted. A fresh-off-the-boat contingent of Cornell volunteers arrived on May 8, 1917, expecting to form their own ambulance section. Andrew explained the need for truck drivers, and to a man, they agreed. Then a group of pre-college youngsters from Andover Academy arrived, also intent on driving ambulances, and they also agreed to drive trucks instead. Then, a group from Dartmouth, and then, from the University of California — truck drivers to a man. The new A.F.S. truck unit was named the *Réserve Mallet* after the French officer in charge, Commandant Mallet. It would grow to 800 men and carry supplies for the French and American armies until the war's end.

Andrew's next problem in the summer of 1917 was the United States Army. Andrew had hoped that the A.F.S. would become an independent unit within the Army with him in command. But politically that was impossible since Andrew had not supported President Wilson's re-election and General Pershing was Wilson's man. Understandably, Pershing favored an ambulance service commanded by military professionals in the Medical Corps. Therefore, the United States Army Ambulance Service would take control of the A.F.S., with a Medical Corps officer, Colonel Jefferson R. Kean, in command, an officer with no ambulance experience. Swallowing his pride, the newly appointed Major Andrew agreed to serve under Kean.[31]

> In the long run, although he did not command the U.S.A.A.S. in name, it was his ideas and timely interventions to bale out the hapless Col. J. R. Kean ... that made for most of the administrative successes that the U.S. Army Ambulance Service had.[32]

6

Other Verdun Ambulance Corps

> Quite independently of the eight sections of the American Ambulance Field Service, it should be said that there are also two independent sections of ambulances in which Americans have served, the Anglo-American Volunteer Motor Ambulance Corps, conducted by Mr. Richard Norton, and a section controlled by the bankers Morgan-Harjes.—A. Piatt Andrew[1]

The American Volunteer Motor Ambulance Corps was the brainchild of Richard Norton, one of the more remarkable characters in the American volunteer effort. Richard Norton was a charismatic leader loved by his men, an energetic organizer, yet a man who had great difficulty dealing with authority. He was, to put it tactfully, "diplomatically challenged" when dealing with people above him in a chain of command, especially people with whom he did not agree. After America entered the war in 1917, Norton's dealings with General Pershing were legendary — they despised each other. General Pershing probably disliked Richard Norton more than he did the Kaiser.

> His quality as leader was greatly aided by his unselfishness and his consideration for all those with whom he came in contact. Added to these qualities was an intense hatred of all deceit and sham and a certain impracticalness in his nature which amounted to quixotry. For those qualities he suffered.[2]

Richard Norton was born in 1872, son of Harvard professor Charles Eliot Norton,[3] described "as the most cultivated man in America." Professor Norton was friend and advisor to many of the nineteenth century's intellectual celebrities, including Thomas Carlyle, Henry Wadsworth Longfellow, John Ruskin and Oliver Wendell Holmes. The learned professor helped found the Archaeological Institute of America — a connection that would determine his son's early career.

The Nortons were part of the intellectual elite of New England. Richard went to Harvard, class of 1892, where he experienced his father's philosophy of education — "to inspire in the men who attended — and especially in those who by reason of inherited wealth were likely to lead leisurely lives — an intellectual purpose and some sense of artistic appreciation." Richard learned both lessons well. After graduation, he spent most of his life abroad as a kind of adventurer, archaeologist and art connoisseur. Following three years studying at the American School of Classical Studies in Athens, Norton returned to America in 1895 for a teaching position at Bryn Mawr College. He must have quickly become bored with teaching coeds because by 1897 he returned to Europe as assistant director of the American School of Classical Studies in Rome and subsequently served as director of that institution from 1890 to 1907. He remained abroad as European art expert for the Boston Museum of Fine Arts until, in 1910, he was charged to lead an expedition excavating the Greco-Roman city of Cyrene in eastern Libya, an area then under Turkish rule. The expedition was under the auspices of The Archaeological Institute of America and the Boston Museum of Fine Arts, both organizations with strong ties to his now deceased father. Although Cyrene was in a dangerous area of Libya, the finds promised to be spectacular; the Boston Fine Arts Museum was very hopeful.[4]

Digging commenced in October 1910. Disaster struck five months later. On March 11, 1911, early in the morning as the men were walking from camp to the digging site, a European at the head of the line, Herbert De Cou, was murdered. Hit by two bullets, he died instantly; his Arab assassins escaped. The intended victim was believed to have been the expedition leader, Richard Norton, who normally was at the head of the line. Norton's handling of this situation revealed two character traits that would recur later during the war years: calm bravery when faced with personal danger, followed by accusations of fault. "Norton could be critical, it seems, of everyone."[5]

Norton saw to the burial of his friend De Cou; they had both been at the American Schools for Classical Studies at Athens and Rome.

> Owing to the inaccessibility of the site, arrangements were made for burial near the camp. The rude coffin was wrapped in an American flag. The service was read by Mr. Norton.[6]

To show the attempt on his life did not intimidate him, Norton completed the season at Cyrene as if nothing had happened. However, Norton was not finished with the assassins; he accused the Italian consul at Benghazi* of the crime, charging that the consul had paid the murders.

> I do not believe that the Italian government had any hand in it, but I do believe that the Italian consul in Benghazi had.[7]

---

*A seaport in northern Libya

The accusation caused a minor diplomatic flap. After the director of the Boston Museum of Fine Arts obtained an interview with President Taft and convinced him to send a gunboat to the coast of Libya as a show of support for the expedition, saner heads in the State Department nixed the operation. At the start of the next digging season (early September 1911), President Taft, under more pressure from Norton's supporters, dispatched the cruiser *U.S.S. Chester* to accompany the expedition as a show of strength. By the end of September, Italy declared war on Turkey and therefore Libya was now a war zone and off limits to American archaeologists. The Italian archaeologists took over the Cyrene dig, and the Greco-Roman loot went to Rome rather than Boston.[8]

> He had a scholar's equipment; had he the temperament? He was, I think, essentially a man of action. That is why he has left so little behind him in an academic way, little if one considers his ability and his knowledge.... He could not fetter himself to a desk; he must be up and doing.[9]

For all his work in archaeology, Norton left relatively little scholarly documentation of his efforts. The academic dictum "publish or perish" was not his. The same attitude applied to his war work; he wrote little in comparison to A. Piatt Andrew. Norton's drivers followed their leader's example. Consequently, the American Field Service has a considerably richer written record (books, published memoirs, magazine articles, newspaper accounts and even photographs) than Norton's American Volunteer Motor Ambulance Corps. Even though the drivers of the two American ambulance organizations got along, their leaders did not. Although Richard Norton and A. Piatt Andrew both had ties to Harvard, they were definitely not pals. In fact, just the opposite, Norton really detested Andrew.[10] It may have been jealousy since the American Field Service certainly was better known to the American public and always attracted more resources and volunteers. Andrew's publicity machine, implemented by his friend Henry Sleeper, achieved real results.

To return to 1914, as war clouds were beginning to darken the European horizon, Richard Norton was yachting in the Mediterranean with his old friend, Allison Armour, the Chicago meatpacking heir. There they chanced upon an old friend of Armour's.

> At Corfu, where Mr. Armour's yacht lay in harbor for a week, the Kaiser's yacht Hohenzollern, was also in harbor. Mr. Armour (an old yachting friend of the Kaiser's) and Richard dined more than once on the Hohenzollern, and another day he went to the place where excavations were in progress, with the Kaiser and his party, "elderly chamberlains greatly bored," as Richard said afterward to us. The Kaiser's friendliness to Richard, whom he had seen on several occasions before, was extreme and before they parted he gave Richard a jeweled scarf pin, the imperial "W" in red stones surmounted by

the imperial crown in brilliants: a strange gift in light of rapidly approaching events.[11]

The Kaiser's crest, the letter *W* surmounted with a crown, would soon be etched on concrete bunkers, military monuments and soldiers' tombstones throughout German-occupied Europe. That summer of 1914, millions of weapons stockpiled throughout Germany were marked with the Kaiser's crest; soon they would be loaded into trains whose destinations in the west were Belgium and France.

Norton was in America when war broke out that August. He immediately sailed for England. His sister Sara Norton[12] remembered him saying, "I'm going back, I'm going to see what I can do."

After a week or two in London, Richard left for Paris, hoping to get a job as a "war correspondent"[13] — but war correspondents, some well known, were swarming there. The battle of the Marne was over — Joffre's victory, which grew in importance as the war progressed — and Richard saw the return of the Marne wounded to Paris. A terrible revelation! There were no adequate preparations then in the armies of the Allies for that flood-tide of suffering which had begun to flow in from the front.[14]

Richard Norton saw what he could do; he cabled his sister, "I am going to organize an Ambulance Corps. See if you can raise funds." He did and she did. His brother Eliot Norton administered the stateside aspect of what would become the American Volunteer Motor Ambulance Corps.

A war-time monument in a German military cemetery in the Argonne Forest; such monuments are rare as most were vandalized after the war. The Kaiser's monogram, the letter *W* surmounted with a crown, is superimposed upon a Prussian cross bearing the date 1914 (photograph by Amanda Klekowski von Koppenfels).

Eliot Norton, a lawyer in New York City, and a brother of Richard Norton, played a large part in the success of the organization. It was he who personally supervised the enlistment of men for service in France as ambulance drivers. No one was permitted to enter this service without having first satisfied Mr. Norton that he would be unafraid, under any conditions, to carry the work of the American Red Cross to the battlefields of France in a creditable way.[15]

In addition to Richard's siblings, the family's connections allowed him to enlist the help of Henry James. In a letter to Grace Norton, Richard's aunt, James described an early meeting in London.

> January 1st, 1915
>
> I can tell you better thus moreover than by any weaker art what huge satisfaction I had yesterday in an hour or two of Richard's company; he having generously found time to lunch with me during two or three days that he is snatching away from the Front, under urgency of business.[16]

James was so impressed with Richard Norton, describing him as "unmitigatedly magnificent," that the seventy-year-old author, agreed, "...to his own professed surprise," to become chair of the American Ambulance Motor Corps. He would be Norton's propagandist, writing advertising copy to raise support for the Corps. His first effort was a sixteen-page pamphlet issued in 1914, written as a kind of open letter "to the Editor of an American Journal."

> Sir,— Several of us Americans in London are so interested in the excellent work of this body, lately organized by Mr. Richard Norton and now in active operation at the rear of a considerable part of the longest line of battle known to history, that I have undertaken to express to you our common conviction that our countrymen at home will share our interest and respond to such particulars as we are by this time able to give.[17]

James confided in a letter to a friend that he wrote the pamphlet, "With all but utterly nothing to go upon I had to make my remarks practically *of* nothing,"[18] and still he managed to stretch "nothing" to 16 pages. The result was not exactly Madison Avenue hype, but it was effective. Based upon the essay, *The New York Times* asked to interview Mr. James, and to the paper's great surprise, he agreed. He had never agreed before. The only requirement he imposed was to transcribe his words and punctuation accurately. The result was a piece that ran a full page praising Norton and his men, ending with an address where funds could be sent.[19] Unfortunately for Norton, he lost his great propagandist just as the battle of Verdun began — Henry James died February 28, 1916. He had only ever given the one interview.

While Henry James was singing the praises of Norton's ambulance corps, in actuality things were not going well. Although initially under the auspices of the British Red Cross, Norton's dealings with the British military left much to be desired. Norton transferred his allegiance to the French, but still "his men met up with the same thing: confusion, hard work, mix-ups, hurt feelings, last-minute change of orders, and fatigue."[20] His was almost a free-lance ambulance corps searching for a niche; time was spent looking for jobs or helping at hospitals, or even distributing Red Cross sundries: socks, shirts, and cigarettes. Moreover, all this driving to and fro always was restricted to far behind the lines. That is until April 1915, when the diplomatic, but persistent, A. Piatt Andrew persuaded French authorities to allow American ambulances to work close to the front lines and be affiliated with French army divisions. The agreement applied to all American ambulance organizations: the American Ambulance Field Service, the American Volunteer Motor Ambulance Corps and the Harjes Formation. Norton's least favorite person, Andrew, had achieved what Norton could not; he had given Norton's American Volunteer Motor Ambulance Corps a real mission.

Norton's ambulance sections generally consisted of 20 large ambulances of various makes: Cadillac, Rolls-Royce, Hudson, Buick, Pierce-Arrow, Ford

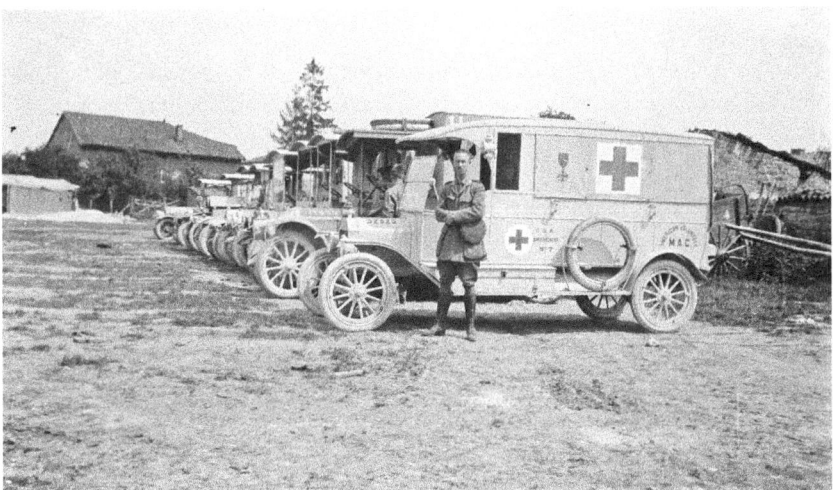

The American Volunteer Motor Ambulance Corps fleet; the AVMAC drove a heterogeneous collection of ambulances of larger and heavier makes such as Rolls-Royce, Cadillac, Hudson, Buick and Pierce-Arrow. The ambulances are easily distinguished from the Model T's because the T's had the ambulance body cantilevered over the rear wheels so that it extended beyond the wheels (see Chapter 6, Kelley ambulance) whereas the larger ambulances had the body within the wheels (courtesy Charlotte Meryman, Meryman family archive).

and Panhard, each car manned by a driver and an assistant; thus a section had 40 men in addition to mechanics, cooks and clerks, making it twice the size of an American Field Service section, since A.F.S. men usually drove solo. Having two men in a car was an advantage, especially when trying to reach a frontline *poste de secours* at night without lights.

> If a road is being shelled it makes passage extremely difficult for cars without light. Shell holes are "hell holes" to get out of, not to speak of the likelihood of a broken axle. It is often necessary for one of the men on the car to get out and walk in front of it with a handkerchief behind his back so that the man at the wheel can find his way along what is left of the road, in and out between the shell holes.[21]

There was another key difference between the American Volunteer Motor Ambulance Corps and the A.F.S. Norton was a "hands-on" manager, out in the field with his men, whereas Andrew delegated his authority to his section heads. Andrew was either at his office in Paris dealing with paperwork, in the U.S. helping solicit funds and recruit drivers, or traveling along the Western Front checking on the needs and wants of his sections. Consequently, Norton's experience of the war was much more immediate, as his letters to his brother Elliot show.[22]

> June 7, 1915
> The biggest battle I've yet seen is under way, we are in the thick of it. It is now 8 A.M., and I've been here since 4. The French are pounding the bottom out of the world in front, and the Boches are doing their best to reply. I write at the dugout at the entrance to the trenches where the wounded wait for us. Batteries are around us and along the road we follow to the hospital. One is some fifty yards from the dugout, and the Boches are trying to find it — not too successfully, for about fifty yards from us there has just fallen a shell.
> We have three groups of four cars out on this work today; the others are doing regular evacuations and service de garde — so we are furiously occupied. Back again from the hospital and waiting for the car to be loaded. It is a wonderful, brilliant summer day, but a strange haze from the bursting shells and the torn earth hangs heavily over the fields. The roads are hidden in the clouds of dust raised by the constant tramp of thousands of men and by the shells[23] of the ammunition wagons.[24]

By fall of 1915, Richard Norton was very pleased with what he had achieved and the role of his ambulance corps in the "big show." In a letter to his brother, he literally gushes with pride.

> October, 1915
> A year ago we started from London with ten cars, and not much more than "hope" for a bank balance. We were wanderers searching for work.

> During this year we have grown into a corps consisting now of some sixty cars, to which the St. John Ambulance and Red Cross Societies render any assistance we ask[25]; and instead of wondering where we were to find occupation, the French authorities have entrusted us with the whole ambulance service of the 11th Army Corps. We have carried during the year just ended 28,000 cases of sick and wounded, whilst during the days of September 25th to October 9th our cars relieved the sufferings of over 6,000 individuals. Besides all this, we have enough money in the bank to carry on for a short time without making a public appeal for more.[26]

But Richard could always find fault.

> February 15, 1916
> There is no doubt that the brains running the automobile service of the army are not the most brilliant in France. French officers with whom I have spoken admit the criticisms I have made, but advance as an excuse the fact that the service is vastly more complicated than was ever imagined before the war. While this is perfectly true, it does not excuse putting persons in command of it who station a convoy such as ours where there is no water for radiators, where the cars sink to their hubs in a swamp, and who do not realize that a considerable amount of essence[27] is needed for keeping our cars in proper condition.[28]

By the first week of June 1916, Norton and his ambulances arrived at Verdun. The Battle of Verdun had been going on for three months and by summer had reached a great intensity. A young driver just arrived from America described his boss, "Norton quite English looking, wore a monocle and waxed his mustache."[29]

The section camped five miles outside of Verdun and served *postes de secours* located on the east or right bank of the Meuse. One of the most dangerous *postes* was in the village of Bras, accessible only at night because of the near constant German shelling. In a letter to his brother Eliot, published in the *Springfield Republican* (Massachusetts), Richard described the perils he and his men faced. They had been at Verdun for only one week and already had two men wounded.

> June 15, 1916
> Since then we have had one car blown to pieces and five others hit. Our Verdun post is shelled every evening, and one of the others was heavily peppered last night. The division has suffered heavily, and I do not think can stay more than a few days more. We can't either, if we go on losing men and cars at this rate.
> Till to-day it has rained steadily, which has added to difficulties. However, we are sticking to it and I think will pull off the work all right.[30]

The carnage had happened in June of 1916 on the road to Bras, then one of the most dangerous *postes de secours* in the Verdun area. An A.F.S. driver also making the Bras run that June, described the chaotic insanity.

> German searchlights (fusees)[31] shot up in the air, showing a line of ambulances beating it for Bras, and soon we saw shells bursting over Bras. Going on into Bras, we found ourselves right in the midst of things, as shells were bursting everywhere, and were digging holes 5 ft. deep in the road.
>
> We were all bunched right in the middle of the town, and spent our time jumping up, and then dropping flat on our faces in the road, as we'd hear a Zing come our way. 50 ft. from us a horse dropped, and at the poste de secours 2 brancardiers[32] were killed. I shall never forget the feeling of scared helplessness that was with me all the time. The shriek of a shell coming your way goes thru you like a dentist's drill. Most of the voitures[33] had lead in them.[34] The wounded, waiting to be taken away, were in a horrible state of fright. Coming back my trio groaned away, and yelled at every bump. A couple of shells burst right in back, and the lead pattered all around, and splattered me with mud. When they exploded, the blessés yelled something awful, and begged me to go faster. One of them coughed a pool of blood on the floor.
>
> I made three trips to Bras before daylight; when we all have to stop, because the road is visible. However the wounded pour in all the time, and have to wait there 18 hours, until we can come again.[35]

A French doctor in the Bras *poste de secours,* no doubt overwhelmed by the situation, requested Norton to send ambulances to pick up badly wounded during daylight hours. Richard obeyed and his section suffered. Rather than just accepting this as a cost of war, he spoke his mind in letters to his brother and sister, knowing the letters would appear in newspapers as they nearly always did. So depending upon the letter cited in the newspaper account, the doctor's order for ambulances was either "extremely stupid" or "idiotic" or "blundering."[36] The articles, when they reached France later that year, must have endeared him to his French colleagues.

Norton's ambulanciers had other problems, the most important being how to stay alive from one day to the next. While Norton was usually at his field headquarters behind the lines, his men were picking up wounded at the front. Sometimes the shelling got so hot on the roads they had to abandon an ambulance and seek safety elsewhere.

> A Frenchman at this moment pointed out the location of an abri by the roadside where we were and into which we could crawl until the shelling stopped.

Inside they found a doctor tending a severely wounded soldier. The story picks up:

A doctor, who was present, stepped forward at this moment to examine the man, but quickly shook his head. At this instant a shell landed about twenty feet from the entrance to our retreat, and the vibration was so violent that it almost shook our teeth out. A great deal of loose dirt between the beams above our heads fell — some of it into the gaping wound of the unfortunate man lying on the floor.

Naturally I began to feel very nervous, for the place in which we were quartered did not impress me as too safe, being only about fifteen feet below the surface, and should a shell land on it I felt that we would stay there a long, long time.

And the shells did come, one after another. It appeared that they were shooting at the dug-out instead of the road now. The place fairly trembled. The doctor fell to his knees and started praying a sort of chant — "My God, my God. I have always tried to serve thee well," etc. I must confess that I was not enjoying myself any too well, for I remember having picked up an old newspaper which I tried to read, but merely turned pages over and over and whistled nervously, wondering where the next one would land.

The doctor turned sharply and addressed me. "You fool, have you no reverence, to whistle while a man is praying?"[37]

When the shelling ceased the doctor and the American crawled out of the *abri*. The ambulance, although left in the open, was undamaged; it was surrounded by fresh craters and jagged fragments of high explosive shells.

French and German wounded sometimes lay side by side on stretchers in *postes de secours* while awaiting transport. In one case, a driver remembered a badly wounded German attempted to bond in someway with a wounded Frenchman next to him, but forgiveness was not possible, the wounds and killing were too fresh.

> He seemed to thirst for comradeship and leaned on and grasped the hand of a hollow cheeked Frenchman on a brancard [stretcher] beside him. The effort was almost too much for him. A little Frenchman came up and shook his fist at him. He replied by pointing to the Frenchman's bandaged head and then to his own hands and legs. Then he [the German] tried to shake hands but the little Frenchman refused. One of the other Frenchmen said to him, "We have the American's working for us but you haven't."[38]

Ambulances moved French, and of course German, wounded from the front to military hospitals, but because the city of Verdun was being shelled constantly, military hospitals were dispersed outside the city. One of the more elegant hospitals was in Le Château des Monthairons, situated a few miles south of the city. The eighteenth-century pile was both a military hospital and the base for American ambulance sections; it was not remembered fondly:

a rather unlovely eighteenth-century château standing in a park built out on the meadows of the Meuse. The flooded river flowed round the dark pines, and at night one could hear water roaring under the bridges. The château, which had been a hospital since the beginning of the war, reeked with ether and iodoform; pasty-faced, tired attendants unloaded mud, cloth, bandages and blood that turned out to be human beings; an overwrought Médecin Chef screamed contradictory orders at everybody and flared into crises of hysterical rage.[39]

The Americans were quartered in one of the farmhouses on the château grounds, sleeping on stretchers propped up from the floor on boxes to keep rats from disturbing sleep. In addition to rats, the place was also full of fleas.

I've been pretty well "bit up." But yesterday I soaked my blankets in petrol and hung them on the line in the courtyard for airing, so I think I left the vermin behind. I also sprayed my clothes, especially my underwear, with petrol, which doesn't make much for comfort, except in so far as the animals are baffled. Flies and mosquitoes are abundant, too. We all have mosquito nets which we put over our heads in the evening, making us look like the proverbial huckleberry pie on the railroad restaurant counter.[40]

It was on the grounds of the château that the most famous baseball series of the First World War was played. A special correspondent to *The New York Times* covered the final game and described it as "unique in the history of baseball."[41] Five ambulance sections competed, with the final game for the championship played between an A.F.S. section and a Norton section. The umpire was one of the Norton men wounded during the notorious daytime run to Bras, and the subject of so much intemperate letter writing, who had recovered sufficiently to join his section, but not to play ball. Equipment was limited; there was only the one bat. Barbed wire entanglements delimited right and left fields, home plate was backed by the Meuse River, and the outfield by a low wall fronting the château. A German plane dropping propaganda broadsides over the diamond interrupted play. At the seventh inning, the Norton team, called away for a mission, all crammed into their Rolls Royce ambulance and left. At end of play, it was Norton team 17 to A.F.S. team 6.

By the end of 1916, the American Volunteer Motor Ambulance Corps merged with the Harjes Ambulance Corps (a.k.a. Morgan-Harjes Unit) to become the Norton-Harjes Formation; it would field three ambulance sections at Verdun by 1917. Its cars were the heavier makes: *e.g.*, Packards, Rolls-Royces, Cadillacs, and the ambulance sections were still twice the size of a typical A.F.S. section because two American volunteers manned each car. But even with the merger, the Norton-Harjes Formation had only three sections of 25 cars each, for a total of 150 volunteers.[42]

America's entry into the war, April 6, 1917, saw a reduced take of volunteers for the Norton-Harjes Formation, but some still came. Most of them sailed aboard the S.S. *Chicago*[43] of the French Line, a twin-screw "second & third-class-only" steamer that plowed the seas monthly from New York (pier 57, North River) to Bordeaux, France. The ship's hold usually was packed with American-made munitions for the Allies. On June 20, John Dos Passos boarded the *Chicago* for France intending to drive for Dick Norton.

Twenty-two years old in 1918 and living in New York City, Dos Passos was an aspiring "red, radical and revolutionary"; he attended anarchist and pacifist meetings and was a passive participant in riots for Bolshi causes.[44] He was anti-war and especially anti–Wilson for getting America into the war. Why he volunteered to drive an ambulance in France is not clear, probably not even to himself. The war was the "big event" of his time, he needed to get to Europe to see it first hand; especially as a writer, he needed the experiences of the battlefield, as they would color his generation—and driving an ambulance was the safest way to share in that experience and be part of the "big event." Besides, it was a way to dodge the draft.[45]

By early August, he was in Lorraine, based in Erize-la-Petite, which he described as "the damndest godforsakenist hole I ever landed in." The village straddled the key road that linked Bar-le-Duc with Verdun, the Voie Sacrée. Erize-la-Petite was quite far from the fighting, more than 20 miles south of Verdun. The gutted buildings that Dos Passos described probably had nothing to do with the battle of Verdun. The village had been in the path of the German invasion of 1914 and presumably had suffered the same fate as Clermont-en-Argonne (see Chapter 2).

From spring through early summer of 1917, the French Army quashed a series of mutinies resulting from catastrophic losses incurred during senseless attacks against strong German positions,[46] and it was only in August of 1917 that French generals dared to go on the offensive again. The planned offensive would be an attempt to regain territory around Verdun that had been lost to the Germans in 1916. Attacks would occur on the left (west) and right (east) banks of the Meuse. Dos Passos' ambulance section served the left bank attack against Mort Homme and Côte 304, whereas Philip Sydney Rice's A.F.S. section was on the right bank in the Douaumont area (see Chapter 5). In light of the mutinies, the French were understandably somewhat anxious about the reliability of their soldiers and watchful of political unrest. It was at this time that Dos Passos sent a truly seditious letter to a friend at home. It included the line, "The war is utter damn nonsense—a vast cancer fed by lies and self seeking malignity on the part of those who don't do the fighting"[47]

Had French military censors read this letter, its inflammatory text would probably have earned Dos Passos a stay in a French prison. The following month, two other Norton-Harjes volunteers, William Slater Brown and Edward Estlin Cummings, were incarcerated for injudicious comments in letters and foolish remarks to French intelligence authorities during interrogations. E. E. Cummings used his prison experience as the basis of his novel, *The Enormous Room*.[48] The enormous room was his prison cell, a space he shared with forty other men.

In August of 1917, things went rapidly down hill for Richard Norton and his ambulance corps. His men were losing faith in his leadership. Cummings uncharitably described him in a letter, "A skinny man, rather lofty, who talks without moving his mouth, has one eye blocked by a monocle; in a word, a pleasant ass and without reason for existence."[49]

In addition to troubles with his men, Norton had troubles with the U.S. Army, which wanted the Norton-Harjes Formation to become part of the United States Army Ambulance Service. Norton would agree only if appointed head of the Service. However, that was not in the cards; General Pershing was adamant. He could not abide Norton. Discouraged about not finding an exalted enough niche for himself in the military, Norton advised his drivers to have nothing to do with Pershing's ambulance service — advice that most followed. He then resigned and went to England.[50] On August 2, 1918, Richard Norton died of meningitis.

> He was such a many-sided character, with such strong traits, that it is hard to say he best fitted into the world before the war.... He was, I think, essentially a man of action.[51]

7

Americans in the Foreign Legion

> People everywhere are in the habit of speaking of men killed in battle as heroes. They all deserve our praise and most were brave fellows; but a distinction should be made between duty and heroism. We Frenchmen who fought in the war, and even those who died, were merely performing a duty required by the laws of our country.... But when men who have no obligation to fight, who could not possibly be criticized if they did not fight, yet nevertheless decide, upon their own individual initiative, to risk their lives in defense of a cause that they hold dear, then we are in the presence of true heroism.—General Gouraud[1]

One man established the legal precedent allowing Americans to fight alongside the French in 1914, Myron T. Herrick, the lame-duck Ambassador Extraordinary and Plenipotentiary of the United States to the French Republic.

In 1912, President Taft appointed Herrick American ambassador to France for the remaining year of Taft's presidency. The previous ambassador, Robert Bacon, had resigned to become a Fellow of Harvard University; evidently, duty to his alma mater was more compelling than being an ambassador.[2] In April 1912, Bacon was on his way to Cambridge, Massachusetts, and his beloved Harvard while Herrick and his family were establishing themselves in Paris. The year passed, Taft was replaced with the election of Woodrow Wilson, who would be inaugurated on March 4, 1913. On February 28, following protocol, Herrick sent his letter of resignation to the new president. Wilson appointed his campaign manager, William F. Combs, to the post of ambassador. Combs arrived in Paris during the summer of 1913 but soon decided there was more money and power available in Washington than in Paris. He immediately resigned and returned home—thus missing a place in history. For the following year, Herrick continued as the American ambassador. In June of 1914, Wilson appointed William G. Sharp as ambassador. Herrick made plans to vacate his post on August 8, but on August 3, France and

Germany declared war, and Herrick's plans changed. Herrick remained at his post as American ambassador until November 28, 1914. During those crucial first four months of the war, he often acted on his own, without State Department consultation.

In August of 1914, the German Army seemed an unstoppable juggernaut; everyone predicted it would soon be at the gates of Paris. The French government panicked and abandoned the city. Nearly all foreign embassies followed the French bureaucrats and fled; only the American Embassy remained. In early September 1914, Herrick and his staff were the only viable government representatives in town. Rumors were circulating that after capturing the city, the Germans intended to hold it hostage, destroying it section by section until the French unconditionally surrendered. Herrick took matters into his own hands and developed a plan to put the city's museums, historical buildings and great works of art under American protection. He intended to meet the advancing German Army in the city's outskirts in order to talk with its commander and, if possible, the Kaiser about protecting the city's cultural heritage. Herrick also had posters printed in French and German to be affixed to houses occupied by Americans.

> Safeguard
>
> The United States Ambassador gives notice that the building in Paris situated at _____ is occupied by Mr._____ an American citizen and hence is UNDER THE PROTECTION OF THE UNITED STATES GOVERNMENT.
>
> The Ambassador therefore asks that the Americans living in said building be not molested and that its contents be respected.
>
> Myron T. Herrick, Ambassador

What Wilson made of such diplomatic corps free-lancing is not recorded, but the French never forgot Herrick's ambassadorial audacity. Fortunately, the German drive toward Paris fizzled that September; the First Battle of the Marne stopped them cold. Trench warfare began soon after.

It was at this time that a group of young American men appeared at the embassy needing legal advice from Ambassador Herrick. They wanted to join the French Army and wondered what impact that would have on their American citizenship. Herrick consulted legal texts and realized that as Americans, they could not swear allegiance to another country, and if they did so, it would jeopardize their citizenship. Moreover, in joining the French Army they would be required to swear allegiance to France.

> I got out the law on the duty of neutrals; I read it to them and explained its passages. I really tried to do more, but it was no use. Those young eyes were searching mine, seeking I am sure, the encouragement they had come in the

hope of getting. It was more than flesh and blood could stand, and catching fire myself from their eagerness, I brought my fist down on the table, "That is the law, boys; but if I was young and stood in your shoes, by God I know mighty well what I would do."[3]

Herrick's answer to their predicament was the Foreign Legion; in the Legion one theoretically swore allegiance only to the Legion, not to France.[4] It was legal nit-picking because the Legion was part of the French Army, but it set a precedent by which hundreds of American volunteers would fight for France. The subsequent ambassador followed the precedent because as Herrick said, "In government affairs a precedent is always useful as a provision against the chance of criticism."

> At this they set up a regular shout, each gripped me by my hand, and then they went rushing down the stairs as though every minute was too precious to be lost. They all proceeded straight to the Rue de Grenelle and took service in the Foreign Legion. These were the first of our volunteers in the French Army. They were followed by others, and in a short time a large group of them had enlisted.[5]

Yet even as late as 1916, there was still doubt among Americans in the Legion about their legal status. In a letter home, a young Legion volunteer, Edmond Genet, wondered what would happen to him when the war ended.

> Have you by any chance read or heard of us Americans who have enlisted here in France for this war being disfranchised by the Amer. Gov't. for disregarding the neutrality and thus being denied the right to vote? I heard yesterday in an indirect way that such was the case. I simply cannot believe it.[6]

Genet was a great-great-grandson of Citizen Genêt, the French ambassador to the United States in 1793 during the French Revolution. With a change of political fortunes in France, Citizen Genêt was ordered home to face arrest and the prospect of the guillotine. Understandably, he chose to stay in America, settling in New York State. His great-great-grandson joined the U.S. Navy after failing exams for Annapolis, serving as an ordinary seaman. In January of 1915, Edmond Genet deserted the navy and took a ship to France to join the Legion. He was eighteen years old. Because of his heritage, he was a celebrity in France. Surprisingly, in spite of his heritage, he could not speak French, although his letters became spiced with more and more French phrases as time passed. Later he transferred to the Lafayette Escadrille in which service he was killed.

If anything characterized the Americans who joined the Legion, it was their variety. They had only one common denominator, the desire to fight for France. The American volunteers included prizefighters, at least one deserter, a poet, journalists, artists, adventurers of every stripe including an elephant poacher, automobile racers, professors tired of academe, less than successful actors, engineers and rich play boys. Some came from wealth, others did not; some were college graduates, others were dropouts; some managed to at least graduate high school and others did not. Some were black, others white; the Foreign Legion was the only military unit of the First World War in which Americans of different races were comrades in arms. However, the diversity of Americans was nothing compared to the rest of the Legion, as noted by Legionnaire Victor Chapman.

> The people I am thrown with are, for the moment, Polish in majority, for they are a crowd which came together from Cambrai. But they are of almost all nationalities and all stations and ages of life. I am most friendly with a little Spaniard from Malaga. He has been a newspaper reporter in London and got tired of doing nothing there, so he enlisted here. So far as I have seen I am the only American (the others having been sent to Rouen a day or two before I enlisted), but I have seen a couple of negroes. There are about thirty Alsatians, a few Russians and a few Belgians, one or two Germans, a Turk, and even a Chinaman arrived this morning. There are Greeks and Russian Jews, and probably many I have not noticed.[7]

Victor Chapman came from a wealthy New England family, graduated from Harvard in 1913, and was studying architecture in Paris when the war broke out. He joined the Foreign Legion in 1914 and later, as a member of the Lafayette Escadrille, was killed at Verdun on June 23, 1916.

After enlisting, the Americans mustered at a caserne or a depot and drew their uniform and equipment; the burden weighed 60 pounds. They were expected to carry it on marches of 20 miles or more.

> The complete trappings are very heavy. The water bottle over one hip, a large bag for grub and odds and ends over the other on top of the bayonet, a box containing 84 cartridges across the chest, the rifle (weighs ten lbs.) and the sack.[8] The sack is about 18 inches square by 5, containing change of linen and personal effects (I bought a water-color box), on top of which are strapped an extra pair of heavy army shoes, and part of the squad field-accoutrement,—such as an ax, a pail or a shovel. I have the last named. Over all is the blanket with a piece of a tent-cloth rolled up and folded about. The sack itself sits at the height of the shoulders, the personal canteen, which is perched above all, is about at the level of the head.[9]
>
> ... Our rifle is all right though. The French use the La Belle, 1886. It has a magazine something like the Winchester—beneath the barrel, and holds 8 shells in the magazine with a cut-off so that the rifle can be fired by single shells injected apart from the magazine. It is not as good or as complete as

7. Americans in the Foreign Legion

On July 4, 1915, at the request of the U.S. Ambassador to France William G. Sharp, the American volunteers in the Foreign Legion had forty-eight hours furlough in Paris. The parents of one of the legionnaires, Mr. and Mrs. Chapman, in Paris visiting Ambassador Sharp, had this photograph made of their son and some of his American comrades. Edmond Genet is seated at center; seated at right is William Dugan. Victor Chapman is standing directly behind Genet. The names of the other Americans are not recorded (*War Letters of Edmond Genet*, edited by Grace Ellery Channing [New York: Charles Scribner's Sons, 1918]).

> our new Springfield rifle but it isn't very bad either. The bayonet is long and needle-shaped. The bullet is solid copper and a trifle larger and heavier than the German one. I was able to do some pretty good shooting at the camp so I guess I can hold my own at the front.[10]

Training consisted of endless hours on the drill field learning and obeying French commands, target practice with the heavy La Belle rifle, digging trenches and saps, advancing under machine gun and artillery fire, tent pitching and field survival, endless mock bayonet charges against straw-stuffed dummies and long forced marches to toughen the men.

> Yesterday we took a seven-hour march that made the most demand on our endurance that has yet been called for. Only one man fell out. We pitched our tents in a high field and went through the entire exercise of bivouacking, taking our sacks inside and lying down six men to a tent. I was sure we were

preparing to spend the night, when the order was given to break camp and in a few minutes all the orderly labor was undone. The company then formed ... and we started back to camp across country, making a wide detour.[11]

One of those that needed toughening was Alan Seeger.[12] Seeger had been living in Paris, trying to establish himself as a writer, when the war broke out. He immediately volunteered for the Foreign Legion; it is very likely he was among those young Americans who visited Ambassador Herrick's office that August. Alan Seeger was remembered as being "slightly built and frail; he was unaccustomed to outdoor life and exercise, and the first few months with the Legion were terribly hard for him."[13] Despite his apparent frailty he had an iron will. In the Legion, he was very much the introvert and did not mix to any extent with his American comrades. When he had free time behind the lines, rather than relaxing with his comrades, gossiping or playing cards, Seeger would slip away and write. He always carried a pencil and notebook in the pockets of his great-coat and wrote down his impressions. Seeger along with 18 other Americans was in Section 1, Company 1 of the Second Foreign Regiment.

Before the war, the Foreign Legion consisted of two regiments, Premier Régiment étranger (First Foreign Regiment) and Deuxième Régiment étranger (Second Foreign Regiment), both based in Algeria. When the war began, because of the large number of volunteers, each of these regiments was divided into four regiments designated as Régiments de Marche, or marching regiments, each with about 4,400 men. Thus, the Premier Régiment étranger consisted of the First Marching Regiment, the Second Marching Regiment, the Third Marching Regiment and the Fourth Marching Regiment, with the same designations for the marching regiments in the Deuxième Régiment étranger. Alan Seeger belonged to the second marching regiment of the Deuxième Régiment étranger, as did most Americans who enlisted in 1914.

Veteran Legionnaires were mixed-in with the Americans to aid with training and assimilation into the Legion. There was considerable ill will, especially in the beginning, between the American idealists and the seasoned Legionnaires. The Americans joined an organization made up, at least in part, of the dregs of Europe, if not the world; many Legionnaires were hiding, or escaping, from something nefarious in their past. Drunkards, thieves, and worse, yet seasoned veterans of many battles in Algeria and Morocco. For many it was their last chance, and for their future, they were not optimistic. As an Englishman who served in the Legion put it,

"If you are thinking of committing suicide it will do you no harm to try the Legion first — it may possibly introduce you to a zest of life that you have never felt, and in any case you can commit suicide as well in Algeria, you know, as you can in London."[14]

By mixing veterans and novices together in the same sections, social differences often led to quarrels that resulted in fights. One such fight broke out after Alan called a huge Serb an imbecile because he disparaged Seeger's poetry. The poet avoided a bad mauling when his friend Bob Scanlon, an Afro-American legionnaire who had been a prizefighter, stepped in. One hard punch to the jaw knocked the Serb unconscious. For a frail poet, Seeger was feisty, and very lucky he had a friend nearby.

The slightest thing could set men off. The most notorious fight was one that occurred in March 1915, when an American was killed. It happened in the courtyard of a ruined château behind the lines and began over a cup of coffee. A veteran was ladling it out and an American attempted to get a second cup, pretending he had had none. The veteran swore that all Americans were cheats and liars and in the heated exchange, he called to a passing friend, an Arab from the machine gun section, for help. The two veterans made scathing comments about the Americans and bragged that each could single-handedly beat seven Americans in a fight. One American, René (Phil) Phélizot, stood up and offered to fight both men. Originally from Chicago, Phil was a well-known African big game hunter, fearless and good with his fists. He and the Arab squared off; a crowd gathered.

> Whereupon, the Arab gripped him by the arms and butted him in the face. They both went down and came to grips, and Phil was gradually getting the best of it.... An Alsacian, a friend of the Arab, broke through the ring and cracked Phil over the head with a bidon[15] [water bottle] full of wine. Figured out in physics, this meant a five pound weight at the end of a four-foot lever, taking into consideration the length of the man's arm and the strap. Phil went down, and a general riot broke loose — our section against the machine gun outfit.[16]

By the time officers stopped the fight, five Americans and six Legionnaires were knocked out. Phélizot was in a bad way, with a fractured skull. He died three days later. The Alsatian was court-martialed, but acquitted. That was too much for the Americans to swallow so they again battled the machine gun section. Only this time they had a target, all concentrated on the Alsatian, stomping his head to pulp from repeated kicks with hob-nailed Army boots. Alan Seeger, Phélizot's close friend, joined the fight. Both had marched together in Paris during August of 1914, carrying American flags and leading volunteers who joined the Legion. Writing home he said, "What we did was pure violence. We reacted with primitive fury."[17] A military inquiry took no action against the Americans — unofficially a case of justified homicide.[18]

During the fall of 1914, the Legion was assigned a sector of the front in Champagne, near the cathedral city of Reims. The Battle of the Marne was over, the German drive for Paris stopped, and both sides were digging in. Trench warfare was in its infancy, there was a lot to learn, and the learning curve was steep and deadly. The Legion's experiences in Morocco and Algeria were of little help in what it was to face on the Western Front. Day and night men dug, thousands of human moles churning through the landscape, digging two parallel underground cities filled "with unspeakably dirty citizens" on each side of No-Man's Land.

> It is two days before Christmas, and just two months that we are here in the front line of trenches with the enemy a quarter-mile before us. Uncle Fred writes he hopes I will not go too near the front! Yet at times one forgets they are there. There are long days of inactivity that become monotonous to despair, and an attack, an ambuscade, a lively cannonade are welcome. When not at that there are trenches to be made, and I have become "miner" — a day labourer.[19]

One of these human moles was Kenneth Weeks of Boston, a graduate from the Massachusetts Institute of Technology. In 1910 he left for Paris to study architecture and there got into writing, had books published, and enlisted in the Legion in August 1914. He was killed June 17, 1915.

Both armies adopted new trench innovations. Barbed wire, an American invention, made its appearance. Initially just plain smooth wire was strung on wooden posts in front of trenches to trip attackers; barbed wire entanglements stopped attackers — or at least severely slowed them. Barbed wire entanglements were initially constructed using wooden posts driven into the ground fronting a trench. Such barriers had two disadvantages: since soldiers often constructed the entanglements at night, the noise made by pounding in the stakes drew enemy fire; and under artillery bombardment, the wooden stakes were often blown to smithereens, collapsing the wire entanglement. To solve both of these problems the Germans invented the screw picket, a device quickly adopted by all the armies. The iron picket was screwed into the ground rather than pounded.

This new technology greatly impressed a Legionnaire from California, Edward Morlae:

> for the stakes to which the wire is tied the Boches had substituted soft iron rods, three quarters of an inch thick, twisted five times in the shape of a great cork screw. This screw twisted into the ground exactly like a cork puller into a cork. The straight part of the rod, being twisted upon itself down and up again every ten inches, formed six or seven round loops in a height of about five feet. Into these eyes the barbed wire is laid and solidly secured with short lengths of tying wire.... When a shell falls amidst this wire protection, the rods are bent and twisted, but unless broken off short

they always support the wire, and even after severe bombardment present a serious obstacle to the assaulters.[20]

Edward Morlae had served in the U.S. Army in the Philippine Islands and, because of his military experience, was put in charge of a section that included many of the Americans. Sergeant Morlae was a cruel martinet despised by his countrymen, who vowed they would do him bodily harm if they met him after the war. Morlae deserted the Legion in October of 1915, turning up at the Boston office of the *Atlantic Monthly*. The magazine paid for and published an article he wrote describing his heroic adventures in the Legion.[21] He also published a book with the Houghton Mifflin Company of Boston, publishers of many First World War memoirs. Morlae survived the Legion and made money from the experience.

In trench warfare, most of the wounds or deaths resulted from head injuries, a result of sticking your head above the parapet. In 1914 and early 1915 neither side wore helmets, the French wore a cloth cap known as a kepi and the Germans had their leather pickelhaube with its distinctive metal spike on the crown. Neither of these head coverings provided protection against shell fragments or shrapnel balls, and the pickelhaube had an added disadvantage — its spike drew the attention of French sharpshooters. Consequently, many German units removed the spike when in the trenches. By mid 1915 the French Army issued the *casque Adrian* (Adrian helmet), a steel helmet that at least protected against nearly spent (low velocity) shell fragments, shrapnel balls and debris kicked up by explosions.

> The casque (helmet) is used by practically all the French troops now to help protect the head from shrapnel and "spent" bullets. They are no protection against "unspent" bullets unless they hit at such a large angle that the metal could possibly cause them to glance off. The casque weighs about 2½ pounds.[22]

Photographs of Legionnaires at the front taken in 1914 show them wearing a kepi, but from mid–1915 onward photographs show men with the *casque Adrian*. The German Army did not introduce a steel helmet until 1916.

The end of 1914 brought more than military adaptations for trench warfare; it witnessed the last instance of large-scale fraternization between the armies opposing each other across No-Man's Land. On December 25, 1914, in many different sectors, the soldiers on the Western Front spontaneously celebrated a Christmas truce.

Perhaps the most fantastic of these Noël celebrations was described by Phil Rader, Legionnaire and seeker of the "main chance."

> I don't know how the truce began in other trenches, but in our hole Nadeem began it — Nadeem, a Turk, who believes that Mahommed and not Christ

was the Prophet of God.... He drew a target on a board, fastened it on a pole, and stuck it above the trench, shouting to the Germans:

"See how well you can shoot."

Within a minute the target had been bull's-eyed. Nadeem pulled it down. In doing so, Nadeem's head appeared above the trench, and we heard him talking across No Man's Land. Thoughtlessly I raised my head, too. Other men did the same. We saw hundreds of German heads appearing. Shouts filled the air. What miracle had happened?

... I think Nadeem was first to sense what had happened. He suddenly jumped out of the trench and began waving his hands and cheering. The hatred of war had been suddenly withdrawn and it left a vacuum in which we human beings rushed into contact with each other. You felt their handshakes — double handshakes with both hands — in your heart.

After supper we heard a sudden blast of music that thrilled us. A little German band had crept into the trenches and announced itself with a grand chord. Then came the unexpected strains of the "Marseillaise." The Frenchmen were almost frantic with delight.

George Ullard, our Negro cook, who came from Galveston, got out his mouth organ and almost burst his lungs playing "Die Wacht am Rhein." The silence in the German trenches was a thousand times more eloquent than the blast of cheers when George had finished. There was no shooting all night until about six o'clock in the morning.

Early in the morning Nadeem jumped out of the trench and began waving his hands again. John Street, an American who had been an evangelist in St. Louis, jumped out with him, and began to shout a morning greeting to a German he had made friends with the day before. There was a sudden rattle of rifle-fire and Street fell dead, with a bullet through his head. The sun was shining down again on a world gone mad.[23]

Phil Rader, an American newspaper cartoonist, deserted the Legion some time after the Christmas truce. In London, he met an American newspaper man who wrote up Rader's stories of life in the Legion, but for some reason they were published under Rader's name. Rader next enlisted in the British Royal Flying Corps. After learning to fly he again deserted, this time showing up in America where he lectured about the war and his experiences. He fell to his death from an airplane while stunt flying.[24]

The following year, 1915, was a bloody one for the Legion; by year's end, the casualties were so high, the Legion was essentially used up and regiments disbanded. Legion regiments had fought throughout a broad stretch of the front, waging ill-conceived assaults against heavily fortified German trench lines. These attacks pitted the brave Legionnaire with rifle and bayonet against emplaced machine guns. Where success occurred, it was trivial and paid for at great cost. Machine guns nearly always had the advantage.

> Little chance one has to last when charging in the face of the rapid-fire guns used in this conflict. They can cut a regiment down in less time than it takes to tell about it, believe me. One can easier run between drops of rain than between the bullets of one of those infernal machines.
>
> An attack only lasts a bare ten minutes (usually less) in this war. Either the attacking party gets across in that time and drives the enemy from their trenches or else is cut down by the mitrailleuses* before it can cover the few hundred yards between the lines. The latter is a pretty likely case.[25]

There were successful raids, of course, and German prisoners captured. The Legion had an interesting way of preparing prisoners for their march to the rear and internment. Legionnaires got out their knives and mingled with the prisoners, slicing off their trousers' buttons, cutting off suspenders, and hacking through belts, even shoes had their laces cut. Thus they reduced the "Kaiser's Best" to a bunch of guys slopping along, hands helplessly in their pockets holding their trousers up, shuffling their feet to keep their boots on, plodding slowly to the rear with a few French soldiers directing them rather than guarding them.[26]

Between suicidal assaults, there were the trenches, home away from home so to speak. The men tried to make them as comfortable as possible, but sometimes it just was not possible.

> The last few days we had in the trenches we were up about to our waists in mud and water. We had a very heavy rain one night and the trenches filled with water. It was misery in the tenth degree. The following morning there were quite a number killed and wounded just because they couldn't keep out of sight on account of the depth of the water while trying to clean it out and we all felt utterly down and out.[27]

The Western Front filled up with corpses: battlefields, trenches, dugouts, road sides, cultivated fields, the grounds around *postes de secours,* nearly everywhere there were dead and decomposing men. They were interred in shell craters, abandoned trenches, collapsed dugouts, shallow graves, mass graves, or not buried at all, just blown to bits and scattered as mulch across the countryside. Rats grew to the size of large cats from feasting on human flesh. In squads and sections there was always work going on dealing with the dead.

> Almost every day there was a wooden tombstone or two to prepare. It was my duty to decorate the tombstone with some sort of design, and a Belgian named Armine always did the lettering. You might find us almost any forenoon working away with a red-hot poker, burning names and decorations on a wooden cross which we had constructed out of any pieces of wood we could find.[28]

---

*Machine guns

Still, the French General Staff persisted with their "do or die trying" approach, and since they were not doing the dying, they kept trying. American legionnaires participated in three of the major 1915 offensives. Between December 1914 and March 1915, in the offensive against the German fortified lines 30 kilometers (18.6 mi) east of Reims, the French managed to push back the Germans only a half mile over a front of five miles at a cost of 100,000 casualties. This was known as First Champagne. Then in a joint attack that summer (May–June 1915) with the British in the Artois region near Flanders, the British sustained 65,000 and the French 102,000 casualties, including Legionnaire Kenneth Weeks of Boston. Weeks was killed June 17, last seen "running towards the third line of the German trenches, his right arm extended and facing the enemy."[29]

Remarkably, in the first half of 1915, there were twenty-two Allied casualties for every nine German.[30] Losses[31] were so great, the original three Foreign Legion regiments to which most of the Americans belonged were, with the addition of new enlistees, reorganized into two regiments. Undeterred by the mounting toll of casualties, the French General Staff planned and executed another pointless blood bath known as Second Champagne. Launched against German lines between Reims and the Argonne Forest, this attack took place during the latter part of 1915, September through mid November, where over a twenty-five-mile long front the French managed to advance only about a mile at the cost of 200,000 casualties which included 30,000 dead, and still the key points remained in German hands.

Why so many failures? The French Army was really inadequately equipped for trench warfare in 1915; it lacked the weapons necessary to breach German trenches, and without breaching the trenches there could be no breakthrough. Deep trenches were best destroyed by plunging fire, weapons that sent a projectile high into the air on an arc that completed its trajectory by dropping down onto the intended target. Modern howitzers and mortars, weapons the French generally lacked, could do the job. French artillery was primarily based on the 75 mm field gun, model 1898. This gun was revolutionary in design in that recoil was absorbed by a hydraulic system that allowed the barrel to slide back and forth on a trough. Since only the barrel moved, the gun remained on target; it could fire 20 rounds a minute and remain on target. Before 1898, artillery guns rolled back with the recoil, and thus went off target. They had to be retargeted with each shot, a slow and clumsy process. The recoilless 75 mm gave a dramatic increase in accurate fire power per unit time. The French Army bet on the 75 mm as its principal artillery weapon. Unfortunately there was a flaw, the gun had a very flat trajectory; consequently shells usually landed in front of a trench, behind a trench, but seldom in the trench where the German defenders were. Before the war, the Germans had adopted the French-inspired hydraulic recoil system for their 77 mm field guns as well as large caliber howitzers, equipping their armies with both. The German Army also used heavy trench mortars (*Minenwerfer*) that utilized hydraulic recoil.[32] The French had few mortars and those it had lacked hydraulic recoil, some were even nineteenth century bronze relics taken from museums.

> The narrower the trench, the better. It gives the least space for German shells to drop in and blow occupants out. The more crooked the trench the better. The enemy has a smaller chance to make an enfilading (raking lengthwise) fire. Here only are narrowness and crookedness virtues.[33]

Legionnaire Bowe, of Canby, Minnesota, was older than most American volunteers. Formerly an evangelist, he could appreciate the virtues of narrowness and crookedness, having railed against them from the pulpit. Bowe had fought in the Spanish-American War, taking part in the capture of Manila and in the Philippine Insurrection, where he won the Congressional Medal. In 1914, Bowe was Mayor of Canby and a prosperous businessman. When the war began he liquidated his business, said farewell to his wife and children, and boarded a ship for France.[34] He survived the war but became a bit radicalized by the experience as the political aphorisms in his memoir reveal.[35]

> Honor, Patriotism, Equality. Those are the level foundation on which democracy rests — not wealth and inequality.
> We must stamp out materialism and save the soul of America.

John Bowe seems to have left America a *laissez-faire* businessman and returned a closet socialist.

Most American legionnaire memoirs dwell on the carnage of Second Champagne, not politics. They describe experiences both heroic and mundane. Some of the latter are surprising. Before an attack, preparations included changing your underwear and writing for the last mail call.

> The gas-masks and mouth-pads were ready; emergency dressings inspected, and each man ordered to put on clean underwear and shirts to prevent possible infection of the wounds.
> One hour before the time set for the advance, we passed the final inspection and deposited our last letters with the regimental postmaster.[36]

Edmond Genet spent the last few moments before going over the top writing to his mother.

> September 22nd, 1915
> My Dear Little Mother,
> There isn't much spare time for me to use in letter writing now but I am using these few minutes to send this — possibly my last. There is a big fight

coming, Mother dear,—that is all I dare say but that little means a lot. Should I get through alive or well enough to write I'll do so the very first chance I get so you won't be held in suspense too long...
Your loving son,
Edmond

An American newspaper mistakenly reported Edmond Genet as killed.[37] He wrote to his mother on October 30, "Don't believe me dead until you hear OFFICIALLY and from the French military authorities." In a letter to a friend, he wrote, "DON'T believe newspaper accounts. 99% are fictitious and the other 1% is misprint." Genet and his regiment were in the worst of the battle; it is remarkable that he survived. After the battle, only 31 men mustered from 2 Legion companies of 250 men each. Later Genet wrote his mother a long and detailed letter describing his near-death experiences.

Somehow we felt that huge shell coming; how, I don't know, but we all just threw ourselves flat into the mud. If I had been one little hundredth of a second late I wouldn't be telling the tale now. I felt that monster hurl directly over my head; the intake of air raised me at least an inch out of the mire which I was gripping with every finger and with all my might. The shell burst not more than three yards behind me and killed four of the section and wounded several others. My heart had one of the quickest jumps of its life.

It is hard to believe that graphic sentences such as those above calmed his mother's anxiety. However, he continues with even more gore and mayhem.

The sight of the dead lying about was awful. Most of them had been literally torn to pieces by the exploding shells....
  We lost men there every day. To protect ourselves as much as possible from the bursting shells we dug individual trenches into the ground just large enough to lie in, but many a poor fellow merely dug his own grave for they are no protection should a shell fall directly into one on top of the occupant. It was hell and nothing less....
  Shells were bursting everywhere. One lost his personal feelings. He simply became a unit—a machine.[38]

The German advantage in artillery literally chewed up the French offensive. The night before the Champagne offensive, Alan Seeger was supposed to have said, "Yes, this is the life. The only life worth living is when you are face to face with death—midway between this world and the next."[39] Alan was a strange fellow.

When the Second Champagne Offensive was finished at the end of November, so was the Legion. Losses were so great that now two regiments became one. The Americans got a choice; they could either stay with what was left of the Legion or move over to the 170th Infantry Regiment, an attacking regiment known as *Les Hirondelles de la Mort,* The Swallows of Death. The majority of Americans transferred to the Swallows. Alan Seeger was one of those who did not.

> Seeger, as usual, silent, mystic, indomitable, appeared not to listen. His thoughts were in the clouds. He had made up his mind to stay. That settled it — no explanation necessary.[40]

8

Rendezvous with Death

> The most famous, and justly so, of the writers among the American Volunteers, was Alan Seeger, whose inspired poems and beautiful letters are so well known to every American with any pretension to knowledge of modern authors and poets, ... — Paul Ayres Rockwell[1]

In January of 1916, having survived the French offensives of 1915, Alan Seeger was finally hospitalized, not with a wound suffered in battle but with bronchitis, an inflammation of the air passages that carry airflow from the trachea to the lungs. Seeger probably had chronic bronchitis, an inflammation that develops from living in an environment where there is recurrent injury to the airways from inhaled irritants. With millions of particles lofted into the air by countless explosions, toxic gas clouds and smoke-filled dugouts, a First World War battlefield was certainly such an environment. Bronchitis causes fatigue, shortness of breath, wheezing and great bouts of coughing. It is very debilitating and can last for months.

After his hospital stay, Seeger recouped his strength at a family friend's home in Biarritz and then later stayed in Paris for a month. He did not return to his Foreign Legion regiment until mid May 1916.[2] It was probably during this period of recovery that he wrote his best known poem, *"I Have a Rendezvous with Death."* Its haunting and prophetic last stanza touched Americans like no other, especially since the poet had already perished when the poem was published.[3]

> But I've a rendezvous with Death
> At midnight in some flaming town,
> When Spring trips north again this year,
> And I to my pledged word am true,
> I shall not fail that rendezvous.

While at the front that May, Seeger received a telegram asking him to compose a poem for reading at the American Decoration Day celebrations

8. Rendezvous with Death

being held at the statue of Washington and Lafayette in the Place des États Unis, Paris, on May 30. Wreaths would be placed in memory of the Americans killed for France. Alan would be granted a forty-eight-hour leave to read his poem. The poet was ecstatic and quickly composed "Ode in Memory of the American Volunteers Fallen for France." Unfortunately, his leave papers were mistakenly granted for June 30 rather than May 30. The events of that day were described in a letter to a Boston lady by Rif Bear, a young Egyptian and Seeger's closest friend in the Legion.

Foreign Legionnaire Alan Seeger, the poet laureate of the American volunteers fighting for France, who died in combat on July 4, 1916, at the Somme. His most famous poem, "I Have a Rendezvous with Death," was published after he had made that rendezvous (*L'Album de la Guerre* [Paris: Illustration, 1923]).

> The eve of the ceremony arrived — I can not recall the date — but no leave came. We were in the trenches and chance had placed me near Seeger in a "petit poste" (the small outlook post in advance of the first-line trench). He confest that he had lost all hope of going, and I tried to find all sorts of arguments to encourage him, that his leave might come at dawn, and that by taking the train at 7 A.M. he could still reach Paris by noon and would have plenty of time, as the ceremony was at two.
>
> The morning came, and instead of bringing the much desired permission to leave, it brought a terrible downpour of rain, and the day passed sadly.[4]

In June, Seeger's regiment, attached to the Moroccan Division, fought in the Battle of the Somme. Seeger was killed on July 4, 1916. Rif Bear described his friend's disappearance.

> The first section (Alan's section) formed the right and the vanguard of the company, and mine formed the left wing. After the first bound forward, we lay flat on the ground, and I saw the first section advancing beyond us and making toward the extreme right of the village of Belloy-en-Santerre. I caught sight of Seeger and called to him, making a sign with my hand.

He answered with a smile. His tall silhouette stood out on the green of the corn-field. He was the tallest man in his section. His head erect and pride in his eye, I saw him running forward, with bayonet fixt. Soon he disappeared and that was the last time I saw my friend.[5]

While Seeger's regiment was at the Somme, his American comrades from the Legion were fighting at Verdun. The first American to fight on that famous battlefield was Frank Musgrave, a San Antonio lawyer remembered as a "long-limbed raw-boned Texan."[6] Musgrave was one of those who had chosen to transfer from the Legion to the 170th Infantry Regiment, "The Swallows of Death." Within a few days, he was badly gassed and wounded (autumn 1915) and evacuated from the front to hospital. After two months in the hospital, he returned to the front, but this time with the 44th Line Infantry Regiment at Verdun. He arrived at Verdun in mid February 1916, just days before the German attack on February 21. As the German juggernaut pushed back the French in those early days of the offensive, they literally annihilated French regiments. The 44th fronted Fort Vaux, taking heavy casualties and eroding away. It would soon also be annihilated. The company to which Frank Musgrave belonged was surrounded; without ammunition and lacking food and water, it surrendered after two days. On February 26, only five days into the battle, Frank Musgrave became a prisoner of war destined for a prison camp near Münster, Germany.[7]

One week later he managed to write Mrs. Alice Weeks, the mother of his late friend and fellow legionnaire Kenneth Weeks, asking for help. Mrs. Weeks' residence in Paris had become a home for many of Kenneth's friends in the Legion when they came to Paris. After her son's death (June 17, 1915), her contacts with his friends were maintained, in fact were strengthened, and they wrote to her often of their needs and aspirations. Their commanders wrote to her of their deaths. She was known as *Maman Légionnaire,* Mother of the Legion. Frank Musgrave had needs: would she please send plain food, especially biscuits, and money to purchase extras in the camp canteen. Other than being a bit hungry, he assured her that he was unwounded and in good health.[8] On March 30, 1916, he wrote again saying he had not heard from her, but to note he had been moved from Münster and was now at Kriegsgefangenenlager, Friedrichsfeld bei Wesel, Rheinland. He added to his wish list, "As to useful things here, sugar, coffee, milk, cocoa are among them, in case you send me a parcel in the future."[9] Another letter, April 16, 1916, states, "Your letter of 21st to hand and as you may suppose was very glad to hear from you." However, the food parcel and money still had not arrived. Finally, on May 21, 1916, good news—packages of food and clothes arrived! "Do not send more money as we work and are paid enough to get on with," but he needed clothing, "just pants, vest and cap."[10] That package arrived June 11. The correspondence and packages continued throughout his stay in Germany. Musgrave was known as "Lucky Frank" in the Legion because of his near escapes with death; his luck held, as he not only survived Verdun but also survived his internment, although with his health impaired.

The Battle of Verdun began on February 21, 1916; soon after the initial German onslaught, the 170th Infantry Regiment was on its way to Verdun. Approaching the city from the west, a long column of tired men, each soldier stooped forward to counterbalance his sixty-pound pack, plodded toward the battle; the roar and flashes of German artillery barrages in the east growing more and more insistent with every mile. To make matters worse, snow blinded the men.

> Suddenly, freakish shapes loom up on the road ahead. They crowd to one side as the column slouches by: old men in queer, heterogeneous apparel — women pushing baby carriages, piled high with household possessions over and above the wailing occupant.
>
> Terror-stricken, dumb, they drift by like startled ghosts; their wide eyes scarcely see the troops. Women, half pushed, half dragged along, calling for killed or missing babies. Lost children struggling to keep up with forced, uneven steps, moaning pitifully for dead parents! "Where do you come from? What's going on?" we shout in passing. But the only answer is a murmur — "The big shells — oh, the big shells!"[11]

After the embarrassingly easy capture of Fort Douaumont in the early days of their offensive, the Germans set a new target — Fort Vaux, a smaller fort about two miles (3.2 km) away. Adapting to the new type of penetrating artillery shells developed in the latter part of the nineteenth century, the French reconstructed and reinforced the fort with concrete, completing the renovations in 1911. Five years later, its new concrete defenses were tested. After the Douaumont debacle, the French were determined to defend Vaux at all costs. The Swallows of Death were ordered to relieve its garrison, the fort served as a sanctuary where wounded were brought from the fighting nearby.

> Soon we are at a huge dark mound, and word comes back that it is the redoubt of Vaux; we are to relieve the present garrison. Then begins a weary wait while they bring out their wounded. Pitiful sights — some of them, hobbling along between two friends, then an endless procession of stretchers — among them the "basket cases." Why they don't put them out painlessly, then and there, is beyond civilized intelligence. Mere trunks, both arms and legs shot off, some of them blind as well, what possible use can they have for life, except the horrible instinct to live.[12]

Fort Vaux immediately after the war; the picket-fence enclosures mark graves. The 170th Division, the Swallows of Death, with its American ex–Foreign Legionnaires, defended the fort and nearby trenches in March 1916.

North of the fort was the village of Vaux. Trenches here were part of the outer defenses of the fort and "The Swallows of Death" manned them. The men ransacked the village to build defensive barricades, strengthened trenches between the houses. Cellars became dugouts and even mattresses served as sandbags. Then the men waited. It was March, cold and wet. "All eyes are strained toward the edge of the slope leading up to the village, expecting each minute to see the grey-green wave of the attack surge over it. Then a heart-stopping whistle."[13]

The attack began with salvo after salvo of high explosive and shrapnel shells ripping into the village, at first gutting the stone houses, then reducing them to a few standing walls, and finally to just piles of masonry and smoking timbers. Men buried alive, men blown to bits. Nevertheless, the defenders waited. Then a mass of German grey-green uniforms appeared through the smoke as the barrage lifted. The French manned what was left of their defenses, and rifle and machine gun fire tore into the advancing Germans, but as soon as one man dropped another took his place and the line seemed impervious. Quickly overwhelmed, the French fired signal rockets calling for an artillery barrage. A battery of 75 mm field guns answered the call. Firing twenty shrapnel shells a minute, they were deadly against massed troops in the open. "The shrapnels cracked like demon whips over all." Sprays of lead shrapnel balls tore great gaps in the German line which faltered and then broke, leaving their wounded behind to face the cold alone.

That the sufferings of the wounded lying out through the long nights of icy wind in the No Man's Land between the lines would be great did not probably disturb the Crown Prince. It is one of the most gruesome facts in the history of the War that the French, peering through the moonlight at what they thought to be stealthily crawling Germans, found them to be wounded men frozen to death.[14]
British observer
French Field Headquarters

But the Germans would not stop; seven times in one day their attacks surged up the slope toward Vaux, and seven times combined rifle, machine gun and field gun fire broke their ranks. Their dead or wounded literally carpeted the slope in front of the village. Letters and diaries collected from German casualties in the vicinity of Vaux and the fort give an insight on the German experience that wintry spring of 1916.[15]

March 9
On the morning of March 9 the 1st Battalion received orders to occupy Vaux village, whose capture had already been announced. The 13th Company was the first to enter the village, in column of fours, without any scouts or advanced guards to screen it. Suddenly it was assailed by a violent machine-gun fire, followed up by a bayonet charge. Our men made off and defended themselves in the houses, where the French slaughtered them with bombs.

Often neither side was sure who controlled Vaux, the village probably changed hands thirteen times that March.

March 10
Since yesterday morning there has been a heavy snowfall: it stops everything and interferes with the operations before Verdun. We can't get away from the cold, the rain, the snow, and the mud, and we camp out in the open. Each man digs himself in as best he can, wraps himself up in his coat and his canvas bag, and freezes all night. To make matters worse, we are constantly under artillery fire which claims a large number of victims every evening, for we have no trenches or shelter.

March 24
There is no need for me to write any more. All the rest may be left to the imagination. Still I want to be hopeful. It's hard, very hard! I am still so young. What's the use? What's the good of prayer and entreaty? The shells! The shells!

April 11
We are in a pit of hell, with artillery fire day and night.... If only this wretched war would end! No one who has any sense can justify such butchery of men.

April 15

I am huddled up in a little hole in the mud, which has to protect me against enemy shell–bursts; and they never leave off for a moment. I have already seen a good many things in this war, but have not been in such a situation as this. Its horror simply beggars description.... On April 11 we made an attack in order to take their trenches. We opened with an artillery preparation on a tremendous scale, lasting twelve hours, and then the infantry assault was launched. The French machine-guns were entirely undamaged, the result being that the first wave of our onset was broken by machine-gun fire as soon as it left the trench. What is more, the French in their turn started such an artillery barrage that another attack was not to be thought of. We are in a first-line trench, about 120 yards from the enemy. The weather is miserable, always cold and rainy.

While part of the 170th defended Vaux village, four companies sheltered inside Fort Vaux. The Germans brought their 210 mm, 380 mm and 420 mm mortars into play and began pounding the fort. The Krupp 420 mm was named *Dicke Bertha* (Fat Bertha) after Bertha Krupp von Bohlen und Halbach; it fired an 810 kilogram (1,700 lb) shell with a specially-hardened point that could penetrate 3.3 ft of reinforced concrete, after which a delay action fuse would set off the huge charge. The impacts of the "smaller mortars" such as the 210 mm or 380 mm were only slightly less destructive.[16] Even a near miss by one of these shells could be devastating. One company of the 170th was sheltering in "bomb-proofs" under the fort's main rampart when a 380 mm shell burst in the dry moat behind it. "Of the two hundred and fifty men, only six survive, and the walls are plastered with blood, brains and bits of smoking uniform."[17]

March 2, 1916

They have just shot away a whole corner of this redoubt — and the damn thing was made of reinforced concrete and steel plates. The devils have been at it for nearly four hours now with an average of one shot per minute at this particular redoubt. I mean one big shell of 210 mm or 380 mm caliber. The little ones only help make a row and sweep the ramparts. Allah knows how long this old box will hold together. We laugh and munch army biscuits and smoke, but there is cold death in the eye of every man.[18]

Ever the optimists, the German general staff had anticipated a triumphal entry into the city of Verdun on March 2, 1916. In fact, Berlin timed the opening of the new German war loan subscription for March 4, two days after the entry and enough time for German newspapers to publish photographs and articles of the victors. The hope was that the victory would inspire German investors to purchase war bonds as they had in August 1915, when the amount raised for the war had been phenomenal. The closing date for the new subscription was March 22.[19] The investment promised a return of 5 percent, but only if Germany won the war. On March 2 the Germans still had not taken Fort Vaux, although they were hammering it mightily. An American correspondent in Berlin wrote, "with almost glacier-like force, irresistibility, and steadiness the vast army of the Crown Prince is slowly enveloping Verdun."[20] But glacial advances are slow, unpredictable, and characterized by retreats as well as advances. And so it was with German assaults on Fort Vaux; advances followed by retreats, with the former always slightly exceeding the latter, until they finally reached the ramparts of the fort. For over three months, from March until June 7 when the fort surrendered, the fighting was relentless. The German Army paid an enormous price for an overvalued piece of realestate. And the French paid an equally enormous price in defending it. The fort's single 75 mm gun turret was nonfunctional and its flanking 75 mm guns had been removed before the battle began. The fort was basically a badger's den of underground galleries and rooms with a poor water supply.

> April 3, 1916
> You can get some idea of how things are with us from the fact that the corps of officers has been entirely renewed. The losses of the regiment are rather heavy, for its position (Vaux tableland) is a rather unpleasant one. Our battalions relieve each other, but the rest-stations are shelled quite as much as the first line.[21]
> A German Lieutenant

In early March, the 170th received orders to leave Fort Vaux and advance toward the village of Fleury, a small hamlet a few miles west of Fort Vaux. Fleury was then in German hands. It should be noted that in the course of the Battle of Verdun, Fleury changed hands many times, until it essentially disappeared, not even a blot on the landscape marking its location when the fighting ended. When the 170th arrived, Fleury had just begun its disintegration; buildings were still intact. The 170th took cover behind a railway embankment from where it charged the village and immediately met murderous fire from German batteries. The Fleury railroad station was hit with shell after shell and began to burn, as did other houses. Greeted by escaped chickens and ducks that fled squawking before them, the French found streets littered with dead horses and cows, "lying on their backs, all four legs stiff in the air." The village was taken quickly, but then the Germans pulverized it with shell fire and the 170th lost heavily. The French soldiers had not had food or anything to drink in two days; the starving men looted the dead, searching for rations.

The soldier-priest Pierre Teilhard de Chardin served as a stretcher bearer during the worst of the fighting around what was left of the village of Fleury. He brought in the wounded, often carrying them on his back. During one of the attacks and counterattacks, he was caught in a seemingly never ending artillery barrage and sought refuge in a shallow crater for two days as shells exploded around him, sometimes as close as a yard away.[22] He witnessed men dying badly, and as a priest, he gave solace during their last moments, heard their last confessions, and officiated at their brief funerals. Even though a priest and supposedly viewing all things in this world as manifestations of God's will, his experience of the battlefield unsettled him.

> Trying to analyze myself, I found once again that when one enters the battle-zone one experiences a sort of transposition in the way one looks at things and judges them, which makes one accept as natural (I don't say pleasant) to see men die and to be exposed to death. One becomes a "war-monad," a depersonalized element in a supra-individual operation.[23]

Before the war, Teilhard de Chardin had studied paleontology, specializing in mammalian fossils. After the war, his research interest focused on human evolution. Perhaps after seeing so much human extinction he needed to understand how mankind arrived at the state it was in. In his post-war writings, he tried to reconcile the scientific basis of human evolution with Catholic theology. He failed. The Vatican banned his books and his teachings. But the book banning was in the future; in 1916 he and his fellows had to somehow survive Verdun.

After Fleury the 170th was ordered to the village of Douaumont, a hamlet a mile west of the fort of the same name and assumed to be in French hands — unfortunately it was not. The French were greeted by German machine guns — and more losses. Finally, they were pulled out of the line, having suffered 80 percent casualties.[24]

A German war correspondent witnessed the fighting around the villages of Vaux and Douaumont:

> But how can we describe the hell on the ridge to the left of Douaumont, upon which for miles the French artillery extended? Upon them the fire of our heavy and heaviest guns was directed. As high as a house, columns of dust, earth and smoke rose from our bursting shells, and it was almost incomprehensible to us that men could live there and fight.[25]

One of the Americans wounded in the fighting around the villages of Vaux and Fleury that March was Eugene Bullard, an African-American who had joined the Legion in October of 1914, when he was only 19 years old, and had later transferred to the 170th. Born in Georgia in 1895, Bullard escaped racist America as a stowaway aboard a German freighter sailing from Norfolk,

Virginia, in 1912. Befriended by the ship's captain, who then hired him as a deck hand, Bullard landed in Scotland with five pounds in his pocket. For the next couple of years he made his living in Britain and on the continent working vaudeville and fighting in the boxing circuit. Compared to America at the time, racially tolerant Europe was heaven for the young American. In a memoir written in the latter part of his life he remembered, "None of the people in the countries which I had gone to in Europe had shown any prejudice on account of my color."[26] He crossed the channel to France and found his spiritual home. Living in Paris when the war began, he joined the Legion that fall.

Eugene Bullard was seriously wounded in the thigh by an exploding shell probably near the village of Fleury. According to his memoir, he somehow made it back to an aid station where a Red Cross Ford ambulance picked him up.[27] Was this ambulance an American Ambulance Field Service Ford Model T and was the aid station the *poste de secours* at Fort Tavannes? Section 2 of the A.A.F.S. arrived in Verdun February 22, 1916, Bullard was probably wounded on March 5, the A.A.F.S. drove the only Ford ambulances then at Verdun and their ambulances were marked with large red crosses painted on their sides. Fort Tavannes was the *poste de secours* for the fighting around the villages of Vaux, Fleury and Douaumont and the A.A.F.S. serviced that area. What is remarkable is that Section 2 may have passed the 170th with its Legionnaire contingent on the road from Bar-le-Duc to Verdun. An American ambulancier, Frank Hoyt Gailor, described it as an African army made up of men of all colors and complexions.

> I knew who and what they were by the curious Eastern smell that I had always before associated with camels and circuses. They were all lined up on each side of the of the road around their soup kitchens, which were smoking busily, and I had a good look at them as we drove along.[28]

Gailor picked up one of their non-commissioned officers who had an injured foot and needed a ride. The man was half–American, half–French and spoke English. What he said sounded like a Legionnaire talking.

> As we talked, I realized that his was a different philosophy from that of the ordinary poilu that I had been carrying. Certainly he loved France and was at war for her; but soldiering was his business and fighting was his life. Nothing else counted. He had long since given up any thought of coming out alive, so the ordinary limitations of life and death did not affect him. He wanted to fight and last as long as possible to leave a famous name in his regiment.[29]

After being moved from the battlefield, Bullard was transported to Bar-le-Duc, a rail terminus 40 miles (64.4 km) south of Verdun. From there he was taken by train to a hospital in Lyon where he would remain for 6 months, first in hospital and later at an out-patient clinic. The United States consul, who had recently learned that a wounded American was being treated, visited him in the hospital. The consul, a white Southerner, was astonished to find a black Southerner in the hospital bed. However, both being Southerners, and outside their native land, a bond developed. It was through the consul that Eugene Bullard met Will Irwin, a correspondent for *The Saturday Evening Post*. The three became friends. Bullard would hobble into town on his crutches and visit the consulate and "on many an afternoon, we three — Southerner, Southern Negro and Northerner — sat and talked war." In the resulting *Post* article Eugene Bullard was Private Gene; the consul was unnamed. Private Gene had been a machine gunner.

> He had fought at Arras; he had been in the charges for Notre Dame de Lorette; he had been wounded in the blasted terrain of Champagne. But all memories of those glorious and horrible old actions seemed to have been dimmed by that terrific fighting at Verdun, and especially by that day when his company held off a German charge until man could hold no more, until he knew the red rage and hot sickness of butchery....
>
> "It was like mowing grass, boss, only the grass grew up as fast as you mowed it. When they got a little start on us and you could rightly see them, they was coming on by fours — four here, four there — *toujours quatre, toujours quatre!* You'd mow them down, and four more would be in their places. You'd look again, and one or two would be way forward. You'd slue the gun around and get them, and four more would be just where you'd fired before, but nearer — and you'd mow them down. *Toujours quatre, toujours quatre!* If you hadn't seen the dead where you'd piled them you'd 'a' got plum disheartened. When you stopped to cool, and the other gun picked up the *feu*, you could see 'em wriggling like worms in the bait box.
>
> "Yassir, I was sick, awful sick! Every time the sergeant yelled, '*Feu!*' I got sicker and sicker. They had wives and children, hadn't they?"[30]

Perhaps Eugene Bullard remembered the kindness of the German sea captain who had helped a young stowaway escape America.

For his bravery at Verdun, Eugene Bullard received the *Croix de Guerre*, but what next, not the infantry as he still walked with a limp because of his wound. As with so many of the American legionnaires, Bullard was attracted to flying. While at Lyon he met the commandant of a nearby military airfield, and with his support Eugene Bullard transferred to aviation.[31]

9

Lafayette's Flyers

To find oneself the sole proprietor of a fighting airplane is quite a treat, let me tell you. One gets accustomed to it, though, after one has used up two or three of them — at the French Government's expense.[1]— James McConnell, Pilot–Lafayette Escadrille

Flying was the most glamorous combat profession of the war. Eugene Bullard's aspiration to become a pilot matched that of many other Americans who had volunteered to aid France. Whether in the trenches fighting or behind them driving ambulances carrying wounded, when airplanes passed overhead all looked up and many wished to be in the cockpit. Fighting an opponent one-on-one in the sky seemed cleaner, a way to escape the mud and gore of the battlefield, and if you survived the aerial duel, you returned to civilization — good food and a soft bed. Flying was very different from ground warfare, where after being an anonymous cog in a mass attack you spent the night in a shell-hole or swampy trench or stretched out in a bloody ambulance trying to sleep amidst the groans of the wounded.

What is remarkable about aviation in the First World War is how fast it developed. A German inventor, Otto Lilenthal, designed the first successful winged gliders. He made over 2,000 safe glides between 1891 and 1896 before being killed in a flying accident.[2] Wilbur and Orville Wright studied the writings of early glider pioneers like Lilenthal before building and experimenting with their own winged gliders. In 1903, the brothers built a motorized glider and carried out test flights at Kitty Hawk, North Carolina. On December 17, 1903, with Orville at the controls, that aircraft achieved a powered flight of 852 feet and was in the air 59 seconds. It was the longest of four flights that day.[3] From that day on all of the brothers' intellectual energies and financial resources were focused on one thing — the development of powered flight. In 1908, in Le Mans, France, Wilbur won the Michelin Trophy with a world record flight of 27 miles (43.4 km), staying aloft for 2 hours and 20 minutes.

The prize of $4,000 and a gold medal "the size of a small can" meant they would be "getting something decent to eat."[4] Always looking for funds to support their work, the brothers were in Pau, France, in the beginning of 1909 demonstrating their machine and giving flying lessons. Among the notables who came to see them fly were Kings Alfonso of Spain and Edward VII of Great Britain. On August 19, 1909, Orville arrived in Berlin to show the Kaiser the wonders of flight. The first flight was at Tempelhofer Field. Kaiser Wilhelm was ecstatic; he loved new technologies, especially when they had military value.[5] A second demonstration was made at Potsdam, this time with the Crown Prince as passenger (see Chapter 3). Orville's father, learning of the royal flight, confided in his diary:

> Orville, at Potsdam, is reported to have flown over 1,600 feet high —1,637 ft. He took up the Crown Prince of Germany, 60 ft. high; gets a present of a diamond and ruby (stickpin) composing the letter "W" and a crown[6]

The Crown Prince was more generous than the Kaiser; the latter gave Orville "an autographed photo of his imperiously decorated self."[7]

Britain, France and Germany all recognized the military significance of the Wrights' invention and assigned their own engineers and inventors to the task of aircraft design. In 1909, a monoplane designed and piloted by the Frenchman Louis Blériot flew across the English Channel making the 21 miles from Calais to Dover in 53 minutes.[8] Piloting a Blériot monoplane, the American aviator Harriet Quimby successfully crossed the Channel on April 16, 1912, the first woman to do so. However, flying was still very dangerous. Quimby purchased a powerful military-type Blériot and entered the Boston Aeroplane Meet that summer and was killed in a crash.[9] The Blériot monoplane flown by Ms. Quimby that fatal day was the prototype for many of the military aircraft of the war.

When the war began in 1914, aircraft evolved quickly, survival in the air became Darwinian with success going to the fastest, most maneuverable and best armed. Protective coloration became important, not to hide from the enemy but rather to distinguish friend from foe. Any airplane flying low doing reconnaissance work or limping home because of engine problems nearly always attracted fire from ground troops. If a plane flew over, regardless of its nationality, everyone shot at it. It was almost a sport, akin to duck hunting, with gunners guessing how far to lead the big bird before firing. Germans bagged their own planes, as did the French and the British. To aid recognition of one's own planes, and thus reduce losses from friendly fire, warring nations adopted national markings on wings and fuselage by the end of 1914.[10] Germany and Austria-Hungary adopted the black Prussian cross to mark their

A Blériot monoplane piloted by the American aviator Harriet Quimby, the first woman issued a pilot's license in America. A fearless pilot, she once said to a reporter, "You see an aviator always thinks no matter how dangerous certain flights may have been to others, his own individual luck will be with him — and he will escape." She perished in an air crash in 1912 (Library of Congress).

planes. The Allies marked their planes with a roundel, a circular target-like insignia with a center surrounded by two concentric rings, the pattern of colors distinguishing the individual countries. The French roundel had a blue center, then a white ring followed by a red ring. The British had a red center then white and blue rings. Later when America entered the war, its roundel was white, blue and red. Allied gunners only fired on planes marked with a box-like black cross, whereas to the other side all roundels were fair game.

The first military use of airplanes was for reconnaissance. However, early in the war airplanes took on new missions and designs evolved for these new missions. Planes became specialized for bombing or destroying other aircraft. Fighter aircraft attacked enemy fighters and, of course, enemy bombers and reconnaissance planes. So began an endless deadly competition as one technological innovation trumped another in the fulfillment of these missions.

The French organized their military aviation into three categories based upon these different missions: *avions de chasse,* high-powered and maneuverable fighter aircraft whose mission was to destroy enemy planes in aerial combat; *avions de bombardement,* large, slow, unwieldy monsters designed for bombing raids; and *avions de réglage,* two-seater scout aircraft designed to fly low over German lines observing enemy dispositions, taking photographs or regulating artillery fire. Scout aircraft had probably the most important and certainly the most dangerous task; while flying long distance reconnaissance alone over German-held territory, they were sitting ducks for German fighters. Although early in the war they were unarmed, eventually two-seaters were armed with machine guns for defense; the pilot could fire forward over the top wing and the observer had a machine gun on a swivel to cover the sides and rear of the airplane.

In late summer of 1915, a scout plane piloted by Corporal James Bach, an American volunteer, was slowly flying reconnaissance deep over German territory. Bach had been in the Foreign Legion but growing tired of trench life, he transferred to aviation. After successfully completing pilot training, he joined the Escadrille MS 38 and went to the front in August. Escadrille MS 38 flew the Morane Saulnier Type L, thus its MS designation. The Morane Saulnier Type L was a two-seater monoplane that had its wing mounted high above the body of the aircraft for better visibility of the terrain below. It was nicknamed the "Parasol" because of its high wing. In 1915 the plane was used for reconnaissance, bombing and fighter patrols. Bombing missions often consisted of dropping large numbers of finned darts (*flechettes*) on German troops, a combination of medieval and twentieth century technologies. Fighter capability was a bit more advanced, the observer firing either rifle, or carbine or Lewis machine gun at the foe.[11]

Corporal Bach was on the back leg of the mission, returning to base. Behind him sat his observer, Lieutenant Giroux. They both spotted a German scout plane coming their way, homeward bound from a similar mission.

The observer in the German plane opened fire with his machine gun,

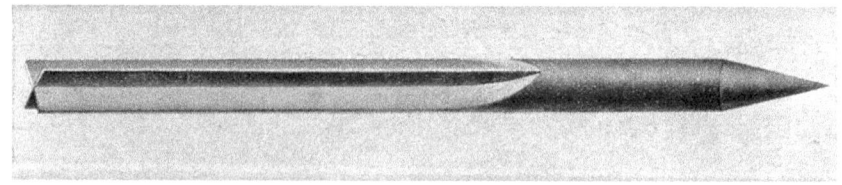

A finned dart (*flechette*) dropped by French flyers on German troops early in the air war. Contained in bombs timed to open a thousand or more feet above the earth, the steel "fountain-pen-sized" darts hurled downward silently and at high velocity on unsuspecting targets. Horses and men were skewered by the hail of deadly steel bolts (*Hamburger Fremdenblatt: Illustrated War Chronic* [Hamburg: Brosckek, 1915]).

slugs tore through the Parasol's fabric, a few slugs hit the engine cowling and one shot passed through the cockpit nearly hitting Bach. Enraged, Bach attacked. In the resulting dogfight, the two planes drifted farther and farther over German territory, but still Bach continued to attack until finally he shot the German scout plane literally to pieces, its wings collapsing as it fell in a steep dive to its doom. This was very likely the first "kill" by an American pilot in the war. The fight had left the Parasol in tatters; it limped for home, crashing just after it crossed the French trench lines. Bach walked away unscratched, his lieutenant suffered a broken arm.

On September 23, 1915, Bach was again in the air, piloting one of a pair of Parasols on an espionage mission. The planes were to ferry a couple of saboteurs behind the German lines. Each plane carried a saboteur in its observer's seat. The Parasols landed on a rough pasture and quickly dropped off their passengers. Turning, the planes took off. Bach's plane got airborne, but the other did not; it became tangled in brush and small trees and flipped over. Bach landed again and picked up the other pilot, but while attempting to take off, his wing tip hit a tree. Now both were stranded behind German lines and both were soon captured. After several unsuccessful escape attempts, Bach spent the war in German prison camps; he was not repatriated until the war's end. James Bach earned the double distinction of being the first American aviator to fly for the French and the first American taken prisoner in the war.[12] He was in captivity so long that the Germans made him Herr Direktor of the Amerikanischer-Kriegsgefangenen-Klub.[13]

Another American aviator flying for the French at the beginning of the war was a rich playboy named William Thaw who would become one of America's most effective air-squadron commanders. A Yale dropout who learned to fly in the United States, William Thaw was known in New York City society for a reckless flight that skimmed under all four of the East River bridges and circled the Statue of Liberty. In the summer of 1914, Thaw was piloting his own airplane on a tour of the resorts on the French Riviera. When the war began that August he donated his plane to the French government and, against his father's wishes, joined the French Foreign Legion.[14] By the end of December 1914, Thaw had transferred to aviation, flying in Escadrille D 6 as an observer in a Deperdussin TT, a two-seater monoplane. Unfortunately the observer sitting in front of the pilot restricted the latter's downward view, thus making landings exciting, but probably no more so than flying under bridges. The poor design of the plane led to its withdrawal from service in the early days of the war.[15] Thaw's job was reconnaissance and defending the aircraft from attack. Before machine guns were mounted on aircraft, defense consisted of taking pot-shots with pistol and carbine.

> About three or four times a week I have to go on little joy-rides in a good machine (we have six 80-gnome Deperdussins) with a good pilot, mark the position of German batteries, and regulate by means of smoke signals the firing of our guns.[16]

By mid–1915, Thaw was a fighter pilot in Escadrille N 65, flying the Nieuport 10, a two-seater biplane. With a crew of two, the plane was seriously underpowered, lacking both speed and maneuverability. The pilot usually flew the plane solo with the forward cockpit empty, making it a de facto single-seat fighter. The plane's only machine gun, a Lewis gun, was affixed to the upper wing so its bullets passed above and clear of the propeller's rotation. The pilot could get to the gun's trigger only by reaching high above his head, while with his other hand he guided the plane. It was a clumsy arrangement at best.[17]

Another wealthy American who volunteered to fly for France was Norman Prince, a Harvard graduate, *cum laude*, 1908, with a law degree from the same institution in 1911. He practiced law in Chicago for two years and during that time became keenly interested in the new field of aviation. Prince took flying lessons and earned his pilot's license in 1912. In 1913, he gave up law and spent the year at his father's residences in France and Massachusetts; when the war began (August 1914), he enrolled in a flying school in Massachusetts to increase his aeronautical skills in preparation for volunteering his services to France. He sailed for France in January of 1915. Rather than immediately enlisting, Prince established himself in a luxurious apartment in Paris and actively promoted an idea that had become an obsession with him — the formation of a volunteer all American fighter squadron. Even with his family's connections in France, the idea went nowhere. Prince enlisted and entered aviation school at Pau in early March 1915. Remarkably, the school occupied land on his father's horse-breeding estate, which Mr. Frederick Henry Prince, Norman's father, had allocated to the French government for the aviation school.[18] By the beginning of May, having successfully completed pilot training, Norman Prince was assigned to the third Groupe de Bombardement flying Voisin 3 bombers. The Voisin 3 was a biplane with its motor mounted in the rear driving a propeller that pushed the aircraft. Fronting the motor was a compartment (*nacelle*) for the observer/bomber and pilot. An 8 mm Hotchkiss machine gun protected the plane.[19] Voisin bombers attacked train stations, artillery positions, air fields and barracks, "but not towns or cities or other localities where the lives of helpless women and children might be endangered."[20] In the summer of 1915, Prince's group was based in Lorraine, near the capital city of Nancy.

> One day six German machines, fully equipped, bombarded Nancy and our aviation field. To retaliate, my squadron was sent out to bombard their field

that afternoon. We started with thirty machines to a designated rendezvous, and fifty minutes later, after getting grouped, we proceeded to our ultimate destination. I had a very fast machine, and reached the German flying field without being attacked. When my observer was aiming at the hangers of the Germans, my machine was attacked by them — one on the left and two on the right. I shouted to my observer to drop his bombs, which he did, and we immediately straightened out for home. While I was on the bank the Germans opened fire on me with their machine guns. My motor stopped a few moments afterwards.[21]

Flying without motive power, an easy target for his German attackers, Prince somehow managed to glide the crippled Voisin back across French lines, landing in a field covered with white crosses of French and German dead.

Elliot Cowdin, another early aviator from a wealthy American family and graduate of Harvard, class of 1907, first volunteered as an ambulancier in the American Ambulance Service, precursor of the American Ambulance Field Service in November 1914. After his tenure of service with the Ambulance Service, Cowdin applied and was accepted to flight school. By May 1915, he was a pilot flying a Voisin bomber and was also based near Nancy.[22]

In December of 1915, Thaw, Prince, and Cowdin obtained leave to visit their families in America. The American press's coverage of the three pilots and the public's enthusiasm for stories about these "knights of the air" or "flying Galahads" finally convinced the French that perhaps Prince's idea of an American fighter escadrille had merit.[23] The publicity generated by an Escadrille Américaine would help galvanize American support for the French cause. So why not pull together the American pilots then serving in various French escadrilles into one unit and reap the publicity harvest? For that reason, on April 20, 1916, the Escadrille Américaine was officially placed on the French roster as escadrille N 124 and its pilots were posted to an airfield at Luxeuil-les-Bains in the Voges Mountains in the Alsace, 35 miles (56.3 km) from Switzerland. The original Escadrille Américaine pilots were Norman Prince, William Thaw, Elliot Cowden, Kiffin Rockwell, Victor Chapman, James McConnell, and Bert Hall. The French commander of the squadron was Captain Georges Thénault. Assigned to N 124 was an army of helpers: including mechanics, chauffeurs, armorers, telephone clerics and medical orderlies. All arrived in Luxeuil-les-Bains with one glaring exception — there were no airplanes.

April 30, [1916]
  As though to aggravate our chagrin at not having the 'planes, the Boche came all the way over and dropped bombs on our field.
  Victor Chapman[24]

After a couple of weeks of frantic telegraphs by Captain Thénault, vans hauling eight disassembled Nieuport 11 fighters entered the airfield. The Americans joined the fitters and riggers in the painstaking job of putting the aircraft together.[25]

> Only four days later, however, Rockwell brought down the escadrille's first plane in his initial aërial combat. He was flying alone when, over Thann, he came upon a German on reconnaissance. He dived and the German turned toward his own lines, opening fire from a long distance. Rockwell kept straight after him. Then, closing to within thirty yards, he pressed on the release of his machine gun, and saw the enemy gunner fall backward and the pilot crumple sideways in his seat. The plane flopped downward and crashed to earth just behind the German trenches.[26]

The Nieuport 11 was a single-seat biplane fighter nicknamed *Bébé*, probably because of its small size; with a wingspan of less than 25 feet (top wing) and a gross loaded weight of 1100 pounds, *Bébé* was fast and had hummingbird-like maneuverability. It was powered by either an 80 or 110 hp nine-cylinder rotary engine. In a rotary, the nine-cylinder engine rotated around a crankshaft that was fixed to the airplane and the propeller was bolted to the engine. There was no carburetor, a mixture of gasoline and high-grade castor oil served as fuel. Castor oil was the only known lubricant able to take the heat and pressure of the cylinders. The oil/gas mixture was sucked from a hollow portion of the crankshaft and fed into the cylinders. Without a carburetor, there was no way to regulate the engine's speed of rotation so it always ran full speed. The pilot managed engine speed by cutting off the ignition so the engine was either running or not. Because of the plane's light weight, the spinning mass of engine resulted in a gyroscopic effect. Since the engine spun to the right from the pilot's viewpoint, it pulled the plane nose down on right turns—an exciting experience for novice pilots.[27]

The Nieuport 11's armament was obsolescent, as the French still did not have a synchronization mechanism allowing the pilot to fire a machine gun through the arc of a spinning propeller. Consequently, the machine gun was mounted atop the upper wing as in the Nieuport 10.[28] In contrast, German fighter planes had the Fokker interrupter gear that allowed firing through the propeller arc, thus permitting a more logical placement of the machine gun directly in front of the pilot, pointing down the centerline of the plane. The period from July 1915 until the French and British developed their own synchronization gears in 1916 was known as the Fokker Scourge (or Fokker Harvest, depending upon one's point of view) because of the advantage German fighters had over the Allies. The first French fighter with such gun synchronization was the Nieuport 17.[29] The Escadrille Américaine (N 124) obtained the Nieuport 17 in September of 1916. Gun synchronization was one of the major technological achievements of the war.

> The propeller turns at the rate of about 1,650 revolutions per minute. Consequently with the two-bladed propeller that we used, the propeller blades were passing 3,300 times per minute in front of the muzzle of the gun. These bullets passed between the blades without ever hitting them.[30]

Prior to flying a mission the machine gun was test-fired to check synchronization, sometimes the bullets chewed off the propeller.

N 124 next went to an airfield in the village of Behonne, about two miles east of the small city of Bar-le-Duc, the railway logistical hub for the battle raging around Verdun. The Americans arriving on May 20, 1916, found lodgings in a villa between Behonne and Bar-le-Duc. During the war, Bar-le-Duc had the reputation of "that little Sodom south of Verdun." The town had all the military amenities: cheap drinks and friendly women. The

Left to right, James McConnell, Kiffen Rockwell, Captain Georges Thénault, Norman Prince and Victor Chapman, members of the Lafayette Escadrille, in front of a Nieuport 11 fighter. The photograph dates to April 1916 during what became known as the Fokker Scourge, a period when German fighter aircraft could fire through the propeller arc and Allied fighters, such as the Nieuport 11, could not. Of the five men in the photograph, only Captain Thénault survived the war (Georges Thénault. *The Story of the Lafayette Escadrille* [Boston: Small, Maynard, 1921]).

Americans soon discovered both in establishments such as the Café des Trois Étoiles.

> But the soldiers were not alone nor lonely. There were almost enough to go around, enough ladies, tawdry little rouge-and-powder cartoons bewildered by the catastrophe of their time and the male hosts of the world, asking very little and giving far too much.[31]

Soon new American pilots arrived, including Raoul Lufberry who became the squadron's leading ace.[32] N 124 now had fifteen pilots and was making its first kills in the Verdun sector.

> Before we were fairly settled at Bar-le-Duc, Hall brought down a German observation craft and Thaw a Fokker.[33] Fights occurred on almost every sortie. The Germans seldom cross into our territory, unless on a bombing jaunt, and thus practically all the fighting takes place on their side of the line.[34]

Because the prevailing wind blew from west to east, aerial dogfights drifted eastward over German territory. Thus, when an Allied plane was shot-up and broke off an engagement the pilot had to fight headwinds as he nursed his crippled plane home. Aerial battles occurred over all of the Verdun battlefield landmarks: on the east or right bank Forts Douaumont, Vaux and Tavannes and on the left bank Côte 304 and Mort Homme. James McConnell, formerly with the American Ambulance Field Service, described Verdun from the sky in 1916.

> Peaceful fields and farms and villages adorned the landscape a few months ago — when there was no Battle of Verdun. Now there is only that sinister brown belt, a strip of murdered nature. It seems to be another world. Every sign of humanity has been swept away. The woods and roads have vanished like chalk wiped from a board; of villages nothing remains but gray smears where stone walls have tumbled together. The great forts of Douaumont and Vaux are outlined faintly, like finger tracings in wet sand.
>
> A smoky pall covers the sector under fire, rising so high that at a height of 1000 feet one is enveloped in its mist-like fumes. Now and then monster projectiles hurtling through the air close by leave one's plane rocking violently in their wake. Airplanes have been cut in two by them.[35]

In their zeal to bring down German planes, some of the Americans took foolhardy risks, sometimes with dire consequences. And they never followed orders.

> A week or so later Chapman was wounded. Considering the number of fights he had been in and the courage with which he attacked it was a mira-

cle he had not been hit before. He always fought against odds and far within the enemy's country. He flew more than any of us, never missing an opportunity to go up, and never coming down until his gasoline was giving out. His machine was a sieve of patched-up bullet holes.[36]

A bullet creased Chapman's scalp, but still he managed to bring his plane back. With a bandage wrapped around his head instead of a helmet, he still continued to fly. On June 23, he made his last flight, the combat occurring north of Fort Douaumont where he "engaged with six or seven German machines and he didn't have a chance."[37] His plane crashed inside German lines. He was the first to perish in the Escadrille Américaine; he was twenty-seven years old. His father, John Jay Chapman, published his letters the following year.[38] The introductory "Memoir" in this volume is unusual in that Victor's father wrote more feelingly of Victor's mother than of the loss of his son. Victor is remembered for his slowness in book-learning, "a morbid child with no apparent talents and a gift of suffering as few natures possess."[39] Mr. Chapman senior was a strange man. When he assaulted a fellow he mistakenly believed had insulted the future Mrs. Chapman, John Jay plunged his own hand into the white hot coals of a stove in remorse for his error, burning himself so severely that the hand required amputation[40] — an act that brings new meaning to giving one's hand in marriage! Perhaps this paternal self-destructive streak partly motivated Victor Chapman's own recklessness.

Chapman was not the only one taking reckless chances. If any traits characterized the Americans, it was their bravery and unfortunate lack of discipline in the air. Although led by a French officer, Captain Georges Thénault, in reality he had little control of his men. The French Foreign Office decreed that punishments were off limits for the Americans. The primary mission of the Escadrille Américaine was to push American public opinion to the side of the French, priming the pump to bring America into the war. If the squadron shot down a few Germans, so much the better, but that mission was secondary. Because of his lack of control, Thénault could almost always be sure that whatever orders he gave on the ground would invariably be disobeyed once the planes were in the air.[41] The Escadrille Américaine flew in formation until someone spotted German planes on the horizon. Then it was every pilot fighting his own war. For example on May 24, 1916, before Chapman's death, Captain Thénault led a morning patrol of five Nieuports from Les Eparges northward toward Verdun. The men's orders were to attack German aircraft only when Thénault gave the signal. As the patrol got near the Verdun battlefield, it spotted a dozen German two-seater observation planes flying low across the landscape, each plane with a pilot forward and a machine gunner behind. Each plane covered the other; it would be suicidal to attack them with only five fighters. Thénault led his men away from the German mini-armada; unfortunately, no one followed him. The Americans turned and flew into the hornet's nest of machine gun fire. Almost immediately, a bullet exploded on Rockwell's windscreen driving pieces of glass and steel into his face, forcing him to flee for home. Then Chapman, hit in the arm by a slug when his plane was peppered, turned for home. Thaw's plane was riddled by machine gun fire. A bullet smashed into his arm; he crashed near Fort Tavannes. French soldiers carried the unconscious pilot to a nearby *poste de secours*. The German planes escaped with little damage.[42]

The squadron spent 113 days in the line at Verdun that summer before being ordered to Luxeuil in the Alsace on September 14, 1916. Squadron 124 had 13 confirmed kills, had numerous planes shot to pieces, a number of its men wounded, one seriously, and one of its own killed. But before Luxeuil, there was Paris, where the men were given three days' leave. They had earned it.

In Paris the Americans made the rounds of the usual airmen hangouts, the Chatham Bar near the Opéra and Harry's Bar, a few steps from the Chatham. The most notable event of the Parisian visit was the addition of a new member to the team, a lion cub purchased from a Brazilian dentist who had offered it in the classified section of the Paris *Tribune*. The beast was soon named Whiskey, after the Americans' favorite drink — whiskey sours. Now the squadron had a mascot, a publicity bonanza for the French. Unfortunately, there would also soon be very bad news hogging the story leads.

At Luxeuil new planes arrived, the Nieuport 17 with an interrupter gear allowing a Vickers machine gun to fire through the propeller arc. Making his first flight with the new plane, Kiffin Rockwell attacked a two-seater German Aviatek. Flying through a hail of bullets to get in position, Rockwell's luck ran out, a slug hit him in the chest, his plane plunged to earth and crashed. He was the second airman of escadrille N 124 to die. Then Norman Prince's plane caught a high tension wire as it was landing after defending Allied bombers returning from a mission against the Mauser rifle manufacturing works in Oberndorf, Germany. His plane somersaulted, throwing Prince from the cockpit with great force. He died of his injuries. Rifle production at the Mauser factory continued as usual. A few days after Prince's burial the Escadrille Américaine left for the Somme.

They arrived at the Somme at the end of October 1916, at the tail end of the battle. The British, French and Germans had suffered 1.5 million casualties since July 1 and were literally punch drunk from the fighting; all combatants called it quits on November 18, the official end of the Battle of the Somme. Rough wooden portable barracks in a sea of slimy mud near an Allied airfield eight miles southeast of Amiens served as billets for the Americans. There were no mess facilities; the Americans were expected to make those arrangements themselves. After previously living in villas and first class hotels, the boys were not happy campers. The weather was cold, rainy and mostly overcast, making flying nearly impossible. Days were mostly spent grumbling. During this time, the unit devised an insignia, a snarling Seminole war chief, inspired by a picture stenciled on a Savage Arms ammunition box. The war chief soon adorned the fuselage of every N 124 Nieuport. With the new insignia came a new name. The Germans had rightfully objected that the Escadrille Américaine was a violation of American neutrality so American Secretary of State Robert Lansing requested a name change. The French obliged, eventually coming up with an even more emotionally charged name, the Escadrille Lafayette or in English word order, the Lafayette Escadrille. The men loved it; the American press became delirious. Fall changed to one of the coldest winters on record, almost too cold to fly. On a jaunt to Paris William Thaw purchased a female lion cub from the Paris Zoo to keep Whiskey company, naming her Soda, naturally.

Then on March 19, 1917, a cold dreary day, James McConnell went on patrol with a new member of the escadrille, Edmond Genet. McConnell did not return; French soldiers found his body near the twisted wreckage of his plane. Among his effects was a letter to be opened upon his death.

> My burial is of no import. Make it easy as possible on yourselves. I have no religion and do not care for any service. If the omission would embarrass you, I presume I could stand the performance.[43]

Finally, on April 6, 1917, nearly two years after Americans began flying for France, America entered the war on the side of the Allies. On April 16, German antiaircraft fire brought down Edmond Genet's plane, giving him the dubious honor of being the first American killed in combat after we entered the war. The year 1917 saw a surge of American volunteers boarding ships for France, almost all wanting to fly, thanks to the Lafayette Escadrille publicity blitz. Nearly 100 Americans entered French flight schools and eventually joined various escadrilles. These Americans were part of what became known as the Lafayette Flying Corps. The Lafayette Escadrille, assigned to help cover the French offensive at the Chemin des Dames, a debacle that resulted in wholesale mutiny of the French Army, then moved to Flanders with the British for the Third Ypres Offensive, the Battle of Passchendale, another notable disaster. Attrition of pilots continued, with replacements coming from the Lafayette Flying Corps. Eventually 38 Americans served in the Lafayette Escadrille, which had an average strength of a dozen, 10 of which were killed either with the squadron or with other squadrons.[44]

Edmond Genet in the cockpit of a Nieuport 17, a French fighter with an interrupter gear allowing the Vickers machine gun mounted in front of the pilot to fire through the propeller arc. As a backup, a Lewis machine gun is mounted on the top wing. Note the metal frame near the end of the Lewis gun, preventing it from being depressed too far and firing into the propeller arc. Genet fatally crashed April 16, 1917 (Georges Thénault. *The Story of the Lafayette Escadrille* [Boston: Small, Maynard, 1921]).

The Lafayette Escadrille returned to Lorraine in August 1917 to participate in the last French offensive at Verdun. Based in Senard, an airfield at the southern edge of the Argonne Forest, the escadrille was no longer flying Nieuports. The old fighter had been replaced by the SPAD 7 built by the *Société pour Aviation et ses Derivées*, whose initials gave the plane its name. Spads were more robust and faster than the Nieuport 17. Escadrille N 124 became SPA 124. The primary mission at Senard was, along with other fighter escadrilles, to protect Allied bombers attacking Dun-sur-Meuse, a small but important railroad yard for the line that brought German troops and supplies to the west bank battlefield. Dun was about 25 air miles (about 40 km) northeast of Senard, so fighters covered the bombers the entire way and back. Needless to say, the Germans vigorously defended Dun, sending very aggressive fighter attacks to intercept the bombers. That August the air above that small town straddling the Meuse River was filled with the screaming motors of diving planes, sprays of machine gun fire, antiaircraft shrapnel shells bursting high above the houses, bombers attempting to target railroad yards and being ripped to shreds in the process. But what goes up must come down: a rain of shell fragments, spent shrapnel and machine gun bullets, pieces of aircraft,

Americans assigned to non-fighter French escadrilles flew planes such as this Caudron R 4, a huge biplane powered by two 130 hp engines. Although originally designed as a bomber, technical deficiencies resulted in this plane being used primarily for long-range reconnaissance. It had a crew of three: a machine gunner seated in the nose, the pilot and then a machine gunner in the rear. Each gunner had twin 7.7 mm Lewis guns on a swivel mount. This armament made the R 4 a dangerous aircraft to attack.

bombs, and sometimes entire planes crashed down on Dun. The sky literally fell on the bedraggled little town, leaving its inhabitants, most of whom were German, understandably upset.

Everett Buckley of Chicago, an aviator with the Lafayette Flying Corps escadrille N 65 made a forced landing in Dun on September 6, 1917.

> I was knocked down by a crowd that had gathered. I was being pretty roughly used when a German military officer rode into the crowd on horseback, slashing right and left with his saber and seriously injuring several Germans. There is no question in my mind that I owe my life to this officer's intervention.[45]

From Dun, Buckley was moved to the nearby fortress of Montmédy, about fifteen miles (24 km) from Dun, where he was held in solitary confinement for 18 days and fed bread and water. Then he was moved to the "Microphone hotel" at Karlsruhe.

> Here I was placed in a room and given supper with several other Allied officers, English and French. In running my hand underneath the table at

supper, I found a card pinned there on which was written: "Be careful, there is a dictaphone in the lamp." Over the center table was a large hanging lamp, and upon investigation, a dictaphone was discovered. It seems that the German idea is to obtain military information by placing Allied officers together in this room soon after capture, giving them a good meal, in the expectation they would exchange experiences and discuss matters which might yield valuable military information as to the location of military units.[46]

After Karlsruhe, he was moved to a series of POW camps in Germany, from two of which he succeeded in escaping, was caught and punished. On his third attempt, he reached Switzerland on July 27, 1918, the first American POW to escape successfully.

Harold Willis of the Lafayette Escadrille had a similar experience. After being shot down over Dun on August 18, 1917, he was taken prisoner, incarcerated at Montmédy, given the convivial meal at the "Microphone hotel" followed by stays at POW camps in Germany. He managed to escape three times; following his last escape, he wandered around the Black Forest for a week before reaching the Rhine River. He entered its cold water and swam 600 feet through hard current to freedom in Switzerland.[47]

With America in the war, nearly all American wartime volunteer organizations in France were being placed under the control of General Pershing and the staff of the American Expeditionary Forces. By the fall of 1917, the days of the Lafayette Escadrille were numbered. On January 19, 1918, Bill Thaw, commissioned a major in the United States Army Air Service, took command of the U.S. 103d Aero Squadron, formed from the legacy of the Lafayette Escadrille. The lions Whiskey and Soda went to a Paris zoo. Of the 152 Americans then in the Lafayette Flying Corps, including the Lafayette Escadrille, 32 opted to remain with the French, many of the rest flew for the United States Army Air Service.[48]

10

Writers and Reporters

> Over in the village the smoke was pouring from a burning house and above the treetops the shrapnel spread their fleecy clouds.
> In the next field I saw a patch of blackened smoke; dirt flew.
> "Run!" shouted the Bavarian Captain, who had been in America. "Run like hell."
> And as we tore pell mell past the ruined house, the artillerymen grinned and waved their hands.
> "Gute Reise!" one of them yelled.
> Pleasant journey![1] — Edward Lyell Fox, American Correspondent with the German Army

The war was fought with the pen as well as the sword, and sometimes the former was mightier. American writers, newspaper hacks and *bona fide* war correspondents all flocked to Europe to tell, and sell, the biggest story of the time. Because the United States was an important neutral, American reporters worked on both sides of the battle lines.

Edward Lyell Fox, a newspaper reporter for the *New York American,* traveled with the German Army in the winter of 1914/1915 just as trench warfare was being established on the Western Front. He witnessed the sad yet proud farewells of troops leaving Berlin for the front. The men resembled marching topiaries: flowers were stuck in rifle barrels, garlands hung from spiked helmets and cartridge belts and knapsacks sported fern fronds. As the trains pulled out, women stood dabbing at the tears in their eyes and waving feebly. For many it was a final parting.

Fox traveled with the troops to the front, somewhere in France. Occasionally German soldiers, learning he was an American, identified themselves as German-Americans fighting for the Kaiser. Not infrequently, they had lived in Brooklyn or the Bronx. Fox always corrected them; they were no longer German-American. They had made their choices and were now German.

At one point Fox toured the firing line in a trench only a few hundred yards from the British. In places, the trench was seven feet deep and it never followed a straight line but rather snaked its way across the battlefield. The zigzags were on purpose; should a section of trench be captured, the enemy could not shoot straight down the entire trench system. His guide was a lieutenant whose orders were to keep the American safe no matter what. Nevertheless, battlefields are inherently unsafe places.

> "It's an attack," he shouted over his shoulder. "Get into one of the dugouts and stay there. And, if they get us, wave your passport if they find you, and yell you're an American."[2]

The lieutenant returned to his soldiers. Fox disobeyed his order and left the dugout to see the fight. The trench was being heavily shelled with shrapnel and high explosives; red hot shell splinters hit the mud with a slapping impact and a hiss as they cooled. Bullets splashed everywhere. He squinted between sandbags on the parapet and saw a line of men slowly walking across No-Man's Land; the line resembled a "monstrous fiery worm" because of the muzzle flashes of rifles. The Germans opened up with machine guns and rifle fire from the protection of trenches and rifle pits.

> I began to notice then, ... that the red wavering lines of fire, which had a way of rushing at you and vanishing to appear again further back, was slower now in appearing after it lost itself somewhere in the mud, and then it became even slower in showing itself and finally when it came, you saw that it had disintegrated into segments, that it was no longer a steady oncoming line, rather a slowly squirming thing like the curling parts of some monstrous fiery worm that had been chopped to bits and was squirming its life away out there on the mud. And it dawned upon you in horror that the fiery red lines had been lines of men, shooting as they had come; and that, when one line had been mowed down, another had rushed up from behind, so on almost endlessly it had seemed until they came broken and squirmed like the others had done, into the mud, and came no more.[3]

When the attack was finally called off, No Man's Land was carpeted with British dead and wounded. Now Fox was amazed to see British machine guns and artillery target No Man's Land as a tactic to prevent the Germans counter attacking across that desolate strip. Then the firing ceased from both sides. The American saw no wounded, only butchered dead.

Fox was given incredible access, including seeing the front from an unarmed German observation plane. Outfitted in warm flying clothing and a steel head protector, he raced to catch his flight.

> I was hurrying across the field towards the aeroplane, its fish-like tail bearing the black inscription "B 604/14," which I later came to know meant biplane number 604 of the year 1914.... I climbed up into the observer's compart-

ment and found myself staring, first at the brown propeller blades only the length of a wagon in front of me, then at the brass petrol tank overhead, and the thick, curving celluloid shield behind, through which I could see the black sleeved arms of the aviator, moving towards the levers.... The brown propeller began to spin, lazily at first, then faster, while the engine that I could have reached forward and touched, began its roaring.... I remembered to pull down my goggles and the next moment I felt a shudder run the length of the machine as it lurched forward, running over the field, to rise slightly, bump gently on its rubbered wheels, and then gliding upward on a gradual slant.[4]

The plane crossed the front, "that patch of blackened land where the pygmies played with death," and continued to the French side, dodging anti-aircraft fire while searching for French artillery batteries. Slowly circling while trying to pinpoint a battery and always alert for enemy fighters, the pilot gave Fox the ride of his life. Finally, the pilot was satisfied, and the plane streaked for home. It arrived near its base after dark; fires marked the landing strip. Fox breathed a sigh of relief as the plane began its approach. But the aircraft had a rotary engine — the landing would be dead-stick

> So we were almost home now — home! — the thought made you grimace — miles away! ... And I heard that most disconcerting of all sounds that you hear in the air, the shutting off of the motor — an instant, and as we slid forward, I felt for the brass handles to brace myself, and no longer sped round by the motor's power, the propeller blades became as the strings of a monstrous harp through which the rushing wind wailed a weird song; and we bolted down.... Gaining in violence, the wind shrieked through the slowly spinning blades, shrieked as though the very air had gone mad; and just when you had begun to doubt that it was beyond human skill to bring an aeroplane to earth through the night like this, you felt a sudden forward horizontal glide, and the next moment the rubber tired wheels were bouncing over the hardened field...[5]

After his adventures on the Western Front, Edward Lyell Fox went with the German Army to the Russian Front.

Probably the most famous American journalist in France in 1914 was Richard Harding Davis, a foreign correspondent who had already covered five different wars around the globe. Reporting on the Spanish American War in 1898, Dick Davis wrote about Teddy Roosevelt's Rough Riders in Cuba, but he did not just write, he picked up a rifle from a wounded trooper and fought. Teddy made him an honorary Rough Rider for his bravery, and Davis' articles helped put Roosevelt in the White House.

Davis was not just a war correspondent but also a celebrity in every sense

The caption reads:
  He: Was that you I kissed in the conservatory last night?
  She: About what time was it?
  Dana Gibson usually had a Gibson girl making light of her male suitor; often Richard Harding Davis served as the model for the hapless male. Despite this, or perhaps because of this, Gibson and Harding Davis remained close friends. This drawing was published in *Life* in 1903 (Charles Dana Gibson. *The Gibson Book* [New York: Charles Scribner's Sons, 1906]).

of the word. By the time he was 26 in the eighteen-nineties, he was the toast of New York City. In addition to being a journalist, Dick Davis was a widely read novelist and short story writer — his short stories and serialized books appeared in the most prestigious magazines — and he had the most recognizable face in America because he was the Gibson man. His friend Dana Gibson, an artist famous for his pen and ink drawings of beautiful and elegantly dressed city women, the Gibson girls, often paired them with a handsome and elegantly dressed city man — Davis was his model. The cover of the May 22, 1890, issue of *Life* showed Davis proposing to a Gibson girl with the following caption under the drawing:

"He: I have three thousand a year. You could certainly live on that.

"She: Yes, but I should hate to see *YOU* starve."

Davis and his wife sailed from New York to England aboard the *Lusitania*; in a letter to his brother Charles, he marveled at the experience.

> On *Lusitania*
> August 8, 1914
> They gave me a "regal" suite which at other times costs $1000 and it is so darned regal that I hate to leave it. I get sleepy walking from one end of it to the other; and we have open fires in each of the three rooms. Generally when one goes to war it is in a transport or a troop train and the person of the least importance is the correspondent. So, this way of going to war I like.[6]

On this voyage, the *Lusitania* would escape German submarine attack, but within a year the ship's luck would run out and a torpedo would find its target. Davis crossed the English Channel to Belgium and beat the Germans to Brussels; he was there when they took the city. Then Davis followed the German invasion through the rest of Belgium. After a brief trip to London, he returned to France and made two memorable visits to Reims in September of 1914.

The cathedral city of Reims is in Champagne. The cathedral was begun in 1211 and substantially completed by 1428. Two hundred years of construction resulted in a colossal structure, a 480 feet long nave flanked by towers, each 266 feet in height; those soaring towers would be the cause of the cathedral's ruin in the First World War. The Germans captured the city in the first week of September 1914, but only managed to hold it for a couple of weeks before the French drove them out. The Germans fell back about 10 miles and constructed a fortified trench system that formed an arc partially surrounding the city in the north and east. Convinced the French were using the cathedral towers to direct artillery fire on their trenches, the Germans responded by shelling the cathedral.

When the German Army had abandoned the city, they left in their wake the flotsam of war, their wounded. French clergy and medical personnel cared for these men in the cathedral. Davis, accompanied by the cathedral's abbot, visited the wounded. A thick layer of straw had been spread on the cold stone for the men's comfort.

> and on the straw were gray-coated Germans, covered with the mud of the fields, caked with blood, white and haggard from the loss of it, from the lack of sleep, rest, and food. The entire west end of the cathedral looked like a stable, and in the blue and purple rays from the gorgeous windows the wounded were as unreal as ghosts.[7]

The Germans shelled the cathedral relentlessly even though it was a refuge for their wounded.

> Shells had torn out some of the windows, the entire sash, glass and stone frame — all was gone; only a jagged hole was left. On the floor lay broken carvings, pieces of stone from flying buttresses outside that had been hurled through the embrasures, tangled masses of leaden window-sashes, like twisted coils of barbed wire, and great brass candelabra. The steel ropes that supported them had been shot away, and they had plunged to the flagging below, carrying with them their scarlet tassels heavy with the dust of centuries.[8]

Davis returned to Paris to file his story but was on his way back to Reims almost the next day — according to the Paris papers, the cathedral had been destroyed!

> The fire started in this way. For some months the northeast tower of the cathedral had been under repair and surrounded by scaffolding. On September 19th a shell set fire to the outer roof of the cathedral, which is of lead and oak. The fire spread to the scaffolding and from the scaffolding to the wooden beams of the portals, hundreds of years old.[9]

The German wounded, many unable to move, were near panic as the cathedral's lead roof started to melt and the straw upon which they lay caught fire.

> Splashed by the molten lead and threatened by falling timbers, the priests, at the risk of their lives and limbs, carried out the wounded Germans, sixty in all.[10]

The priests then had to defend the Germans from the citizens of Reims who wanted to kill the prisoners in retribution for the destruction of their cathedral and city.

Davis returned to Paris to write his story.[11] The pointless bombardment of the cathedral would continue for four years and become one of the symbols of German barbarism. The Huns from the east were blowing to bits Europe's historical and cultural heritage.

Edith Wharton passed through the city on August 13, 1915, on her way to the Alsace. She briefly noted:

> When the German bombardment began, the west front of Rheims was covered with scaffolding: the shells set it on fire, and the whole church was wrapped in flames. Now the scaffolding is gone, and in the dull provincial square there stands a structure so strange and beautiful that one must search the Inferno, or some tale of Eastern magic, for words to picture the luminous unearthly vision.[12]

To Mrs. Wharton's eye, the Prussian pyrotechnics improved the old cathedral's appearance — the black soot evidently enhanced the sculpted relief of the remaining statues! A pen-pal of Edith's, Henry James, wrote her in 1914, when the German bombardment of the cathedral was first reported.

> Lamb House, Rye
> September 21st, 1914
> Dearest Edith,
> Rheims is the most unspeakable and immeasurable horror and infamy — and what is appalling and heart-breaking is that it's "for ever and ever." But no words fill the abyss of it — nor touch it, nor relieve one's heart nor light by a spark the blackness; the ache of one's howl and the anguish of one's execration aren't mitigated by a shade, even as one brands it as the most hideous crime ever perpetrated against the mind of man.[13]

Henry was really upset!

Other Americans also witnessed the cathedral's destruction, but they did so from the German side. Irwin S. Cobb, a staff writer for the *Saturday Evening Post,* saw the cathedral from an observation balloon tethered over German lines. He had been given permission to go aloft in a *Drachen,* which he described as a seventy-five foot long, oily-looking yellow frankfurter filled with very flammable hydrogen gas with a riding car attached.

> It was not, strictly speaking, a riding car. It was a straight-up-and-down basket of tough, light wicker, no larger and very little deeper than an ordinarily fair-sized hamper for soiled linen. Indeed, that was what it reminded one of — a clothesbasket.[14]

He climbed into the basket accompanied by a German artillery observer; the German's first instruction was "no smoking"! Soon the duo was 1200 feet above the earth, the basket swaying gently in the wind. The observer noted where German shells fell and telephoned corrections to a switchboard.

> For once in my life — and doubtlessly only once — I saw now understandingly a battle front. It was spread before me — lines and dots and dashes on a big green and brown and yellow map. Why, the whole thing was as plain as a chart. I had a reserved seat for the biggest show on earth.[15]

But there could be a stiff price to pay for the gallery seat. Cobb learned that a French fighter aircraft had attacked a previous balloon at the same site; the balloon exploded and the balloonist burned to death in mid-air. After telling this sobering story, the observer got a telephone call — a French fighter was hiding up in the clouds, preparing to attack. Cobb anxiously scanned the sky. Anti-aircraft guns instantly blazed into action, defending the *Drachen* by sending up a curtain of exploding shrapnel shells. As the guns roared and through the fog of gun smoke, the balloon began its slow descent. Six big draft horses harnessed to a cable and drum pulled the gas bag down to earth and safety. When finally on *terra-firma*, Cobb had this to say about the risks of ballooning, "On observation balloons, in time of war, no casualty insurance is available at any rate of premium. I believe those who ride in them are also regarded as unsuitable risks."[16]

A less risky enterprise followed the aerial adventure, a tour of the German trenches fronting Reims. The trenches were from seven to eight feet deep with a shooting step below the parapet. The men had dug caves into the walls of the trenches and constructed cozy shelters; some had doors salvaged from nearby houses and one bore a sign lettered in chalk, "Kaiserhof Café." Cobb saw the cathedral city in the distance under a haze of smoke.

> we could, with the aid of our glasses, make out the buildings in Rheims, some of which were then on fire — particularly the great Cathedral.
> One of the towers had apparently been shorn away and the roof of the nave was burned — we could tell that. We were too far away of course to judge of the injury to the carvings and to the great rose window.[17]

Another American, Edwin F. Weigle, a twenty-six-year-old photographer representing the *Chicago Tribune* visited the front not far from Reims. An expert in the then new communication technology of motion pictures, his mission was to film the war from the German side. The *Tribune* had struck a deal with the German high command that half of all profits made by showing the films would be donated to help crippled and blind soldiers.[18] Weigle gives another excuse for the bombardment of Reims.

> That night an attack was made on the Kaiser's palace[19] by a daring French aviator. The aviator dropped several bombs near the palace and they exploded within 200 yards of where His Majesty was sleeping. The aviator was driven off by machine guns and in retaliation for his daring act the Ger-

mans proceeded to fire 500 shells into the city of Rheims. German aviators then dropped proclamations into the French trenches warning them that if another attempt was made on the Kaiser's life they would retaliate by pouring 1,000 shells into Rheims.[20]

Excuses aside, there probably was no real reason to bombard the cathedral. From the German viewpoint, there just was not a good reason not to. A German directive issued early in the 1914 campaign made this clear.

> The more terrible you are, the quicker you will cross, and the speedier the victory! Spare only the railway stations. They will be more use to us than cathedrals.[21]

Another German officer, Major-General von Ditfurth, made the point a bit more brutally:

> It is of no consequence if all the monuments ever created, all the pictures ever painted, and all the buildings ever erected by the great architects of the world were destroyed, if by their destruction we promote German victory over her enemies.[22]

Remarkably oblivious, some would say stupidly oblivious, to international public opinion, the Germans marched to their own drummers — the world be damned! The French were savvier, for them the destruction of the

Germans score a direct hit upon the transept of Reims cathedral. The shelling of the cathedral became the public relations fiasco of the war. A pointless waste of artillery shells with only one consequence, it convinced the neutral countries that the Kaiser and his cronies were barbarians (*L'Album de la Guerre*, Paris: Illustration, 1923).

cathedral was a publicity bonanza. What better example of new German *Kultur* than the destruction of Europe's heritage. Reims became an obligatory stop for all foreign journalists and important visitors.

In December 1916, a tour for six American journalists and a munitions manufacturer from Bridgeport, Connecticut, left Paris for the cathedral city. Among the journalists was Mabel Potter Daggett representing the *Pictorial Review*, a New York City publication with four million female readers. Ms. Daggett described herself as a feminist and suffragist. She got to the front by literally blackmailing the French press bureau, the *La Maison de la Presse*.

> Other American publications may offer Maison de la Press other facilities for reaching the American public. But none of them can duplicate the facilities presented by the Pictorial Review, the leading champion of the feminist cause.... Is not France interested in what she shall read there?[23]

As the party approached Reims, they found the road leading into the city screened with cloth curtains hung on wires fifteen feet high to keep the numerous auto convoys of visitors from being targeted by German artillery. In the distance, the sound of explosions told of the continued bombardment of the city. This element of danger sharpened senses as the touring cars passed through the city gate. The party entered a ghost town, their footsteps echoed through deserted streets and everywhere scenes of desolation appeared. They slowly picked their way to the square fronting the cathedral with its famous statue of Joan of Arc. Although the cathedral was slowly being wrecked behind her, the Maid of Orléans on her horse triumphant was untouched.

A priest led the Americans on a tour of the cathedral, their shoes crunching on the shards of stained glass that littered the nave. The roof had been recently torn open by a shell and birds were roosting on the transept rail. Statues of saints had toppled to the floor and smashed into pieces. Nothing seemed immune from destruction, except the equestrian statue of Joan of Arc fronting the disintegrating pile. Perhaps Ms. Daggett felt that was appropriate, since this war was caused by male foolishness.

After the day's tour, the Americans returned to Paris, excited by what they had seen. Now that was real war! Ms. Daggett had mail waiting at her hotel.

> I am standing at the window with a Christmas card in my hand, thinking pleasant thoughts of the faraway city called New York where there is still peace on earth, good will to men, when down the Rue de Rivoli passes a motor lorry piled high with black crosses. There are fields in France that are planted with black crosses, acres and acres of them. After each new push on the front, more are required, black crosses by the cartload![24]

Now that was real war!

About 60 miles (96.5 km) southeast of Reims is the Lorraine town of Stenay. It was here in November 1914 that an American reporter named Karl von Wiegand, a representative of the Hearst press, interviewed Crown Prince Wilhelm, the Kaiser's son and heir. Wiegand was the first American reporter ever granted such access. It was the scoop of the year.

The Crown Prince, commander of the German Fifth Army at the age of thirty-two, had established his headquarters in Stenay in mid September 1914. Needing a place to live, he commandeered the Château des Tilleuls (see Chapter 3). Wiegand met with the Prince at the château and since the Prince spoke English more comfortably than Wiegand did German, their discussions were in English. The resulting article[25] was pretty much a puff-piece; the Crown Prince came across as everyone's friend, except perhaps Britain's, and stated he would love to visit America and learn to play baseball. There is nothing included that might be the slightest bit controversial, perhaps because Wiegand was the head of United Press in Berlin, with special access to the Kaiser's entourage, and he intended to keep the position. In 1958, von Wiegand remembered that during the interview the Crown Prince declared, "We have

The Château des Tilleuls in Stenay served as Crown Prince Wilhelm's residence from September 1914 to February 1918. Here the American reporter Karl von Wiegand interviewed the prince in November 1914. The château survived World War I only to be gutted, as this photograph shows, in World War II (courtesy Mme. Bergeret, owner of Château des Tilleuls, Stenay, France, personal collection).

lost the war. It will go on for a long time but it is lost already."²⁶ This quote was not the only omission from the article. Wiegand also omitted any mention of the Prince's marital infidelities, already ongoing at Château des Tilleuls in September 1914. Weigand could not have missed meeting Blanche D., the Prince's favorite, as she was the only one of his mistresses permitted to visit the château.²⁷

Karl von Wiegand was in Berlin in February of 1916 and thus missed the first onslaught of the battle of Verdun. Richard Harding Davis missed it as well, but he was in America.

> February 28, 1916
> The attack on Verdun makes me sick. I was there six weeks ago in one of the forts but of course could not then nor can I now write of it.²⁸

Davis died of a heart attack on April 11, 1916, never getting a chance to write about Verdun.

Based upon a German officer's eyewitness account, von Wiegand described the massive German artillery barrage that obliterated the French lines opening the battle.

> Hour after hour, day and night, the thunder of the big guns in what was perhaps the greatest artillery duel in the history of the world, rolled in from around Verdun like the ponderous roaring of gigantic waves continuously breaking on some rockbound shore. The roar of battle was at times heard 200 kilometers or about 124 miles.
> Several stories high smoke, earth, and débris shot into the air where the biggest shells exploded. Each time it seemed as if an unusually gigantic wave had broken there on the cliff. It was impossible to conceive how human beings could live through that fire.²⁹

By the end of March 1916, von Wiegand was at the German lines north of Verdun from where he confidently predicted, "...with almost glacier-like force, irresistibility, and steadiness the vast army of the Crown Prince is slowly enveloping Verdun."³⁰ He got it wrong of course; the Crown Prince's army never took Verdun. Karl von Wiegand was very pro–German, even going so far as to write and publish German war-poetry.

> Since I was one of the peerless
> Of the German warriors bold,
> Be thine a brow as fearless
> As thy father's was of old.³¹

Not exactly Robert Frost, but perhaps it lost something in translation.

Numerous Americans visited the French side of Verdun in 1916; probably one of the most interesting was Walter Hale: actor, illustrator and writer.

Sponsored by the American Relief Clearing-House in Paris, Hale planned to produce a documentary film showing the city's devastation in order to raise relief money in the States. A camera crew from the *Section Cinéma* of the French Army would shoot Hale exploring the city — or what was left of the city. It was Hale's second visit to Verdun; he had been there before the war as a tourist and thus could contrast the pre- and post-bombardment city. The party left Paris heading for Bar-le-Duc, the first stage in their journey. Included in the party was Hale's dog Toby.

> Our expedition on this occasion comprised the private motor of the Director-General of the American Relief Clearing-House in Paris and a second car carrying Lieutenant C_ of the Section Cinéma of the French Army and his assistants.[32]

They spent the night in the military city of Bar-le-Duc where, after dinner, Hale took his dog for a walk near the railroad yard.

> I stood near the siding in the rain. Artillerymen were preparing the runways for a battery of "75's" that had just arrived on flat-cars. The nose of each gun leaned over the breech of the one ahead, like the bristling quills of a porcupine.[33]

From Bar-le-Duc, the group traveled the *Voie Sacrée* to Verdun.

> Here was the long succession of troops and trucks, the jumble of close-following carts, the jangle of artillery harness as the heavy guns lumbered forward, and the weaving of flying officers' cars through the openings that suddenly appeared in the endless procession. Into this tangled caravan our small entourage threw itself and was swept with it.[34]

Arriving in Verdun Hale sought out the hotel where he had stayed during his visit in 1910.

> Indistinctly I recollect the little Hôtel des Trois Maures, at which we stopped, the quay-side whereon I sat and sketched the interesting old houses across the river, the somnolent fisherman on the bridge who watched me at my work, and the American motorist who helped me repair a recalcitrant stand-pipe in my engine.[35]

Hale found his old hotel but it had changed considerably, "shattered window panes, the tops of its chimneys blown off, and its walls and shutters punctured with shot holes." With German heavy artillery batteries less than ten miles away, Verdun was an easy target. First incendiary shells set houses afire and then shrapnel shells kept the firemen from dealing with the blazes.

In Verdun, a young French captain who had been educated in England and had rowed in the Henley Regatta guided the film crew. Getting bored with filming Walter and his dog walking aimlessly around smoldering ruins, the officer and the cameraman came up with something more artsy. A skiff similar to a racing-shell was found and all agreed, Walter being hesitant, upon "the novelty of a motion picture showing a French officer who had stroked a crew at Henley rowing a correspondent from overseas on the Meuse at Verdun." The cameraman set up on the right bank with the sun behind him to shoot the boat as it passed the city ruins on the left bank. Shells were falling in the city as the intrepid boaters pushed off. Walter was terrified but he could not refuse, it would be ungracious to his hosts.

> When the captain had added his weight further forward, we showed a three-inch freeboard above the hurrying stream. So unstable was the craft that if we dodged or ducked a shell we would probably have to swim for it. From the opposite bank the operator commenced his "panoram," as it is known in the vernacular of his profession.[36]

The captain put his back to the oars and off they went. The agreed upon turning around point came and went, Walter was panicking, the shells were falling, and the captain kept rowing — he was doing what he loved. Finally, the skiff turned, and after a long pull against the current, a wobbly Walter finally reached the dock where his journey on the Meuse had begun.

Walter retuned to America with a film and a great story; the captain returned to the Verdun battlefield — no one knows whether the Frenchman survived the war, but Walter did not; he died in 1917 of cancer.[37]

Coverage of the war during the period of American neutrality was very biased; nearly all the major newspapers and magazines supported the Allies. To present another viewpoint, pro–German supporters in New York founded a national weekly magazine, *The Fatherland*, its first issue coming out in August 1914. *The Fatherland*'s editorial policy was fair play for Germany and Austria-Hungary; its editor and founder was George Sylvester Viereck, a thirty-year-old Germanophile who would later become a Nazi apologist and be imprisoned from 1942 to 1947 as a Nazi agent. *The Fatherland* immediately found its niche, reaching a weekly circulation of over 75,000. It sold for five cents a copy and developed a number of unique marketing tactics for yearly subscriptions, for example boys could earn a free baseball bat (what could be more American) if they could get their parents or friends of their family to sign up for a two dollar yearly subscription. If one was not interested in baseball, there was a free Hindenburg teaspoon for a subscription. However, it was not all smooth sailing. The editor was astonished to learn that the trustees of the Public Library of Passaic, New Jersey, withdrew *The Fatherland* from its reading room. "Banned in Passaic" sent Viereck into a tizzy of indignation and self-righteousness.[38]

The Fatherland Easter 1916 cover; the German rabbit has all the eggs from the Verdun battle while the wounded Allied rabbits sadly look on. After mid-summer, *The Fatherland* no longer mentioned Verdun (University of Massachusetts, Amherst, W.E.B. Dubois Library).

Many of *The Fatherland* advertisers were brewers, the most prominent being Anheuser-Busch, brewers of Budweiser beer. Their advertisements often had a pitch against the growing prohibition movement in America. They must have been pleased to read the following:

> You notice that the men who have been foremost in the fighting around Verdun are the Brandenburgers, the Badeners, and Rhinelanders. These men come from provinces where more beer and wine are consumed than probably any other territory in the world. You can draw your own conclusion from this, as to whether the moderate drinking of beer or wine destroys the wholesome strength of the people or breaks down manly virility, as your fanatical prohibitionist says they do.[39]

The article then takes a swipe at American women who evidently are slaves to cigarettes and cocktails; they are not like good German Frauen who start their day with a stein of beer for breakfast. Other advertisers included agents offering German war loan bonds at 5 percent, tax exempt in Germany and payable after 1924; Hungarian war bonds at 6 percent, payable after 1921 (also tax exempt in Hungary); jewelers selling "*Kriegs-Schmuck*" such as scarf pins, hat pins, broaches, and watch fobs with the Kaiser's likeness; and publishers peddling books favorable to the German cause, usually written by German-Americans or Irish-Americans with a visceral hatred of England. One of the more unusual classified ads offered a course in lip-reading to make silent films more interesting.

Most of the articles in *The Fatherland* were polemics against American arms trafficking with the Allies, or vitriol about anti–German articles in New York newspapers. Adolph S. Ochs, owner of the *New York Times*, was a special demon. Articles dealing with details of the ongoing war were scarce and, when published, were mostly fantasy.

> **Germany's Victory at Verdun**
> The German General Staff planned to take Verdun within six months. Since that time the German army has proceeded slowly, methodically, invincibly against the French stronghold. According to last reports from Germany, the Germans are at present three weeks ahead of their schedule. In other words, unless other unforeseen circumstances arise, Verdun will fall within five months and one week after the siege was begun. The present operations against Verdun began about three months ago. Accordingly, we look for the fall of the great fortress by August, 1916.[40]

After July 1916, the Battle of Verdun was no longer a subject that merited comment in *The Fatherland*. The German army's assault came to an end that October, having run out of steam; the city of Verdun remained in French hands.

The American correspondent Granville Fortescue was one of those Francophiles that Viereck and subscribers to *The Fatherland* abhorred. Fortescue was the illegitimate son of Robert Roosevelt, President Theodore Roosevelt's uncle. Robert had established a satellite family with an Irish immigrant named Marion Theresa O'Shea; the surname Fortescue was invented. When Robert's wife died, Robert married Ms. O'Shea and adopted their children (there were three). Granville and Teddy Roosevelt were first cousins and both shared a love for adventure; Granville was a member of Teddy's Rough Riders, served in the army during the Philippine Insurrection and then as a military aid in Teddy's White House. He was always quick with his hands. In 1909, while aboard the North German Lloyd steamship *Kronprinzessin Cecilie,* he throttled a gambler for cheating at dice.[41] When the war broke out, Granville became a reporter for the *Daily Telegraph* of London and described the German invasion of Belgium and France for British readers.[42] He traveled with Richard Harding Davis on the memorable trip to Reims in September 1914.

Of the many articles he wrote during the war, the most egregiously pro–French essay was published in *National Geographic* in 1917.[43] It could just as well have been published in *The Fatherland* with a bit of editing, i.e., changing the French bias to a German one. He began the piece by arguing that France in the early nineteenth century and Greece during the age of Pericles had much in common. Fortescue then discussed military matters. French soldiers were said to be better fighters because they were more emotional than Germans. French soldiers were better led; their officers more caring of their men.

> The greatest crime in the officer's calendar is wantonly to waste the life of a subordinate. Circumstances may call for the last sacrifice at times, but short of this condition the French commander husbands the lives of his men as a miser his pieces of gold.[44]

Fortescue then unfortunately cited General Nivelle as the commander-in-chief responsible for all this caring. In April of 1917, Nivelle, disregarding advice from his staff and members of the French government, launched one of the bloodiest offensives of the war against a sector of the front known as the Chemin des Dames ridge. To validate the correctness of his decision he ordered repeated suicidal attacks against nearly impregnable German positions, always hoping to break through but the break-through never happened. Nivelle's stubbornness cost the French 270,000 casualties, including tens of thousands of deaths. This military debacle became known as the infamous "Nivelle Offensive" and was yet another example of a pointless bloodbath on a grand scale, one of many in the war. The Nivelle Offensive's only tangible result was to incite wholesale mutiny within the French army—the men had had enough caring![45]

Always protesting that it was not his fault, General Nivelle was fired as commander-in-chief and replaced by General Pétain, whose primary job was to bring back the French army as a credible fighting force. Pétain restored discipline and order by using both the carrot and the stick, i.e., punishing the leaders of the mutiny, sometimes with death, while promising better food, more leaves and an end to pointless offensives. As a test of his new army, Pétain decided to engage the enemy at Verdun; he had been successful there in 1916, perhaps his luck would hold in 1917. Thus the August 1917 Verdun offensive came about, an offensive that involved nearly all of the American volunteer organizations on the Western Front: the Lafayette Flying Corps attacked Dun-sur-Meuse; American Field Service and Norton-Harjes ambulances picked up wounded in the hills north of Fort Douaumont; and the French Foreign Legion, with the few surviving American volunteers, attacked Cumières, an obscure village located between an infamous hill known as Mort Homme and the Meuse River. Far behind the lines, safe from enemy fire, Pétain invited honored guests to watch the revitalized French army in action. One of the guests was General John J. Pershing, an officer who would soon be spending a lot of time in Lorraine.[46]

11

Lafayette, We Are Here!

Just before the gangplank was lowered the band on the first transport played "The Star Spangled Banner." The men on the ship stood at attention. The crowds on shore only watched. They did not know our national anthem yet. Next the band played the "Marseillaise" and the hats of the crowd came off. As the last note died away one of the Americans relaxed from attention and leaned over the rail toward a small group of newspapermen from America.
 "Do they allow enlisted men to drink in saloons in this town?" he asked. — Heywood Broun[1]

On July 4, 1917, a crowd of French and American notables gathered in an ancient cemetery[2] on the outskirts of Paris. They had come to commemorate the historically close link between France and the United States, a link forged during the American War of Independence when France supplied the revolutionary army with money, arms, soldiers and her navy. One man, the Marquis de Lafayette, embodied French aid. General Pershing, Commander-in-Chief of the American Expeditionary Forces, walked stiffly to the grave of Lafayette, saluted, and laid a wreath of flowers. Chief spokesman for the United States Army, Colonel Charles E. Stanton, a fluent French speaker and an eloquent orator, gave the address. Unfortunately as he began to speak, a fly-over of very low, and very loud, military aircraft drowned out much of what Colonel Stanton said.[3] But his concluding line was memorable: "Lafayette, nous voilà!"

Lafayette, we are here! It was a great line and Pershing wished that he had said it: "Many have attributed this striking utterance to me and I have often wished that it could have been mine. But I have no recollection of saying anything so splendid."[4]

Pershing never anticipated becoming commander of the overall American war effort in France. On May 3, 1917, less than a month after America entered the war, he received a telegram from his father-in-law, Senator F. E. Warren, "Wire me to-day whether and how much you speak, read and write French."[5]

Being an ambitious man, Pershing naturally overstated his linguistic abilities. He optimistically believed that at best he might get command of a division, around 25,000 men. There were many generals above him on the seniority list for overall command. He jumped ahead of them all, some said because of his senator father-in-law but that was just bitterness and envy. Pershing turned out to be the best man for the job. The position was not about being America's foremost warrior, or even being the oldest or most senior, but about being able to comprehend and solve the very complex problems involved in transporting, sustaining, training and arming over a million American soldiers for combat on the Western Front in France. It was an unprecedented task for the American army and one for which the American government was totally unprepared.[6]

On May 24, 1917, President Wilson summoned Pershing to a meeting; it would be his only meeting with the President for the course of the war until Wilson showed up in France after the Armistice.

> Mr. Wilson spoke of my recent expedition into Mexico and inquired about my acquaintance with France. I had naturally thought that he would say something about the part our Army should play in the war in coöperation with the Allied armies, but he said nothing.[7]

On May 26, in a letter from the War Department, the president designated Major General Pershing "to command all land forces of the United States operating in Continental Europe and in the United Kingdom of Great Britain and Ireland." Two days later Pershing boarded the *S.S. Baltic*, bound for the war. Accompanying him were only 190 men: 59 officers, 67 enlisted, the rest civilians (clerks, interpreters and three reporters). Onboard, plans were initiated that would eventually bring a million soldiers to France. In their spare time, Pershing and his staff took French lessons.

> The interpreters organized the officers into groups of different grades from those well-grounded in West Point book French to those who did not know how to ask the way or for something to eat, ... General Pershing was in the first grade.[8]

At home, although Congress passed the Selective Draft Act on May 18, 1917, assuring Pershing would have the men for his new army it had accomplished little else.

> I was really more chagrined than astonished to realize that so little had been done in the way of preparation when there were so many things that might have been done long before. It had been apparent to everybody for months that we were likely to be forced into war, and a state of war had actually

existed for several weeks, yet scarcely a start had been made to prepare for our participation.⁹

Although America did not enter the war until April 6, 1917, the path to war had begun on February 3 when President Wilson severed diplomatic relations with Germany over its policy of unrestricted submarine warfare. That act alone should have alerted the War Department to begin preparations for war, but according to Pershing not much happened. Then there was the *Laconia* sinking. On Saturday, February 17, the Cunard liner *Laconia* left New York harbor for Liverpool carrying 73 passengers, 200 crew and a large cargo of munitions and war materiel. Eight days later the *Laconia* was torpedoed, about 200 miles off the Irish coast. As luck would have it, one of the passengers was Floyd Gibbons, a reporter for the *Chicago Tribune*. He survived and filed one of the most influential stories of the war.

> Five sharp blasts sounded on the Laconia's whistle.... Those five blasts constituted the signal to abandon ship. Every one recognized them.¹⁰

That night at 10:30, the ship shuddered as if she had hit a large immovable object. Soon she began to list as cold North Atlantic water poured in through the breach in her hull. Emergency rockets with red flares were launched with the hope that nearby ships would see the distress calls — none did. Since the torpedo hit on the starboard side, the ship listed that way as more and more water flooded in. The life-boats on that side easily swung clear of the ship's hull as they were literally suspended over the water. Gibbon's life-boat was on the opposite side.

> The list of the ship increased. On the port side, we looked down the slanting side of the ship and noticed that her water line on that side was a number of feet above the waves. The slant was so pronounced that the life-boats, instead of swinging clear from the davits, rested against the side of the ship. From my position in the life-boat I could see that we were going to have difficulty in the descent to the water.¹¹

First the bow line jammed and the life-boat hung at 45 degrees bow up. When the bow line was freed the stern line jammed, again the life-boat hung at 45 degrees, only this time stern up. The terrified passengers clung to their seats as the boat see-sawed its way down.

> Then bow and stern tried to lower away together. The slant of the ship's side had increased, so that our boat instead of sliding down it like a toboggan was held up on one side when the taffrail caught on one of the condenser exhaust pipes projecting slightly from the ship's side.

> Thus the starboard side of the life-boat stuck fast and high while the port side dropped down and once more we found ourselves clinging on at a new angle and looking straight down into the water.[12]

The life-boat finally reached the water right side up and the survivors immediately cut away entangling lines so it would not be pulled under when the *Laconia* sank. Then another torpedo struck.

> The ship sank rapidly at the stern until at last its nose rose out of the water, and stood straight up in the air. Then it slid silently down and out of sight like a piece of scenery in a panorama spectacle.[13]

Near Gibbon's boat the submarine surfaced, "a black hulk, glistening wet." An officer emerged and asked the name of the ship and its tonnage for his log. The officer assured the survivors a British patrol ship would pick them up soon; the submarine then disappeared into the black waters of the Atlantic. The German officer was correct; a ship did pick them up. However, not all survived; a mother and daughter perished, both were Americans.

> a wave came and washed both Mrs. Hoy and her daughter out of the boat. There were life belts around their bodies and they drifted away with their arms locked about one another.[14]

The *Laconia* story ran in all the major American papers and was instrumental in pushing public opinion toward war with Germany.

Although the War Department may have been lethargic in responding to the changing situation in February of 1917, there was at least one American who seemed sure that America would soon join the Allies. He was George Viereck, editor of *The Fatherland*. Viereck realized what he had been publishing would soon be called treason; patriotic vigilantes might even lynch him.[15] It was time to change editorial policy. When the February 7, 1917, issue appeared President Wilson was on its cover, a place previously reserved for the Kaiser or his apologists. The next issue saw a name change, *The Fatherland* metamorphosed into *The New World—The American Weekly* with a lead article by William Jennings Bryan. The following issue's cover saw another name; *The New World—The American Weekly* became *Viereck's New World*. Still not satisfied, Viereck made yet another transformation in the following issue. On February 28, *Viereck's New World* was renamed *Viereck's The American Weekly*. Remarkably, through this nomenclatural turmoil Anheuser-Busch continued to advertise with Viereck. Advertisements from agents selling German war bonds disappeared, replaced by ads promoting stock in oil and mineral companies—sure winners in a war economy. Advertisers of Kaiser Wilhelm or General Hindenburg photographs now offered pictures of George Washington or Woodrow Wilson instead. America entered the war on April 6 and the following week's issue declared:

> We have opposed the war.
> Our side has lost.
> We stand behind our government.

One could not help but wonder, "Which government — Berlin or Washington?"

In March, the slide to war was accelerated by more lost ships and the newspaper publication of a telegram from German Foreign Secretary Arthur Zimmerman to his ambassador in Mexico. In this communication, Zimmerman outlined a mad contingency plan if America entered the war. Mexico should join with Germany and, should they be victorious, Mexico would be rewarded with the states of New Mexico, Texas and Arizona. The notorious Zimmerman telegram could be said to have been the final German provocation that pushed America into war.[16] On April 2, President Wilson delivered his war address to Congress and four days later Congress declared for the Allies. By the end of May, Pershing and his staff were aboard the *Baltic* on their way to England. Pershing met with King George at Buckingham Palace on June 9, was entertained at the houses of other members of the royal family, and finally left for France on June 13. In France, there was another round of diplomatic functions, culminating in the ceremony at Lafayette's Tomb on July 4.

Both the British and the French pushed to have American soldiers integrated into their respective armies as replacements for the catastrophic losses of 1916/1917. Pershing was adamant: Americans would fight only in an American army led by American officers under his command. Pershing's hard-headedness on this point resulted in considerable angst among the Allied high commands.

> In the midst of the various opposing opinions and schemes of the Allies, the idea remained fixed in my mind that the morale of our troops, their proper training, and their best strategical use all demanded their concentration into an American army instead of being allotted beyond our control as replacements in the ranks of the Allied armies.[17]

The French were the first to realize that they must accommodate Pershing. In late April, Joseph Joffre, Marshal of France and former commander-in-chief of the French army, paid an official visit to America and quickly sensed the mood of the Americans. He returned to France and convinced his military bureaucracy that the American government would never sacrifice its soldiers as replacements for the blunders of foreign generals. The French accommodation guaranteed that the American army would fight beside the French army rather than the British army in the great battles of 1918.[18] The French would train the Americans in the kind of war being fought on the Western Front and they would equip the Americans, but the Americans would fight in their own army. The French equipped the American Army with machine guns, artillery, aircraft, and tanks; the British supplied helmets and trench mortars.[19] Even the premier American weapon, the Model 1903 Springfield rifle, was in short supply.

> As it was impossible, because of manufacturing difficulties, for our factories to turn out enough Springfield rifles within reasonable time, the Secretary, after hearing the facts, decided to adopt the Enfield rifle[20] for our infantry. It was then being manufactured for the British in large quantities at private factories in our country and a slight modification of the chamber only was necessary to make it fit our ammunition. More than 2,000,000 of these rifles were manufactured during the war.[21]

Pershing and the Allies faced another decision, where would the American army fight. What sector of the Western Front would become the American sector? Pershing realized that the sector should not be dependent upon the English Channel ports, as that gave the British too much control, nor should it be between the British and the French, as that could restrict the American sphere of activity.[22] The only available ports on the west coast of France capable of accommodating large vessels were St. Nazaire, Bassens (Bordeaux) and La Pallice; from these ports the main railway lines ran eastward, converging on Neufchâteau in Lorraine, a region of France that included the Argonne Forest, Verdun and the St. Mihiel Salient, places where the French had fought horrific battles in the recent past. Now, because of its access to ports and railroads, Lorraine became the American sector and the American Army would fight on those same battlefields. The American Expeditionary Forces (A.E.F.) established its headquarters in Chaumont.

Pershing settled on Chaumont as his headquarters almost by chance. On August 3, 1917, Pershing and General Harbord, A.E.F. chief-of-staff, were exploring the countryside searching for a suitable location. General Harbord recalled the day:

> We left at an hour early enough to miss the newspaper correspondents who had followed us from the day before, and ran to the old town of Joinville, and thence to Chaumont, a thriving city of about 20,000 people, a railroad center, and having a fine drive around the old ramparts which once formed part of the walled stronghold in other days.
>
> We lunched at the Hôtel de France, were driven around the city by a French general afterwards, and at about two started for Paris.[23]

Pershing realized that Chaumont had what he had been looking for. Its location was ideal; the railway lines from the principal A.E.F. seaports (St. Nazaire, La Pallice and Bordeaux) converged on Chaumont before continuing to Lorraine, and it had a military installation that seemed most suitable. Three very large concrete barrack buildings, forming three sides of a large parade ground, became the "Pentagon" of the A.E.F. during the war.[24] Pershing's office, in the center building on the second floor overlooking the parade ground, had whitewashed walls without decoration except Liberty Bond posters and maps, a plain oak desk, a stove and a few plain chairs for meetings. The key adjectives were nearly always "austere" or "plain" when describing the commander's office. The public image was of a Spartan general leading his men and, albeit in a different way, sharing their hardships. The actuality was very different; First World War generals lived regally. General Pershing's residence was a large château about five miles from Chaumont. A reporter described it as a beautiful castle surrounded by spacious grounds and parks for strolling.[25] Most First World War generals, including of course Crown Prince Wilhelm, resided in commandeered châteaux. How else could one deal with the stresses of the job?

If there was a weak point to Chaumont, it was communication; A.E.F. headquarters relied on the French telephone system to communicate with seaports, railroad yards, warehouses and other A.E.F. installations, as well as Paris and London. Without doubt, the French telephone lines were overtaxed; although the Americans eventually laid their own lines to ease the burden, the monolingual, and often impudent, French switchboard operators drove the Americans crazy. Pershing acted quickly to solve the problem.

> Instead of trying to train men of the Signal Corps, I requested that a number of experienced telephone girls who could speak French be sent over, and eventually we had about 200 girls on this duty. Some doubt existed among the members of the staff as to the wisdom of this step, but it soon vanished as the increased efficiency of our telephone system became apparent.[26]

After settling the communications conundrum, Pershing and his staff turned to the problem of troop morale for the thousands of American soldiers arriving in France. What they needed was a doughboy newspaper.

> By my direction, the question was taken up by Colonel Nolan and the result was the *Stars and Stripes*— the official newspaper of the A.E.F. This publication was under the management of Lieutenant G. T. Viskniskki, who assembled as editors of the various departments a remarkable group taken entirely from the enlisted personnel of the Army. From the start, no official control was ever exercised over the matter which went into the paper — it was

entirely for and by the soldier. The first number was issued on February 8, 1918, and its success was immediate. Before the Armistice its circulation grew to more than 500,000. I do not believe that any one factor could have done more to sustain the morale of the A.E.F. than the *Stars and Stripes*.[27]

The first "editor" brought in by Lt. Viskniskki was Private Hudson Hawley, a Yale graduate and ex-newspaper man. Hawley served in the 101st Machine Gun Battalion, edited the battalion newspaper, *The Tripod*, and was in trouble with his commanding officer over its irreverent content. He jumped at the chance to join the *Stars and Stripes* office in Paris. Hawley was responsible for writing most of the articles in the first issues of the *Stars and Stripes*. It is said that *The Tripod* served as the model for the *Stars and Stripes*.

Private Harold W. Ross joined the editorial staff; after the war, he founded and edited *The New Yorker*. Another notable editor, Alexander Woolcott, was the former drama critic for *The New York Times*. He became the front-line battle correspondent.[28] Since the war certainly had drama, star players and bit-parts, the appointment seemed appropriate.

The *Stars and Stripes* was self-supporting, its funding coming from subscriptions and advertisements. However, not all advertisements were acceptable. The following were deemed inappropriate for doughboy eyes: advertisements for artificial limbs (too depressing), advertisements for naughty French postcards (too arousing), and advertisements for alcoholic beverages (too tempting). Sex and booze were a perennial anguish for Pershing due to American prudishness and the growing temperance movement. He was always reassuring wives and mothers at home not to worry.

> Engaged in healthy, interesting exercises in the open air, with a simple diet, officers and men like trained athletes are ready for their task. Forbidden the use of strong drink and protected by stringent regulations against sexual evils and supported by their own moral courage, their good behavior is the subject of most favorable comment, especially by our Allies. American mothers may rest assured that their sons are a credit to them and the nation.[29]

Reassurances aside, reality was very different. Paris and other French cities teemed with temptation. The war had been on going for four years; consequently most of the men were either dead, wounded or at the front. There were many lonely and accommodating women. Although a topic soldiers did not write home about, there is one anonymously published memoir.[30] Excerpts from it give a flavor of what it was like to have leave in "gay Paree" during the war years.

> Wed. Jan. 30, 1918, Paris. To Hôtel Edouard Sept. Took stroll.... All but raped. Zig-zig — nothing else but. More danger in French skirts than

Boche shells. But danger well advertised. Nobody need fall unless one gets behind himself and pushes. From the Opéra to the Etoile a million girls all whispering: "Will you sleep wiz me?" C — and E — fell for the first ones they met.[31]

Sat. Feb. 9, 1918, To big city for weekend. Dinner at Continental.... Streets full of whores. Like gnats on a July night. R — and E —, great swordsmen both, insist danger's overrated. French girls regularly inspected, and if you're careful, you'll be O.K., etc. Maybe — and then, maybe not.[32]

Sun. June 16, 1918.... Six months since I've seen children. Probably forgotten me. Lucky if they have.[33]

For those too low in the chain of command to get leave in Paris, there were always French publications for titillation. The pictures and drawings, especially corset advertisements, in *La Vie Parisienne* and *Le Sourie* were much sought after. Most doughboys could not read the French text, but a picture was worth a thousand words.[34]

By the late fall of 1917, four American divisions had arrived in France: two U.S. Army divisions, 1st and 2nd (which included two regiments of Marines) and two National Guard divisions, the 26th from the New England states and the 42nd made up of Guard companies from twenty-six states. These four divisions would be the veteran divisions of the A.E.F. All four trained with French instructors and finished their training occupying quiet sections of the front. By the spring of 1918, they were ready to engage the Germans.

Behind the lines, the Salvation Army and YMCA established canteens where the men could eat doughnuts, get cigarettes, and write letters home, preferably to their mothers or wives. American volunteers, many of whom were women, ran the canteens. Both Christian organizations espoused temperance; they were there to protect American soldiers from demon rum — or French cognac or French wine or French beer. A Salvationist clearly identified the problem from her perspective:

> It will be remembered that the French habit of drinking wine was ever before the American soldier, and with 165 francs a month in his pocket, he became an object of interest to the tradespeople, who encouraged him to spend his money in drink.[35]

Canteens, or huts, were established near the lines to lure the men away from local *estaminets* where alcoholic drinks and loose women were available. A typical week's program at a YMCA canteen included the following events[36]:

Sunday. Hot chocolate and cookies
Religious Service with special music
Song Service. More chocolate
Monday. French classes
Hot chocolate and jam sandwiches
Tuesday. Boxing and wrestling matches
Hot chocolate and sardine sandwiches
Wednesday. Band concert
Hot chocolate and jam sandwiches
Thursday. Movies
Hot chocolate and cookies
Friday. Sing fest with solos
Hot chocolate and jam sandwiches
Saturday. Stunt program
Canned fruit and cookies

Hot chocolate or not, there was no competition with demon rum or French cognac or French wine or French beer! Katharine Morse, a YMCA volunteer from Smith College bemoaned:

> If I were God I would lay a blight on every grape-vine in France; then I would sink every still, wine press, distillery and brewery to the bottom of the sea.
>
> We have had pay-day. It happened Friday. The total results didn't make themselves evident immediately; it was instead a cumulative effect, a crescendo, beginning Friday and reaching its climax yesterday. On these three days, out of the twenty-five hundred men stationed here, twenty-four hundred and ninety-three, I could take my oath, have come into the canteen and leaned over the counter, drunk;—that is to say, visibly and undeniably under the influence of liquor. When a lad, as some half dozen did ... came into the canteen entirely and unmistakably sober, one welcomed him as a drowning man does a spar. For a moment one had come in touch with something stable in a reeling world.
>
> I have learned to gauge the stages. When a man looks you squarely in the eye and declares vociferously, "Never took a drink in my life!" he is very drunk indeed. And there is always someone nearby to wink and comment; "He must have joined the gang that pours it down with a funnel."[37]

In spite of occasional breaches of decorum, particularly following payday, doughboys valued the canteens and especially the charming American women who ran them. For the women, their "boys" were very special.

> I shall never forget those long brown files drawn up against the dim grey houses. Five hours hence and those very boys would be in the front line trenches, face to face with the enemy. We passed Company A. I called out to them to be sure not to stick their heads over the top, and not to dare to take

off their gas-masks before they were ordered to. Never did I realize how much those boys meant to me. Each face I saw flashed some vivid unforgettable association to my mind. "When you come back," I called, "I'll be waiting for you with the hot chocolate ready." They smiled and waved Good-bye to me.[38]

By the spring of 1918, the Americans were ready to engage the Germans. The first to see significant action was the 26th, the Yankee Division. In April 1918, the New Englanders were assigned a fifteen-mile-long segment of trenches on the southern side of the St. Mihiel Salient; this sector had been held by the French since the fall of 1914, and more recently in 1918, by the U.S. 1st Division. The trenches skirted the village of Apremont la Forêt, whose ruins the Germans had fortified. The German and French armies had occupied the area for nearly four years. The No-Man's Land between the opposing lines resembled a garbage dump "with ten million bottles and rusty cans thrown over the top." Behind the trenches battlefield graves were marked with wooden crosses. Because the trenches had been stable for so long, stone tombstones had replaced some of the crosses. The Germans held the hills with stoutly constructed deep trenches, cut into bedrock in some places, often with spe-

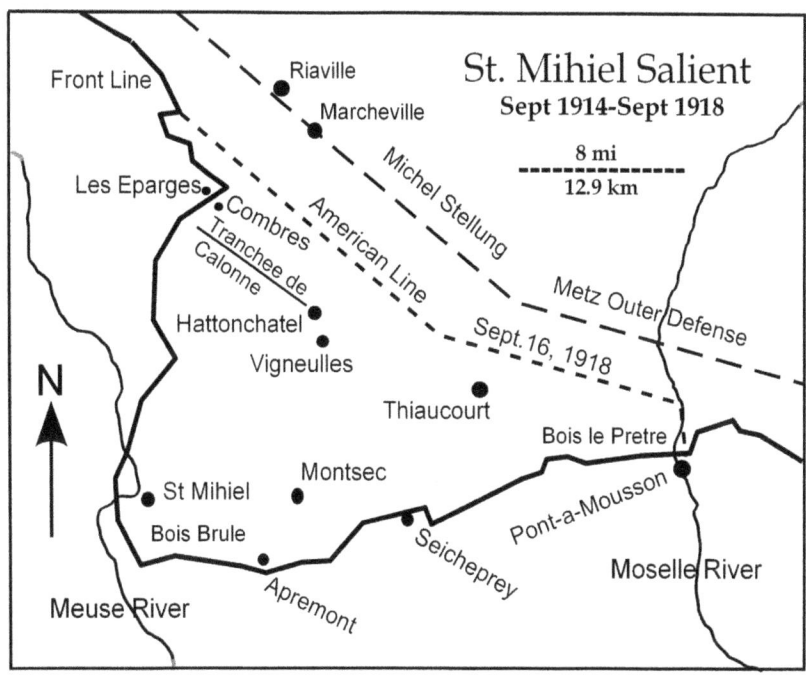

St. Mihiel Salient.

cialized concrete fortifications for added protection. The French held the flat land facing the hills; their trenches were more rudimentary, often being only deep ditches that filled with water after a rain. The Americans inherited the "deep ditches."

On April 10, the Germans attacked the American lines near Apremont in force. They hit the "deep ditches" held by the Massachusetts 104th Infantry Regiment. A force of 800 attackers followed a devastating artillery barrage of gas and explosives. Thus began the four-day battle of Bois Brulé, or burned woods, a fight closer in tactics to the Minutemen of Lexington and Concord than to the U.S. Army of 1918.

> All through the afternoon and evening of the 12th the struggle continued — the Germans holding stubbornly to the sections of trench they had entered, only to be fiercely assailed by the Americans, who, in turn, would be checked by well-placed hostile artillery fire. It was a fight of sections and platoons, in a tangle of broken trenches, twisted wire, and thick underbrush, where organized control was difficult and unified direction impossible, where individual grit and fighting ability counted for everything.[39]

Many men performed extraordinary feats at Bois Brulé, but one man, a noncombatant, stood out. Reverend John De Valles, the Catholic chaplain for the 104th Infantry, literally lived in No-Man's Land for four days during the fighting. He cared for the wounded, often carrying them to safety on his back, gave solace to the dying regardless of faith, and manned a stretcher. When his hands lacked strength, he tied the stretcher to his wrists with wire. With bleeding wrists and suffering from gas exposure, he crawled back into No Man's Land again, and again. For his heroism in action, he received The Distinguished Service Cross. When the fight ended, the Americans had suffered 37 dead and 75 wounded but had regained their trenches and captured 36 prisoners. Acknowledging the bravery of the Americans, the French decorated the colors of the 104th Infantry Regiment with the *Croix de Guerre.* For the first time in history, a foreign power decorated an American military unit. That decorated flag still hangs in the Massachusetts State House in Boston.

A week after the fight near Apremont, the Germans struck again. This time the attack was 10 miles (16 km) to the east of Apremont, at the small village of Seicheprey, near the American front-line trenches. Approximately 350 members of the 102nd Infantry Regiment, formerly the Connecticut National Guard, held the destroyed town while the main body of American troops occupied second-line trenches about a mile behind the village; Seicheprey was literally an isolated forward outpost. The sector was relatively quiet, with only sporadic artillery fire and small trench raids occurring. Then on

April 20, the quiet life changed! Early that morning, at 3:05 A.M., the Germans unleashed Operation "Kirschblüte" or cherry-blossom. A massive bombardment of high explosive shells, shrapnel and gas shells targeted areas behind Seicheprey — isolating the village. An inferno of fire and deadly mustard gas engulfed the American second-line: trenches collapsed, dugouts vanished, communication lines destroyed. Seicheprey was cut-off from help; nothing could get through the storm of steel and lead.

> This bombardment, however, was far more intense than any previous artillery fire by the enemy on the American line and the whole back area of Seicheprey as far as Mandres and beyond was drenched in a death-dealing shower of shells and gas.[40]

Then, at the worst of the bombardment, the Germans attacked — 3,500 German troops, including a specially trained, elite storm trooper battalion equipped with trench mortars, machine guns and flame-throwers, surrounded the 350 Americans. The Americans fought courageously but were outgunned and outnumbered.

> To the men in the Sybil trench,[41] however, there was nothing to do but wait. And the first they knew that the infantry attack was on was when the Germans swarmed over and into the trenches and the dugouts.
>
> There were not very many men who came back from that trench. The odds were 350 to 3,500 but the Connecticut boys gave all they received and more. It was a fight with bayonets, with clubs and rifles, with fists, with bare hands, until by sheer force of numbers, the Connecticut boys were over whelmed and those who escaped from the trench were those whom the Germans overlooked in the dark.[42]

Even chaplains fought; Father William Farrell went to the assistance of an artillery battery when four gunners were killed. Even wounded, he carried ammunition and kept the gun firing. The commander of the Yankee Division, General Edwards, recommended Father Farrell for a commendation. General Pershing thought otherwise. Chaplains did not man artillery in the American army, it was against the rules, and Pershing was a rules-book man. Farrell was reprimanded for actions unbecoming a man of the cloth.[43]

By mid-morning it was over; 188 Americans (5 officers and 183 men) marched off to German prisoner-of-war camps.[44] Interrogating the Americans, the Germans were surprised by the radical (realistic?) political views of some of the POW's.

> Quite interesting, too, is the following deduction in regard to the war which seemed to prevail generally among the American prisoners:
> Their political views fully coincide, maintaining that America, i.e., Big

Business, merely entered the war for the purpose of recovering the money advanced to the Entente nations.[45]

American fliers captured by the Germans also said "...that the United States entered the war for financial reasons only."[46] Evidently not everyone believed President Wilson when he declared that America had entered the war "to make the world safe for democracy."

American casualties in Seicheprey and the lines behind it included 81 dead, 187 wounded and 214 gas victims. Only 30 Americans escaped the village. German casualties were 52 dead, 145 wounded, 6 missing.[47] Although the Americans were able to retake Seicheprey the following day, the battle was by most measures a German victory. The men from Connecticut had fought bravely, but ordered to hold an indefensible position, they had paid dearly. The Germans paraded their captives through the towns of the St. Mihiel Salient and printed post cards (*Feldpostkarten*) showing the American POW's. *Feldpostkarten* were one of the main ways German soldiers corresponded with their families at home, so the news of the victory spread. But the victory was short-lived, within six months the same Connecticut National Guard regiment would be instrumental in pinching off the salient and capturing thousands of German POW's.

This German *Feldpostkarte* or field postcard shows American soldiers captured in the spring of 1918. Common subjects for both French and German field postcards, photographs of enemy prisoners of war helped uplift the folks at home (Massachusetts National Guard Museum and Archive, Worcester).

When German artillery began to pummel the lines behind Seicheprey in the early morning of April 20, a Salvation Army canteen was in the path of the barrage. Located only a mile and a quarter behind the trenches, the canteen was run by two sisters, Gladys and Irene McIntyre; Gladys was a graduate of the Pratt Institute of Brooklyn and Irene, of Mount Holyoke College in Massachusetts. Exploding shells awakened the sisters; they dressed, donned their helmets, strapped on gas masks and went to work making hot coffee, chocolate and donuts for the soldiers. Cooking came to a halt when the canteen was hit by gas shells and had to be abandoned.[48] Myrtle Turkington[49] and Stella Young joined the McIntyre sisters and the foursome moved their canteen farther behind the lines to an encampment known as L'Hermitage. On the canteen's Victrola one song, "Just Another Little Drink Won't Do Us Any Harm," was played over and over until a German six-inch high explosive shell found the Salvationist tent.[50] Because of the proximity of their canteens to the fighting, the Salvation Army ordered that its women be armed with revolvers.[51]

Closer to the lines, three miles behind Seicheprey, a Civil War veteran whom the men called Dad ran a Salvation Army canteen in a house in the village of Mandres.[52]

> For some little time the boys enjoyed this hut, but on one occasion the Germans sent over a heavy barrage; they hit the hut, destroying one end of it, scattering the supplies, ruining the victrola.[53]

Determined not to leave his boys, "Dad" moved the canteen into a cellar beneath the ruins of a nearby house.

> This cellar was vaulted and had been used for storing wine. It was wet and in bad condition, but with some labor it was made fit to receive the men; and tables and benches were placed there, the canteen established and a range set up.[54]

Knee deep in mud, Dad sold eggs, fruit and donuts to the soldiers in spite of the near constant shelling by the Germans. Dad's wine cellar was remembered as a dank hole that smelt like a pig sty.[55] The YMCA established a canteen at Ansauville, about five miles from Seicheprey. The Germans soon targeted the conspicuous white tent and blew it to bits. The shell-shocked YMCA secretary reopened in a nearby cellar.[56]

It was under the auspices of the YMCA that vaudeville arrived at the front behind Seicheprey. The young American Elsie Janis gave the first show. The twenty-eight-year-old Miss Janis was a celebrated musical comedy star, well known in both Europe and America. Using her fame and connections to cut through American and French military red tape and her own money to fund the tour, Miss Janis, her mother and her piano accompanist left Paris in early May 1918. Passing through the ruins of Verdun, they continued toward the St. Mihiel Salient and the trenches held by the Yankee Division. On May 21, a few miles behind Seicheprey in the village of Lagny, Miss Janis gave the first of her many performances to very enthusiastic doughboys.

> This crowd were just out of the trenches and between the joy of still being alive and the excitement of seeing a girl from home they very nearly went mad. I thought the French inhabitants of Lagny looked rather scared. Perhaps they thought the Yanks might decide to throw the village houses in the air as they did their overseas caps.[57]

The following day she was asked to give a special concert for men who had seen her sing the day before but were now badly wounded from a night raid.

Elsie Janis entertaining the troops near Seicheprey in May 1918; she is singing from the divisional boxing ring. She toured the front at her own expense with her mother and her piano accompanist. Miss Janis was known as the "Sweetheart of the A.E.F." (Elsie Janis, *The Big Show* [New York: Cosmopolitan, 1919]).

went to the hospital, gave one show for the fellows who could move about in the "hut,"[58] then went through the wards to see the boys from last night's raid. Poor kids! they had just gone in and were settling down when the Huns put on a gas show and got some of them quite badly, but they tell me that seventy dead Germans were counted — hanging on the barbed wire at dawn today, so that's not so bad for beginners.[59]

Elsie Janis, known as the sweetheart of the American Expeditionary Forces, was really special for the Yankee Division, coming as she did after they had a hard fight and lost many. The men renamed the division in her honor, affixing a large sign to her motor car as she left: "Elsie Janis Division."

While Miss Janis entertained the troops in the St. Mihiel Salient, the German Army made ready its own entertainment for the Allies. On March 3, 1918, a crucial event occurred that changed the course of the war. Bolshevik Russia and Imperial Germany signed the Treaty of Brest-Litovsk, bringing fighting to an end on the Eastern Front. Essentially Germany had won the war on the Eastern Front. Now the German high command could move over 900,000 veteran troops from the east to the Western Front. The Germans finally had the advantage in man power over the Allies, or at least until the Americans arrived in force. That spring and early summer, in an all out effort to break the Western Front before the Americans arrived, the German army launched a series of hard hitting offensives against the British, trying to cut them off from their Channel ports, and against the French, threatening and hopefully capturing Paris. A desperate gambler throwing his dice and wagering all, and ultimately, losing everything, is probably the best analogy for the motivation and results of the German High Command's actions in 1918.

12

Gott Mit Uns[1]

"Well, we ought to win because we have God with us, but now that the Allies have America — ich weiss nicht!" — German Prisoner of War[2]

Among the warring parties in 1918 there was one monarch who earnestly believed he ruled by Divine Right and that, of course, was Kaiser Wilhelm II. In an address to his people before the war, he summarized this view, "I regard my whole position as given to me direct from Heaven and that I have been called by the Highest to do His work."[3] He was dangerously sincere, some would say to the point of madness, in his belief the Almighty had appointed him to lead Germany to victory. It was his destiny.

> His belief that God is on his side is deep-rooted. Whenever he goes to the front the imperial banner — orange, black embroidered with a cross, and bearing the legend "God with us"[4] — goes with him. He has had that motto inscribed on the belt buckles of his soldiers. He has given every soldier in the army a little pocket Bible. He is accompanied by a chaplain wherever he goes.[5]

In the spring of 1918, it seemed as if the Kaiser's prayers had been answered. The Eastern Front collapsed with a German victory, and now nearly a million men were available to crush the French and British on the Western Front. Germany would win the war before the Americans arrived in force. Or so he hoped!

The German offensives began in March of 1918. On March 21, they launched Operation Michael, a massive attack against the British line between Arras and St. Quentin. The British collapsed, losing 160,000 casualties; the French lost 70,000; more than a thousand artillery pieces were abandoned. Caught in the chaos of the retreat were 11 women of the Smith College Relief Unit.[6]

> They have lost their equipment, to be sure, but they have saved the lives of hundreds of French women and children and old people. Each girl was

charged with the evacuation of a village, and each one stuck to her post and rescued her people in spite of shell fire. We have believed for a long time that American college girls were equal to any emergency. We have never had a finer example of their courage and ingenuity than that which this small band of Smith girls has given us. Major Perkins wants more like them in France.[7]

Initially Operation Michael succeeded beyond expectations and by its end on April 5 the Germans had captured 1,200 square miles. But the real estate captured lacked strategic value and the cost had been too high, over 200,000 German casualties.[8] As Michael ran out of steam, the Germans launched Operation Georgette on April 9, again against the British, only this time farther north, near Flanders. The push achieved an initial success, opening a thirty-mile gap in British lines, but in the end could not win the hoped for jackpot. The British remained in Flanders. Georgette ended on April 29.

The next, and last, major German offensive began as a gigantic feint to draw French forces away from the British. This feint was to be a prelude to another offensive against the British in Flanders.[9] Winston Churchill called the feint the surprise of the Chemin des Dames.[10] On May 27, an army commanded by Crown Prince Wilhelm, of Verdun fame, attacked over a fifty-mile (80.5 km) front centered on the Chemin des Dames

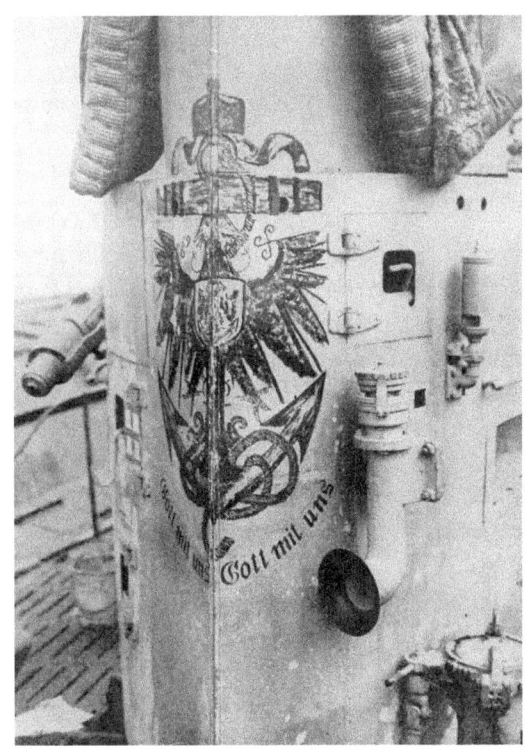

A German U-Boat exhibited in the Brooklyn Navy Yard after the war. The conning tower carries the emblem of the German navy; beneath the anchor is the Kaiser's motto, *Gott mit uns*. *The Outlook* (1919) published the photograph and included a comment on the motto, "a characteristic piece of German arrogance that was not omitted from these piratical craft" (*The Outlook*, Volume 122, 1919).

ridge. The French were caught napping, their lines disintegrated. Responding to the French collapse, more and more German troops funneled into the attack. What began as a feint turned into one of the major German offensives of the war. In a few days of relatively easy fighting, the Crown Prince's army achieved a breakthrough into open country beyond the trenches, the goal of nearly every offensive of the war. By June 3, the Germans had advanced 30 miles (48 km) and established a bridgehead across the Marne River near the city of Château Thierry. They had destroyed seven French and British divisions along the way, capturing sixty thousand prisoners. The French army seemed to be unraveling. The Germans were only 50 miles (80.5 km) from Paris.

> As a result of the German successes against the French, something akin to a panic prevailed in Paris. Probably a million people left during the spring and there was grave apprehension among the officials lest the city be taken. Plans were made to remove the French government offices to Bordeaux and we¹¹ were prepared to move those of our own that were in Paris.¹²

The huge triangle of territory the Germans had captured in less than a week became known as the Marne Salient and was the setting for the Second Battle of the Marne. The French petitioned Pershing for help and, seeing their dire need, he ordered American divisions in France to the Marne Salient to fight alongside the French army. The idea of a separate American army waging war in its own sector, for which Pershing had argued, was put aside; the German juggernaut grinding through the Marne Salient had to be stopped first.

The U.S. 2nd Division, which included a brigade of U.S. Marines, went into action on June 6 at Belleau Wood, near the apex of the salient. The fighting lasted 19 days, during which time the Marines sustained fifty percent casualties, but by June 25 Bois Belleau was in American hands. An American reporter, Floyd Gibbons, armed with a notebook instead of a rifle, marched with the first wave of attacking Marines. In the previous year, 1917, Mr. Gibbons survived the sinking of the *Laconia* by a German submarine, but he almost did not survive the battle at Belleau Wood. A machine gun bullet shot away part of his left shoulder, another bullet smashed through his arm. A third bullet tore out his eye and resulted in a compound skull fracture. He filed his first report with the *Chicago Tribune* before getting wounded; it was published while he was in hospital. What a publicity bonanza for the Marine Corps. In his memoir, he fleshed out the story.

> In the dense woods the Germans showed their mastery of machine gun manipulation and the method of infiltration by which they would place strong units in our rear and pour in a deadly fire. Many of these guns were

located on rocky ridges, from which they could fire to all points. These Marines worked with reckless courage against heavy odds, and the Germans exacted a heavy toll for every machine gun that was captured or disabled, but in spite of losses the Marine advance continued.[13]

The fighting was terrific. In one battalion alone the casualties numbered sixty-four per cent. officers and sixty-four percent. men. Several companies came out of the fighting under command of their first sergeants, all of the officers having been killed or wounded.

I witnessed some of that fighting. I was with the Marines at the opening of the battle. I never saw men charge to their death with finer spirit. I am sorry that wounds prevented me from witnessing the victorious conclusion of the engagement.[14]

The Germans, on the receiving end of the Marine attacks, also had their eyes opened by the ferocity of the Americans.

Their morale is inexhaustible, and they are imbued with a spirit of implicit confidence. Significant are the words of one prisoner: "Kill or get killed." All the attacks in Belleau Wood in July were executed briskly and without hesitation.[15]

Pershing committed nine American divisions to fight along side the French in the Second Battle of the Marne. Of the nine divisions, four were U.S. Army, the 1st, 2nd, 3rd, and 4th and four were National Guard, the 26th from New England, the 28th from Pennsylvania, the 32nd from Michigan and Wisconsin, the 42nd from twenty-six different states, and one, the 77th, was a National Army division made up of draftees from greater New York City. The Second Battle of the Marne was the turning point in the war. In fifteen days of fighting, the Allies captured thirty thousand German prisoners and regained most of the Marne Salient, although the bulk of the German army managed to escape. Of more importance, Allied psychology had changed, in part because of the Americans. Now led by Marshal Ferdinand Foch,[16] the newly appointed Supreme Commander of the Allied Armies, the Allies would attack, and attack again. The great Allied offensives of 1918 began at the Marne that July; they would not stop until the war's end in November. After the war, Marshal von Hindenburg reflected that the Marne was the beginning of the end of the German army.

Although the fighting in the Marne salient had saved us from the annihilation our enemy had intended, we could have no illusion about the far-reaching effects of this battle and our retreat. From the purely military point of view it was of the greatest and most fateful importance that we had lost the initiative to the enemy.[17]

After the Second Battle of the Marne, the Allies divided the Western Front into sectors from which their respective national armies would launch offensives against a still formidable foe. The American sector was Lorraine. Pershing's First Army would finally go into action there under his leadership. He finally had his American army; he had now joined the exclusive club of First World War battle commanders, a club that unfortunately included notable failures who squandered their troops' lives shamelessly. How Pershing would be judged remained in the future.

> The final decision that the First Army would undertake the reduction of the St. Mihiel salient as its first operation was transmitted to army headquarters on August 10th, and the army staff immediately began the development of plans for the concentration of the troops necessary for its execution.
>
> It was certain that the psychological effect on the enemy of success in this first operation by the American Army, as well as on the Allies, our own troops, and our people at home, would be of signal importance.[18]

The St. Mihiel Salient was a two-hundred-square-mile triangular bulge, a thorn in the French line south of Verdun. The Germans had captured the salient in the fall of 1914. In 1915, it was the scene of very costly French attacks attempting to pinch it off, all of which failed. Mrs. Wharton had witnessed one such attack at Les Eparges on the northern base of the salient and an American Field Service ambulance section worked at Pont-à-Mousson at the southern base of the salient. After 1916, minimal fighting occurred in the salient until 1918. The German army employed its men usefully, using the time to construct fortifications. Trenches were lined with concrete, deep underground shelters were built of reinforced concrete, even field hospitals were built of concrete, concrete machine gun pill boxes were sited at critical topographical junctures; the German army had a passion for concrete. When not mixing concrete, the soldiers carved elaborate funerary monuments for their military cemeteries.[19] Bavarian-style villages were constructed in woodlands, reminding the men of home since many of the troops were Bavarians.

For Pershing the salient was the prize; where the French army had failed after so many costly efforts, the American army would triumph. He and his staff assembled an overwhelming force. Although over a half million American soldiers would be used in the attack, none of these troops was nearby, most were still at the Marne.

> Our divisions were scattered and it seemed doubtful whether sufficient rail or truck transportation could be found to bring them in the area, together with the corps and army troops and auxiliaries, before the rainy season, which usually starts about the middle of September and which, it was said, might seriously hinder operations in that sector....

A luxurious German trench in the St. Mihiel Salient; three German officers on the firing step are casually observing the landscape beyond the parapet. All is neat and tidy since there had been no serious fighting in the Salient since the end of 1915. The doorway leads to a *Mannschafts-Eisenbeton-Underständ* or MEBU, an iron-reinforced concrete shell-proof dugout built under the parapet. They usually had bunks, furniture (taken from nearby villages), a wood stove for warmth and cooking and could be very cozy, giving protection from the weather and, of course, artillery fire. MEBUs were homes away from home for soldiers at the front. They typically had two entrances; if shell fire destroyed one, escape was possible. If both were blocked, the MEBU became a tomb (*Der Weltkrieg in Seiner Rauhen Wirklichkeit* [Oberammergau, Germany: Herman Rutz, 1926]).

> The actual movement for the concentration of the more than one-half million men, whether by rail, truck, or on foot, generally took place at night. The troops bivouacked during the day in forests or other sheltered places hidden from observation of enemy airplanes, resuming the movement at nightfall.[20]

The area near the salient became a beehive of activity for the coming offensive, scheduled for mid September. Soldiers installed miles of telephone and telegraph lines, transported over a million artillery rounds, constructed railway spurs for railroad guns that French crews manned, prepared hospitals to accommodate the wounded, built a safe water supply for the incoming troops, established airfields within striking distance of the salient, prepared thousands of tons of road building materials to construct roads across No-Man's Land and repaired roads leading to the salient. There were arrangements made for traffic control and the camouflaging of staging areas, roads and materiel from German planes.[21] Pershing and his staff planned for almost every contingency they could imagine except one — the possibility of canceling or significantly reducing the operation if the Allied high command deemed it no longer strategically significant.

> On August 30th, the day when I assumed command of the sector, Marshal Foch, accompanied by Weygand, his Chief of Staff, came to my residence at Ligny-en-Barrois and after the usual exchange of greetings he presented an entirely new plan for the employment of the American Army.[22]

Pershing was furious, as the new plan canceled St. Mihiel and broke up the American First Army. In his memoir, the arguments and counter arguments with Foch cover eleven pages![23] In the end Pershing prevailed, but to do so he struck a Faustian bargain with Foch, a bargain that would cost American lives. The American Army would pinch off the St. Mihiel Salient as planned and then almost immediately undertake a new major offensive in the Meuse-Argonne, 60 miles (96.5 km) away. The Meuse-Argonne offensive was a formidable task, and, it has been said, using military resources and time in the St. Mihiel Salient resulted in a considerable human cost in the Meuse-Argonne.[24]

> Our commitments now represented a gigantic task, a task involving the execution of the major operation against the St. Mihiel salient and the transfer of certain troops employed in that battle, together with many others, to a new front, and the initiation of the second battle, all in the brief space of two weeks. Plans for this second concentration involved the movement of some 600,000 men and 2,700 guns, more than half of which would have to be transferred from the battlefield of St. Mihiel by only three roads, almost

entirely during the hours of darkness. In other words, we had undertaken to launch with practically the same army, within the next twenty-four days, two great attacks on battlefields sixty miles apart.[25]

In the summer of 1918, the salient was defended by only 23,000 German soldiers, most of its defenders having been sent north in response to the British and French offensives. The date for the American attack was set for September 12. Four days earlier the German high command ordered the evacuation of the salient; it was no longer worth defending.[26] On September 12, 1918, after preliminary artillery softening, seven divisions, the U.S. 1st, 89th, 2nd, 5th, 90th, 82nd and 42nd divisions, attacked the southern flank of the salient; the 42nd had Brigadier General Douglas MacArthur as its Chief of Staff. A force of 267 French tanks commanded by Lieutenant Colonel George S. Patton led the charge. Simultaneous with the attack in the south, the northern flank came under attack. Two divisions, the 4th and 26th, the Yankee Division, took part in this attack. In the air, Colonel William "Billy" Mitchell led an air armada of nearly 1,500 planes and 20 observation balloons. The Americans had complete control of the skies. A key part of the plan was to pinch off the salient, trapping German men and supplies. The two critical divisions were the 1st and the Yankee Division. The 1st would push from the south and the Yankee Division from the north, meeting in the town of Vigneulles, a German supply depot in the middle of the salient.

At 8:00 A.M. on September 12, the Yankee Division went over the top. From the small village of Les Eparges, the infantry pushed into the hills. Numerous battles had been fought near Les Eparges (see Chapter 1) so that in 1918 the countryside was a maze of old trenches, dug-outs, craters, barbed wire entanglements, abandoned equipment and numerous war graves. Fortunately, in 1918, these fortifications were lightly held, their few German defenders being keener on surrendering and surviving the war as POW's than dying in combat. By the end of the first day, Yankee Division infantry reached the Tranchée de Calonne.

The Tranchée is not a trench, but rather a fifteen-mile-long (24 km) road that leads into the heart of the salient. It is a road with American connections. In the eighteenth century, Charles Alexandre de Calonne built the road for an easier access to his château. Calonne was controller general of finance for King Louis XVI and bankrupted France in order to help underwrite the cost of the American War of Independence. Colonne's creative financial machinations were, some say, the catalyst for the French Revolution. However, in September of 1918, those historical allusions were far from the minds of the doughboys as they marched down Calonne's straight road. Leading the march into the heart of the salient was an infantry regiment (102nd) made up of the Connecticut National Guard. This was the same regiment that had been hit so hard at Seicheprey earlier in the spring, now they were paying the Germans back. The Connecticut men set a brisk pace as they marched through the night. Resistance was light, just a few pesky machine guns; mostly the Germans surrendered, happy to be out of the war, and were sent to the rear under light guard. The Connecticut regiment met the 1st Division on the morning of September 13 in Vigneulles, thus pinching off the St. Mihiel Salient. Ironically, the 1st Division began its drive for Vigneulles from Seicheprey. The salient had been erased in less than two days; there was little German defense. Overall, in the St. Mihiel drive, the Americans captured 16,000 German prisoners at a cost of 7,000 American casualties.

> German gunners, two miles back of the line, with no fresh shell holes about their positions, had not even taken the camouflage off their guns to fire into our advancing infantry, but had deliberately avoided action, apparently to assure their safety. This, taken with other incidents, which confirmed observation, indicated the reason for the slight resistance. There was no use of an observer going any further. It was not a battle. It was a field day for every division. Our troops did not require direction. All they had to do, along the whole length of our line of assault, was to keep on advancing to their objectives, cleaning up machine-gun nests on the way.[27]
>
> A German major marching to the rear at the head of a prisoner column at St.-Mihiel passed a marching column of American infantry. "Those men are all young and fresh and vigorous," he complained. "We can't do it, but I wish I had had a 1914 battalion behind me. You wouldn't have had such a pleasant afternoon."[28]

Meanwhile at the apex of the salient, General Pershing and his French colleague General Pétain were celebrating the "victory" by touring the destroyed town of St. Mihiel. September 13, 1918, was Pershing's fifty-eighth birthday. The closure of the St. Mihiel Salient was the perfect birthday gift, two hundred square miles of France liberated.

Pershing now had to move his entire army 60 miles (96.5 km) to the Meuse-Argonne for a new offensive to begin in less than two weeks. But what if he didn't? Why not continue the offensive from the base of the salient to Metz, only 15 miles (24 km) away. Metz was a very important target; the Metz-Sedan railway link was critical in transporting troops and supplies to German-occupied northern France and Belgium. Capturing Metz would turn the hollow victory in the salient into a prelude for something much more strategically significant. After the war there would be endless discussions published by professional and amateur military theorists about whether or not Pershing should have been allowed to attack Metz.[29]

12. Gott Mit Uns

Metz was probably the most strongly fortified city in Europe. After its capture in the Franco-Prussian War, German military engineers, recognizing the city's strategic importance, set to work ringing it with fortifications. From the eighteen seventies until 1914, the heights surrounding the city were developed into a vast complex of forts, including dispersed protected batteries of 150 or 210 mm guns in armored rotating turrets, underground bomb-proof

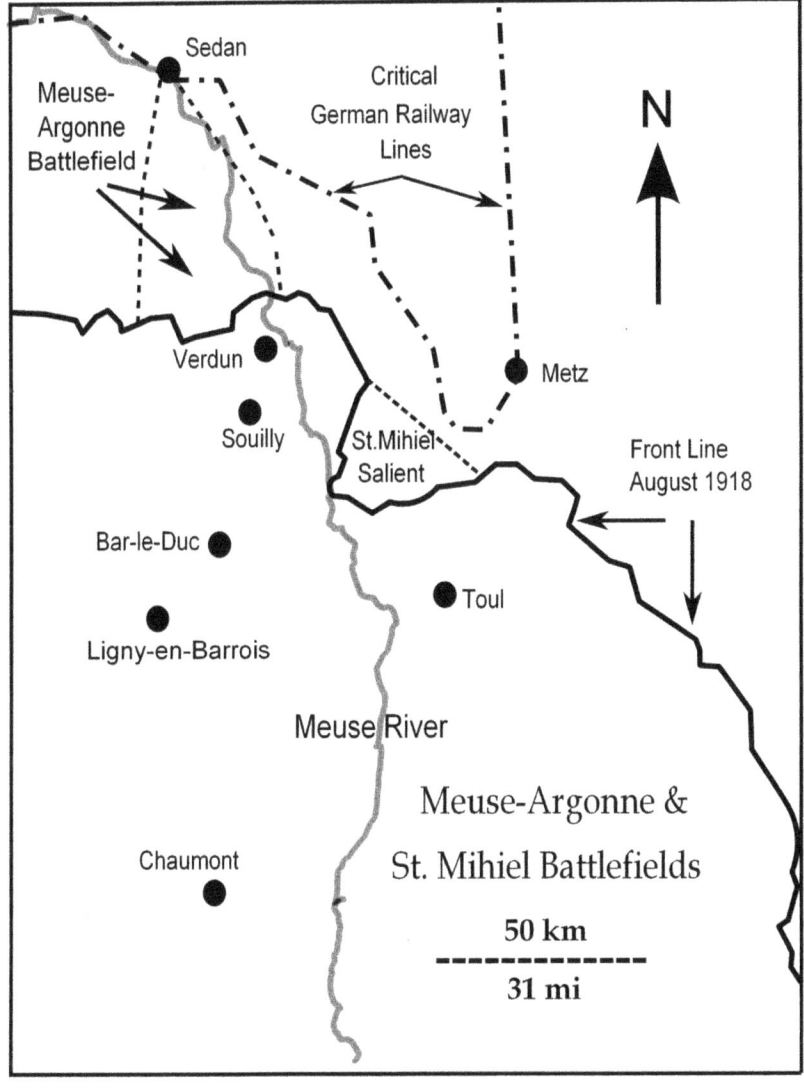

Meuse-Argonne and St. Mihiel Battlefields.

shelters and barracks, all interconnected with a network of tunnels.[30] Some of the fortress complexes covered over three hundred and all were camouflaged against aircraft reconnaissance. As military arsenals for offense evolved in the late nineteenth century, German engineers adapted. German forts became huge areas of defended real estate. Metz was perhaps nearly impregnable in 1918. In 1944 German troops, fighting from these pre–First World War defenses, held out against General Patton's Third U.S. Army for nearly three months, even though offensive weapons in the Second World War were orders of magnitude more effective than those of 1918.[31] However, in September 1918, the possibility of a Metz attack worried the German high command.

> To all appearances, an attack against so strong a fortress as Metz could not be considered tempting to the enemy. However, there was one possibility. The enemy might know that Metz had already been stripped of a great part of its defensive artillery for the reinforcement of our field army. It was natural enough for the enemy to invade the country to the northwest of Metz. There, the Briey-Longwy Iron Basin constituted one of the main sources of our armament. Of special importance to us were the railroad connections leading from Metz.... If these lines were actually disturbed, or even only threatened, communications with the armies in the west would be seriously interfered with. By flattening out the St. Mihiel triangle, Pershing's army got closer to these vulnerable points of our position.[32]

Could Pershing have advanced from the St. Mihiel Salient on September 13, 1918, and taken Metz? Probably but only if its defenses were lightly manned, which they may have been. Metz's fortifications were backed by a network of strategic railways whose purpose was to move in a vast army should the city be attacked, if such a German army was available in the fall of 1918.[33] General Hunter Liggett, who commanded a Corps that fought in the salient that September, concluded that taking Metz was an impossible dream.

> Under the conditions that existed on September 12, I thought then and think now that Marshal Foch was exceedingly wise to limit us to the immediate task of flattening out the salient and protecting our rear for another attack to the westward. I find no support for the theory that so skilled and indefatigable a soldier as the German, with years in which to do it, had neglected his defenses in any section of the Hindenburg Line, or that he was without reserves. The ease and rapidity with which Von der Marwitz threw reserves into the Meuse-Argonne, near at hand and ten days later, answers that, in my judgment. This latter battle was a greater surprise of the two, yet from the third day on they held us up until we paid in blood for every yard we gained.[34]

But perhaps General Liggett was wrong.

In anticipation of treating wounded from the upcoming Lorraine battles, the A.E.F. established a dozen hospitals in the old cathedral city of Toul, a city located between St. Mihiel and A.E.F. headquarters at Chaumont. Toul, surrounded by double walls and moats from an earlier era, gave its name to the Toul Sector, which included the St. Mihiel Salient. In the fall and winter of 1918, Toul was described as "...humble in size, its buildings insignificant, its streets crooked, dirty and ill paved, under the prevailing winter skies had a gray dinginess as its dominant color note."[35]

The American Red Cross, perhaps anticipating Lorraine would become the American sector, had established a presence in the city in 1917. Red Cross nurses who arrived then treated war refugees rather than soldiers. Most of the refugees were children who had lost their parents in the turmoil of war; the children in some instances had literally become feral, begging or stealing food.

> We arrived at Toul at 10 P.M. and, after a night's rest at the hotel, went to the French Barracks, and saw the children. Here we found 500 of them in a most shocking condition, with about fifty mothers in the same state. The children were dirty, their bodies covered with every description of sores, and ragged hair infested with vermin. Their lack of knowledge relative to sanitary or toilet arrangements was incomprehensible. Our first act was to give them all a bath, and they never had had a bath before; in fact, never having had all their clothing removed at one time since birth, we met with considerable opposition. Incidentally, the French peasants do not remove their underwear upon retiring. We found giving them the first bath a difficult problem. The only bathing facilities were the soldiers' shower bath. Never before have I heard such shrieks as the children gave when undressed and during the bathing process. When we finished their baths, our uniforms were saturated with water, making it necessary to undergo a complete change of clothing....
>
> During the entire time I remained in Toul, we were having air raids from the Germans, and the siren was blowing as often as ten times during the day. We could hear the bombardment and see the flares and searchlights every night.[36]

By the end of September 1918, as the Meuse-Argonne battle began to extract its human toll, the beds in the military hospitals in Toul would fill with American wounded. However, before that battle could begin there was much to do. After the successful closure of the St. Mihiel salient on September 13, 1918, Pershing had to begin another offensive just 13 days later in the Meuse-Argonne. An army of 600,000 men, 3,000 artillery guns, 90,000 horses and 900,000 tons of munitions and supplies had to be moved more than 60 miles (96.5 km) over narrow dirt roads. Horse-drawn artillery, wagon trains, endless convoys of trucks crawling tailgate to bumper clogged every road, with everything moving in slow motion when movement was possible. Columns of infantry trudged along the sides of the roads, leaving the way clear for vehicles, even though walking was often faster. The traffic jams were incredible. The traffic density was so great that trucks sometimes took 16 hours to cover the 60 miles (96.5 km). And to keep the Germans from deducing where the Americans would attack after St. Mihiel, the movement of men and materiel occurred only at night.

Georges Clemenceau, Prime Minister of France, toured the salient after the American victory. He had been strongly against the formation of an independent American army, thus no doubt Pershing was gloating a bit. All went well until the party reached the St. Mihiel town of Thiaucourt and got bogged down in a massive traffic jam. Clemenceau, known for his Gallic wit, commented: "They wanted an American Army. They had it. Anyone who saw, as I saw, the hopeless congestion at Thiaucourt, will bear witness that they may congratulate themselves on not having had it sooner."[37]

> At times roads were blocked for hours. Shadowy lines of vehicles two and three abreast stood motionless or hitched forward a yard at a time. Men and horses and guns, tons of ammunition, tons of food, tons of equipment, were jostled and pressed onward in a movement that had to be as swift as it seemed slow.[38]

To add to the confusion as the Americans approached the battlefield, the traffic became multidirectional. The Americans were replacing French divisions who held the front. These divisions and their supply trains were now struggling away from the front against the current of American traffic. In addition, American divisions and their supply trains were crossing routes as they headed to their assigned sectors of the front. To an outside observer the roads between Bar-le-Duc and Verdun in those last two weeks of September appeared to be a seething mass of movement punctuated by curses.

General Pershing moved his field headquarters to the Meuse-Argonne. He selected for his base the village of Souilly, about 20 miles behind the front. Souilly straddles the "Sacred Way," the road that played such a critical part in the Battle of Verdun in 1916. Souilly had served as the headquarters of General Pétain and his staff; it was from here that Pétain had directed the defense of Verdun, stopping the German juggernaut. An American journalist visiting it in the spring of 1916 at the height of the battle left this description.

> Few towns have done less to prepare for greatness than Souilly. It boasts a single street three inches deep in the clay mud of the spring — a single street

through which the Verdun route marches almost contemptuously, the same nest of stone and plaster houses, one story high, houses from which the owners have departed to make room for generals and staff officers.[39]

Pétain's headquarters was in the only large building in the village, the *Mairie*, the town hall/school house. His office was on the second floor, in what had previously been the mayor's office.

Think of the Selectmen's office in any New England village and the picture will be accurate: a bare room, a desk, one chair, a telephone, nothing on the walls but two maps, one of the military zone, one of the actual front and positions of the Verdun fighting. A bleak room, barely heated by the most primitive of stoves.[40]

In contrast, Pershing's headquarters was sumptuous. Pershing arrived in Souilly aboard his luxurious ten-car train, known as "the Commander-in-Chief's Field Headquarters Train."[41] The train pulled into a railway siding hidden in a grove of trees near the village. Captain Earl Thornton, a former Chicago hotelman, skippered the train. His charge was the care and comfort of the General. One of the cars had a generator and telegraph and telephone apparatus, connections with the outside could be made five minutes after stopping if lines were available. Then the office car for conferences, followed by General Pershing's own car with his bedroom, dressing room, library and four compartments for visiting notables, then dining and sleeping cars for officers, cars for enlisted, and finally the automobile car that contained two large autos for local travel. Captain Thornton especially remembered that Pershing was very particular about breakfast: fruit, wheat cakes, boiled eggs, toast and tea. Enlisted men scattered on foraging expeditions throughout the countryside for fresh eggs — "one œuf here, two œufs there." After breakfast, Pershing went to the office car for meetings with staff, reading reports, sending messages and issuing orders. Luncheon and dinner were formal affairs with place cards, each man seated according to rank. Before retiring, regardless of the weather, the General took his daily constitutional, a brisk walk up and down the train's length for an hour.

In 1918 and 1919, the train traveled more than 75,000 miles conveying Pershing and his entourage to meetings and conferences. He lived in what his doughboys would have described as luxury. He even had a lover in Paris, Micheline Resco, who, when Pershing met her in 1917, was twenty-three years old, thirty-four years his junior. Whenever the "Commander-in-Chief's Field Headquarters Train" was in Paris for A.E.F. business, he visited Mademoiselle Resco surreptitiously at night. Using one of the autos from the train, with the two windshield signs, the American flag and four stars out of sight, Pershing sat up front with the chauffeur so as not to be recognized on visits to her apartment at 4 rue Descombes for an evening of romance. Mademoiselle Resco was probably the best kept American secret of the war![42]

In Souilly, once Pershing arrived, preparations went into high gear for the upcoming Meuse-Argonne battle. Unfortunately, the earlier St. Mihiel affair had a cost that would now be due, a cost that would be paid in unnecessary American casualties, a cost that Pershing recognized.

> As we have seen, some of our most experienced divisions, the 1st, 2d, 26th and 42nd, were used at St. Mihiel. This prevented their transfer to the Meuse-Argonne in time to open the fight, and compelled the employment of some divisions which had not entirely completed their period of training. Four of the nine divisions that were to lead the assault were without their own artillery and had brigades of that arm assigned to them with which they had never previously been in contact.[43]

13

The Fog of Battle

> Gentlemen, we have reached the time we have all been looking for, we are about to engage in the most serious business ever undertaken by man, and no one can tell who will come out of it. Gentlemen, may God be with you.—Major General A. Cronkhite, 80th Division, U.S. Army[1]

The battle began on September 26, 1918, and so did the feint. Coincident with the American attack in the Meuse-Argonne, one American division, the 26th or Yankee Division, launched an assault from the northern base of the St. Mihiel Salient against the outer defenses of Metz. The plan was to deceive the Germans into believing that the entire American army was attacking from the salient with Metz as its target. If the ruse succeeded, the Germans would hold reserves near Metz, rather than reinforce their Meuse-Argonne front. On September 26, an infantry regiment made up of the Connecticut National Guard (of Seicheprey fame) attacked the Michel Stellung, the outer fortification of the Hindenburg Line that ran along the base of the salient, the first line of the Metz defenses. Incorporated into Michel Stellung were the ruins of two small villages: Marchéville and Riaville. Those two villages were the objectives of the Yankee Division. The Michel Stellung lived up to its promise; its attackers faced a storm of steel. Machine guns sent deadly sprays of lead that scythed down their targets. The Germans repulsed the Riaville attack. The Marchéville attack was successful. The New Englanders fought their way into the village and managed to clear it. Pershing ordered them to hold Marchéville for 24 hours while the main attack in the Meuse-Argonne launched. Now it was the New Englanders' turn to defend Marchéville. The Germans counterattacked, virtually trapping the Americans. When the order finally came to abandon the village, they had to fight their way out. By then, the Meuse-Argonne attack was in full gear and the need for deception over. The ruse succeeded, for during the first couple of days of the Meuse-Argonne attack the Americans found the German lines undermanned. The German command believed that the Meuse-Argonne was the feint!

> The enemy's plan therefore succeeded. His clever preparations, and especially the fact that our attention was deflected too long by developments at St. Mihiel, led to the insufficiency of our forces now surprised to the west of the Meuse.[2]

So why attack in the Meuse-Argonne? What was the strategic significance of this piece of French real estate? The answer was railroads. East of the Western Front the German army moved men and supplies on a railway system roughly paralleling their lines; the French called it the *voie de rocade* and it

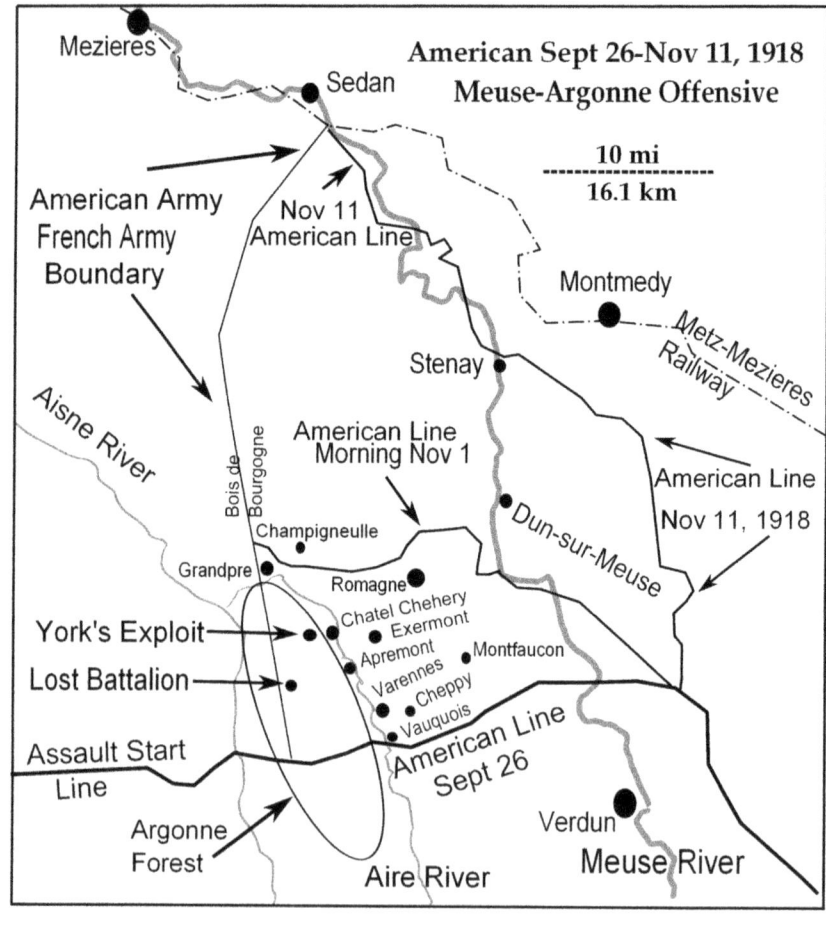

American Meuse-Argonne Offensive.

gave the Germans a great logistical advantage. Railway lines out of Luxembourg and Strasbourg fed the *voie de rocade*. From Metz tracks ran west to Conflans and then northwest to the fortress town of Montmédy, then to Sedan and to Charleville-Mézières and on to Lille in the north. Branch lines led to areas near the front.[3] Foch planned a Franco-American attack to cut the line near Sedan. The French would attack from the Champagne, west of the Argonne Forest, and the Americans from the Meuse-Argonne, both attacks converging upon Sedan. These attacks were part of a series of offensives Foch launched, all within days of each other: September 26, the Franco-American drive toward Sedan; September 27, the British attack between Péronne and Lens; September 28, the Belgian, British, and French offensive in Flanders; September 29, the French and British offensive between La Fere and Péronne.[4] The German lines were to be hit in multiple places. The German concern soon became not how to use the *voie de rocade* to move men in to plug the breaches, but rather how to keep the railways secure as lines of retreat.

The preparatory bombardment of the Meuse-Argonne battle opened at 2:30 A.M. on September 26; "H" hour at 5:30 A.M. was when the Americans went over the top. Troops assembled at their jump-off positions a couple of hours before.

> We had two hours to wait. It was cold and damp, and I hugged the ground to keep from shivering. We were tired to the bone, but we could not sleep. Indeed, who wanted to sleep in such a scene as that. It cannot be described, it can only be felt. The big guns behind us were booming and lighting up the sky with their flashes, and the Boche was answering back, and we could hear the great missiles of death singing over our heads in a multitude of monotones. Just before dawn the lesser guns opened up like the barking of many dogs, and then the whole world was filled as if with the noise of great machinery grinding out death.[5]

At "H" hour, the young soldiers entered a surreal world; the battlefield they would fight in was a churned-up graveyard of past battles. For the more reflective, it was as if they could see their own future in the skeletons littering the battlefield; some were still clothed in tattered uniforms, others disarticulated by explosions. Bones seemed to be everywhere.

> The front from one end to the other was indescribably broken up. French and Germans had fought for four long years in the Argonne and about Verdun. Men had dug trenches and shell fire had filled them so many times that the area no longer seemed like the face of the earth. Masses of tangled barbed wire, mine craters, abandoned trenches, swamps, flooded creek bottoms, gaunt dismantled forests, uprooted graves, skulls remaining from the

battles of 1915 and 1916, castaway equipment, gun wheels, marked that wide belt of bleak, unhuman destruction.[6]

The American front ran east to west, stretching 20 miles (32 km) from the Meuse River in the east to the hills of the Argonne Forest in the west. Nine American divisions faced five under-strength German divisions. Since American divisions were twice the size of German ones, the Americans had a four to one advantage in manpower. The front crossed *Le Mort Homme*, Côte 304 and the woods at Avocourt, places where hundreds of thousands of French and Germans had perished during the Battle of Verdun in 1916 and 1917. In the west it faced the Butte de Vauquois, a decapitated hill fought over since the fall of 1914 in a seemingly endless game of "king of the mountain" by the French and Germans. The nearby town of Clermont-en-Argonne served as a staging area for American troops, the same town Edith Wharton visited in 1915, and later described in a letter to Henry James (see Chapter 1). The American front then crossed the river Aire and ended in the hills of the Argonne Forest, a tangled maze of trenches, barbed wire and fortifications fought over since the early days of the war.

German soldiers in gas masks awaiting an attack; one soldier mans a light machine gun and the other is priming a stick grenade. The desolate battlefield is littered with German and French equipment. The trench appears to have been collapsed by shell fire so that it is more of a crater than a trench. The earth is raw and living plants are absent (Massachusetts National Guard Museum and Archive, Worcester).

13. The Fog of Battle

Going "over the top" that morning of September 26 was akin to entering another dimension. Not only did the Americans enter a charnel house of previous battles where landmarks had disappeared, but nature conspired to further confuse them — a thick fog had settled over the landscape. Units soon disappeared into the fog and smoke; green American divisions, led by officers without sufficient training or combat experience, soon became disoriented, and then outright lost. It was literally the blind leading the blind.

> Whole battalions, led by commanders with a poor sense of direction, wandered from their proper line of advance, sometimes to bring up in another division's sector or to find themselves moving southward.[7] Battalions lost their companies and platoons escaped from their companies. The most energetic and resourceful platoon or company commander could not keep constant control of a widely deployed attack line, only the nearest men of which he could see....
>
> Many platoons went their own way the entire forenoon without having seen another American unit or without having any sort of idea where they were. The constant effort to seek contact with the flanks of adjacent units became a more engrossing occupation even than dealing with the enemy.[8]

Units passed German strong points, unaware they had until fired on from behind. Some of the doughboys had been in the army only six weeks and had never received any rifle training; they got trained quickly "on the job" if they survived the first day. Men attacked in groups rather than in spread out formations, German machine guns felled entire platoons in one sweep. After the opening barrage, American artillery fired blindly rather than by direct observation, thus machine gun nests had to be smothered with American flesh rather than taken out by artillery fire.[9] But still, in spite of the chaos and inexperience of its soldiers, the American surge was unstoppable that first day. Perhaps their inexperience was an advantage; rather than waiting for orders, they just went ahead. Soldiers joined with others from different units and under the leadership of a nearby officer or non commissioned officer or even a charismatic private kept fighting.[10]

> The attack moved northward with undiminished momentum. Platoons which had wandered into the sector of some other regiment than their own, or even some other division, stalked machine gun nests as cheerfully as if still at home. Officers who had lost their own commands gathered up groups of enlisted men who had lost their officers and went ahead.[11]

By the second day, the battle became even more *ad lib*. Nine divisions advanced against the enemy; over a quarter of a million men were somewhere out there fighting, but where? Communications with them were scanty. Wireless communication was technically possible but in its infancy. Wireless operators often heard transmissions from the Eiffel Tower in Paris but not their own corps headquarters. Telephones were the primary means of communication in the American army of 1918, but its cloth-covered telephone lines were not waterproof and thus grounded out when wet. Some units rolled up German wire, which was waterproof, for reuse. Runners were sent out, but German snipers got many of them. Pigeons were tried; cages of birds and instructions for their care were delivered to field officers. One told his Signal Sergeant:

> "Take those damned birds, and if the Adjunct wants to write any notes to the corps you can send them."
>
> That was the last I saw of the pigeons, but the Adjunct told me that he sent a couple of messages by them, but if these were ever delivered we never heard. I learned afterwards that some of the outfits were eating their pigeons and I have always regretted that I did not use mine to better advantage than I did.[12]

The experiences of the division that took the Butte de Vauquois, the hill of Edith Wharton fame, illustrate the problems the men dealt with in the first days of the offensive. The 35th Division was composed of National Guard units from Kansas and Missouri; its most famous member was an artillery officer who would go on to become the 33rd president of the United States, Lieutenant Harry S. Truman. The objective for the first day of the attack was Vauquois Hill, considered the most formidable German defensive position facing any American division on the entire Meuse-Argonne front. Prior to the day of the offensive (September 26), officers were given an intelligence assessment of what Vauquois held in store.

Confidential Report On Vauquois Hill[13]

Confidential	1st Army Corps, U.S.
Not To Be Taken Into	Second Section, G. S.,
front line trenches	September 22, 1918

VAUQUOIS

VAUQUOIS may be taken as the perfect example of German fortification, combining an elaborate trench system with the use of mines.

(1) The trenches, during the day, are occupied by sentinels, as few as are absolutely essential. The garrison is in deep dugouts affording protection from our largest shells. These are very comfortably equipped, having electricity, water supply and kitchens close at hand. All necessary supplies are brought in by a railroad. On the slightest signal, everyone can be at his post of combat.

(2) The fortress of VAUQUOIS, dominating the plain for 100 miles, is one

of the points on the front where the Germans have installed themselves with great thoroughness.

In the defensive system of VAUQUOIS, mines figured very prominently throughout 1916, and the beginning of 1917. Since the month of June, 1917, mining activity has steadily decreased. At the present date galleries are known to be in existence, but there have been no recent explosions.

From captured documents dated December, 1917, it appears that VAUQUOIS must be held at any cost.

If the tactical situation eventually necessitates a retirement the Commandant of VAUQUOIS is ordered to blow up all mined galleries....

Americans believed 18 officers and 1,370 men held Vauquois. On September 26, the hill was actually defended by only 75 men commanded by a nineteen-year-old lieutenant.[14] This Teutonic "forlorn hope" was ordered to fight to the death for Kaiser and country. It did not. The Americans left their lines at 5:30 A.M., in a thick fog that shrouded the landscape; the Americans mistakenly fired smoke shells to obscure their attack but this only intensified the gloom, making it impossible to tell friend from foe at 25 yards. After some desultory attempts at defense, the Germans decided not to fight to the death and surrendered. Vauquois fell in less than 40 minutes. Vauquois was not unique; most of the German front line facing the Americans that morning was lightly held and offered little impediment. Places where thousands had perished over every contested acre in previous years now fell relatively easily to the Americans on the first day of their offensive.

The first real fighting the Kansas-Missouri boys saw that day was three kilometers (1.8 mi) north of Vauquois near the village of Cheppy. German defenses included machine gun nests sited at strong points near and in the village; the Americans, pinned down for three hours, were taking many casualties until eight tanks commanded by Colonel George Patton literally came to their rescue. His tanks swung out of column and into line facing the enemy and in a few minutes of firing, their one-pounders blasted the machine gun nests and their crews to bits. Surprisingly the Germans had been defending Cheppy with some American-made weapons.

> A battery of enemy guns captured in the woods near Cheppy had been made by the Bethlehem Steel Works[15] for the Russian Government, the inscription stated. From Russia they had been brought by the Germans to this front, and now, through the fortunes of war, had come back into American possession.[16]

Patton, directing his tanks while following them on foot, sustained wounds from machine-gun fire just north of Cheppy and was out of the battle. However, his tanks were not. They turned west and helped the 35th liberate Varennes, a largish town straddling the Aire River.[17] After Varennes, the tank regiment was pretty much out of the Meuse-Argonne battle also, most of its tanks being either destroyed or down because of mechanical failures.[18] Without the tanks, the 35th was in trouble because it essentially had no artillery support — its artillery initially could not reach the fighting because of impassable roads[19] and when it did, it was used ineffectively.[20] The 35th continued its attack northward, taking villages and pushing back the Germans but with unnecessary casualties.

> The failure of liaison and all mechanical means of communication cost the lives of many brave men in the front lines in the course of the battle. If the troops located machine gun nests or battery positions, as happened many times, the fact was immediately reported. The Intelligence section worked out the map co-ordinates to ask the artillery to shell the spot. This would have resulted in silencing the battery which was driving furrows through our ranks. The wire from regimental headquarters (if regimental headquarters was located) would get no answer from the brigade, and through brigade headquarters was the course which the appeal to the artillery must take. Runners would be dispatched. If they were not killed or wounded en route, they probably would find the agile brigade headquarters had moved from the shell hole in which it had last been seen, and there would be no one there to tell where it was gone. The search for the headquarters would continue while the battery or machine gun would continue to take its toll of American lives.[21]

"Very" pistols, issued for signaling, helped to resolve the problem; different colored rockets fired from the pistols allowed communication with artillery batteries. Unfortunately, the ammunition for the pistols was the wrong bore! When the correct ammunition arrived, included was a code list: *e.g.*, six white balls in a rocket meant send a barrage, one white and one green meant something else, two reds and a blue meant something else, and so on. However, the new ammunition included only "yellow smoke." There was nothing on the code list about "yellow smoke!"[22] The French soldiers, subjected to their own army's foul-ups for four years, dealt with such situations using *Système D*. "D" stood for either *se débrouiller* or *se démerder*. The former meant you untangled the situation yourself, whereas the latter meant you got out of "the shit" yourself. Pershing's offensive in the Meuse-Argonne relied upon a considerable dose of *Système D*.

Sometimes *Système D* was not sufficient for success. On Sunday, September 29, 1918, at five-thirty in the morning, the Kansas-Missouri boys were ordered to attack the dismal little village of Exermont,* a German strong point. The attack would be made, as usual, with insufficient artillery. And

---

*It still is a woebegone hamlet.

what artillery fire there was shelled the wrong part of the battlefield![23] Visiting the division the day before, Pershing reportedly said, "Well, make it tomorrow morning regardless of cost."[24] The attack finished the 35th.

In a driving rain, the Americans advanced on Exermont. The Germans responded with a devastating barrage of high explosive shells, shrapnel and gas shells. Scything back and forth, machine gun fire came as a horizontal hail-storm of lead. Without American artillery to take out German batteries and machine guns, it was a German turkey shoot. After a couple of hours of being targets, the American lines broke and the men ran.[25] *Système D* in this case was *se démerder*.

The 35th was not the only division overwhelmed by the fury of German artillery and machine gun fire in the Meuse-Argonne. The 5th Division had an even more violent baptism coming into the line to take over from the 80th.

> It appears they went over the top between six and seven o'clock of the morning ... they met such unexpected and violent resistance in the front which I had turned over to them and had come under such galling fire from the enemy's machine guns and artillery that they broke and came back a distance of nearly two kilometers, and suffered, I am told, in three days' time, fourteen hundred casualties, five hundred of which were killed.[26]

The 5th Division came into the line during the second American attack in the Meuse-Argonne, which began on October 4. In the first, September 26–30, the Americans went through the first German defensive position, the *Giselher Stellung*,[27] before the Germans could move in reserves. By September 30, the reserves had arrived and the offensive slowed considerably. Even so, the green American divisions had made remarkable progress, pushing the Germans back over 6 miles (about 10 km) in the sector of the battlefield between the Meuse and the foothills of the Argonne Forest. In doing so, they captured the heavily fortified hill Montfaucon, where the Crown Prince had an observatory built from the ruins of the Montfaucon village church. There he was supposed to have watched the fighting on Mort Homme and Côte 304 in 1916, from a very safe distance of course. The only place that the American offensive stalled was, not surprisingly, in the Argonne Forest itself, a rugged range of wooded hills running north south bounded by the Aire River in the east and the Aisne River in the west. Steep ravines, some 750 feet deep, traversed the forest from east to west. Earlier in the war, the French had stopped the Germans at a line running midway through the forest; it was here the American September 26 offensive jumped off. At this point the forest is about 5 miles (8 km) wide and 10 miles (16 km) long, ending at the town of Grandpré where there is a gap through which the Aire River swings west to join the Aisne.

The region was a natural fortress beside which the Virginia Wilderness in which Grant and Lee fought was a park. It was masked and tortuous before the enemy strung his first wire and dug his first trench. The French had burned their fingers on the German half of it in 1914 and let it alone thereafter; the enemy had been content to do the same, but had strengthened his half leisurely in the ensuing years, with all the ingenuity of skilled military engineers The underbrush had grown up through the German barbed and rabbit wire, interlacing it and concealing it, and machine guns lurked like copperheads in the ambush of shell-fallen trees. Other machine guns were strewn in concrete pill boxes and in defiles. On the offense, tanks could not follow, nor artillery see where it was shooting, while the enemy guns, on the defense, could fire by the map.[28]

There were two ways to take the Argonne: either by fighting down the Aire valley east of the forest and taking Grandpré, thus forcing the Germans to withdraw rather than be cut off; or by attacking into the forest directly from the jump-off line. Such a frontal attack was considered suicidal, as it would play into the German defenses.[29] Pershing, hedging his bet, chose both approaches, frontal into the forest and down the Aire valley.

The 77th Division, a draftee division from New York City, advanced into the forested labyrinth on September 26; it bogged down after a few days. Responding to Pershing's pressure to move forward regardless of cost, two battalions were ordered to push through a temporary gap in the German defenses on October 2, to establish a kind of beachhead on Charlevaux Brook 1,300 yards beyond American lines. Major Charles Whittlesey, a New York attorney and graduate of Williams College and Harvard Law, led the attack battalion; Captain George McMurtry, a New York stockbroker and Harvard alumnus, commanded the reserve battalion. Together, the two battalions totaled 456; they would become known collectively as the "Lost Battalion." The battalions broke through one of the defensive lines of the Giselher Stellung and advanced up the broad Charlevaux ravine.

After heavy fighting we penetrated the German line, gaining our objective just at sundown. We were located on the northern slope of a bleak, unsheltered ravine. Some of the men stood guard while the others dug themselves into the hillside for shelter from shrapnel and bullets. Then night settled over the forest, and we were ordered to be as quiet as possible, as any noise would give away our position to the Hun.[30]

On the steep north side of the ravine a road had been cut high up on the slope. The Americans decided to spend the night there and wait for reinforcements. The site was ideal since the road cut formed a defensible line and the bivouac area lay on the reverse slope of a hill with respect to incoming

German artillery fire. German batteries were to the north and thus shells passed over the reverse slope and hit beyond the Americans. The men dug shallow funkholes[31] in the stony terrain and took up position below and parallel to the road in an oblong formation; the site became known as the pocket.[32]

> On Thursday, October 3, we tried to send messages through, but found our runners at the nearest post either killed or captured. Patrols were sent out to reconnoiter, and then we knew that we were completely surrounded; surrounded on a bleak, unsheltered ravine, with the German Army on a cliff above, and with a powerful German detachment deeply entrenched on the other side of the ravine. Enemy troops were so close that we could hear the calls and orders of the men. If we showed ourselves in the openings of the wooded forest, we could be reached by German machine guns, rifles and trench-mortars.[33]

The Germans had the Americans trapped and soon laid siege, attacking across the cliff-like road cut a number of times. They were always driven back but always by fewer and fewer defenders as American casualties increased. German snipers and machine gun fire continually took their toll. The German high command was amazed at American determination, surrendering was just not an option.

> When on the defensive, the American, even in desperate situations, proves himself absolutely tenacious. For example, one American battalion, although

A concrete German village in the Argonne Forest used as divisional headquarters for the 77th Division during the saga of the Lost Battalion. It is known as the *L'Abri du Kronprinz*; the royal furnishings included a piano and wine cellar.

surrounded and having suffered extreme losses from artillery, machine guns, and flame throwers, resisted for days.[34]

On October 3 and 4, the 77th sent forces in an attempt to reach the pocket; each time they were driven off with considerable loss.[35] On October 4, American artillery mistakenly fired on the pocket. Whereas the pocket was protected from German artillery fire by being on the reverse slope, it was on the forward slope with reference to American artillery fire, and thus a sitting duck! The barrage lasted an hour and a half; the Americans suffered 35 needless casualties.

> Everywhere about us the ground was heaving and shooting up. You can imagine our excitement. It had a Wall Street panic beat a hundred ways. It was a case of lambs with us all. Some stayed in their holes, others ran to the left, others to the right. The sergeant-major ran to the right, and the only traces we found of the poor lad after the barrage was his hat and gat (pistol). Under this deadly fire we suffered many casualties. The groans of the wounded and the dying all the time made the place an inferno.[36]

The woodland on the slope was blown to smithereens, resulting in the pocket being more open to German observers and snipers.[37] The Americans had run out of food and were nearly out of ammunition. After dark, they gathered rifles and ammunition from German dead, hoping to find German rations as well. On October 6, an air drop of food and ammunition was attempted, but it landed outside the pocket.[38]

At sunset on the sixth, one of the stranger stories associated with the Lost Battalion began to unfold. Eight or nine American soldiers attempted to sneak through German lines and make contact with their support lines.[39] Machine gun fire killed or wounded most; one of the least seriously wounded was an eighteen-year-old private named Lowell R. Hollingshead. Captured and taken to a dugout, he faced an interview by Lieutenant Heinrich Prinz, a German officer who had worked six years in Seattle for a German company. Lieutenant Prinz arranged food for his American captive, gave him a cigarette, and had a doctor tend his wound. He then ordered Hollingshead to return to the pocket under a white flag of truce and deliver a letter to Major Whittlesey. Recognizing that the bearer of unpleasant news often becomes a victim, Prinz extolled the virtues of Private Hollingshead as a good soldier and patriot before suggesting that the Americans surrender. Fortunately, Hollingshead is not a German name or all the praise would have seemed suspicious!

The Demand for Surrender

To the Commanding Officer — Infantry, 77th Division.

Sir: — The bearer of this present, *Private Lowell R. Hollingshead,* has been taken prisoner by us. He refused to give the German Intelligence Officer any answer to his questions, and is quite an honorable fellow, doing honor to his Fatherland in the strictest sense of the word.

He has been charged against his will, believing that he is doing wrong to his country to carry forward this present letter to the officer in charge of the battalion of the 77th Division, with the purpose to recommend this commander to surrender with his forces, as it would be quite useless to resist any more, in view of the present conditions.

The suffering of your wounded men can be heard over here in the German lines, and we are appealing to your humane sentiments to stop. A white flag shown by one of your men will tell us that you agree with these conditions. Please treat *Private Lowell R. Hollingshead* as an honorable man. He is quite a soldier. We envy you.

The German Commanding Officer.[40]

Private Hollingshead crossed back to the pocket and delivered the letter to Major Whittlesey at 4:00 P.M., October 7. Whittlesey's response was to ignore it.[41] Soon after, not seeing a white flag, the Germans launched their final and most desperate attack — it failed. At about seven that evening a relief force from the 77th Division fought its way into the pocket, saving the Lost Battalion at last. Of the 456 trapped soldiers, approximately half were able to walk out; 69 were dead or missing; the rest seriously wounded.[42] Perhaps the last casualty of the Lost Battalion was Whittlesey himself; in late November 1921, he boarded a ship bound for Havana, Cuba. On the evening of November 28, he jumped over the side to perish in the cold waters of the North Atlantic. Whittlesey's suicide brought closure to a journey that had begun on October 2, 1918, in the Charlevaux ravine. Since the war's end, mothers, widows and wounded soldiers had besieged him with calls asking for help. Earlier in the month, on November 11, 1921, Armistice Day, Whittlesey had been a pallbearer in ceremonies for the burial of the Unknown Soldier at Arlington National Cemetery.[43]

Perhaps his orderly, Private Robert Manson, wrote the most fitting remembrance of Charles Whittlesey.

> Our casualties increased on the fourth day. The Major, however, was as cool as ever. His hourly message to the men was, "Be patient, help will come." As I watched him from my hole in the ground, I said to myself, "How calm he is." I realize now why they call him "Cool Charles" in civil life.[44]

14

Attack, Attrition, Pursuit

> In Champagne and the western bank of the Meuse a big battle had begun on the 26th of September, French and American troops attacking with far reaching objectives. West of the Argonne we remained masters of the situation, and fought a defensive battle. Between the Argonne and the Meuse the Americans had broken into our positions. They had a powerful army in this region, and their part in the campaign became more and more important.—General Erich Ludendorff, First Quartermaster General, Imperial German Army[1]

Three periods divide the American battle for the Meuse-Argonne: September 26–30, the initial attack; most of the month of October, the period of attrition when the American army fought a series of costly offensives as it approached and finally breached (in places) the formidable Kriemhilde Stellung; and the final period, November 1 to the Armistice (November 11), when the American offensive caused the precipitant retreat of the German Army from the Meuse-Argonne.[2]

Pershing had hoped to reach the Kriemhilde Stellung in the initial September attack, but he had asked too much of his inexperienced army and had greatly underestimated the tenacity of the German defense. By the beginning of October, the American attack bogged down short of its goal. Pershing recalled the time as the low point of the war.

> The period of the battle from October 1st to the 11th involved the heaviest strain on the army and on me. There was little time to make readjustments among the troops heavily engaged, without giving the enemy a respite in which to strengthen his defenses and bring up reserves. The battle could not be delayed while roads were being built or repaired and supplies brought up. The weather was cold and rainy and not the kind to inspire energetic action on the part of troops unaccustomed to the damp, raw climate.[3]

Probably Pershing's biggest headache during that time was the fate of the Lost Battalion. If it could not be relieved in time and was annihilated, or worse yet, if it surrendered, there would be a blot on Pershing's record and a public relations fiasco for the A.E.F.[4] The solution to the problem came from General Hunter Liggett, at the time the commander of First Corps, which included the divisions fighting in or near the Argonne Forest. Liggett's idea was to push down the Aire River valley beyond where the Germans surrounded the Lost Battalion and then launch a flank attack westward into the hills. The hoped for response was that the German units surrounding the Lost Battalion would withdraw because their supply lines were threatened and they themselves could be cut off.[5] If the German units withdrew, relief units of the 77th Division could reach their surrounded comrades. In essentials, Liggett's plan worked.

The first division to begin the plan's implementation was the 28th Division, the Pennsylvania National Guard. The division began its drive from Varennes, a town straddling the Aire. The first objective was Apremont,[6] a heavily defended village on the Aire four miles (6.4 km) north of Varennes. A road from Apremont ran west across the Argonne Forest, where the Lost Battalion was fighting for its life below a road-cut. To flank the Germans the Pennsylvanians had to make their way past Apremont, a task easier said than done as it turned out. The village was heavily fortified with snipers, and machine guns seemed to be everywhere. After the war, veterans remembered that there was a time in "ensanguined Apremont" when the water running in the gutters was bright red with blood — and not all of it was German blood.[7] American losses were very heavy; it was the most costly battle fought by the 28th in the war.

> There were instances of companies emerging from the combat in command of corporals, every commissioned officer and every sergeant having been put out of action, and in at least one instance, a battalion was commanded by a sergeant, the major, his staff, the commanders and lieutenants of all four companies having been incapacitated.[8]

After Apremont, the fighting moved to a heavily fortified ridge known as Le Chêne Tondue, located near where the road leading to the Lost Battalion entered the hills. The fighting here held up the division for four days. After capturing the ridge, the Pennsylvanians advanced into the edge of the Argonne Forest to the small town (or large village) of Châtel-Chéhéry, located two miles (3.2 km) north of Apremont in the foothills of the forest. The village served as a railroad depot for the German system in the Aire valley; 7 locomotives and 268 cars were captured. The Germans had attempted to destroy the engines before retreating, but the Pennsylvanians were familiar with the workings of steam engines. They soon repaired four engines and the railroad was back in service for the American army. Also captured was an electrically powered sawmill with a large store of prepared lumber and a number of electric power plants which were soon working. Probably the strangest find had connections to the 1916 battle of Verdun and its German commander Crown Prince Wilhelm.

> Near Châtel-Chéhéry, in the depths of the woods, the soldiers found a hunting lodge which prisoners said was occupied for a long time by the German Crown Prince. They said that, unmindful of the great tragedy such a short distance away and for which he was at least partly responsible, he entertained parties of gay friends at the lodge and went boar hunting in the forest. That he was more or less successful was attested by several large boars' heads on the walls.[9]

With the taking of Châtel-Chéhéry along the forest's eastern edge the stage was set for the second act of Liggett's plan, a deeper flanking attack into the forest proper. The 82nd, a draftee infantry division, made this attack into the Argonne just at Châtel-Chéhéry. Units of the division marched from Varennes on the night of October 6–7, but the German Army had already begun pulling out of the Argonne Forest. German commanders had divined that a flank attack was coming. On October 8, the 82nd jumped-off to fight its way west a mile and a quarter into the forest. Its mission was to sever a narrow-gauge military railway that carried supplies to the German troops south of Châtel-Chéhéry, including the area of the Lost Battalion.

During the war 60 cm (about 2 ft.) gauge railways were the primary method of moving ammunition, supplies, construction materials and men to the battlefields from depots far behind the lines. In turn, normal gauge railroads supplied these depots. Invented in 1875 by a Frenchman, Paul Decauville, for transport on large agricultural estates, especially those in French colonies, the war saw the adoption of 60 cm Decauville railways by all belligerents on the Western Front. When an army captured a section of the front, it had the bonus of the foe's Decauville railway tracks since they were conveniently the same gauge! Decauville tracks were prefabricated; 5 m track sections, including rails and steel cross ties (sleepers), weighed only 100 kilograms (220 pounds), and men could quickly assemble them into a railway spur following an advance, much like assembling a giant model train set. Pulled by small locomotives, steam or gasoline engine powered, the trains readily crossed muddy terrain because the Decauville track-way sections distributed the heavy loads keeping them from sinking. In contrast, heavy trucks in the same terrain eventually so rutted dirt roads as to make them impassable. Often a track-way was sited on an old dirt road, using the road as a convenient track bed. On October 7, at 9:45 P.M., the 164th Infantry Brigade of the 82nd

A Decauville railway somewhere in the Argonne Forest; such 60 centimeter (23.4 in) gauge lines moved men and supplies to the active front and were used by all sides. In the photograph a German troop train with its officers in the first car awaits an engine (*Die Wochenschau* [Berlin: W. Girardet, 1916]).

Division was ordered to make "a powerful thrust for the purpose of cutting the road and railroad about two kilometers (1.2 mi) west of Hill 223."[10] Hill 223 is next to and just north of Châtel-Chéhéry. Unfortunately, the "thrust" was pointless; the Lost Battalion had been saved about three hours earlier at 7:00 P.M. Regardless, the "thrust" proceeded as planned. On October 8, at 6:00 A.M., the 328th Infantry Regiment, a regiment of the 164th, attacked.

> The 328th Infantry was charged with the duty of driving hard, straight west, to cross the rail road at the nearest point. A rolling barrage was provided for, which was to advance at the rate of 100 meters in three minutes until the railroad was reached. The barrage was then to stand 300 meters beyond the railroad until ordered to stop.[11]

Thus began one of the most incredible individual achievements of the war because a member of the 328th Infantry Regiment was Corporal Alvin C. York.

In 1919, George Pattullo interviewed Corporal York for *The Saturday Evening Post*. Pattullo was in the Argonne after the Armistice when he got a tip that York had been involved in something that would make a great story. The A.E.F. had made little of York's exploit since York somehow did not fit Pershing's notion of the ideal A.E.F. hero. Pattullo's *Post* article catapulted York into fame. *The Saturday Evening Post* had two million readers in 1919. The article made Pershing very sore at Pattullo — whom he felt had blindsided him.[12] Pattullo introduced Corporal York and his exploits to America in his lead paragraph, and America went wild over the homespun hero.

> Alvin C. York, comes from Pall Mall, Fentress County, Tennessee, and is second elder in the Church of Christ and Christian Union. The sect is opposed to any form of fighting; they are conscientious objectors. But York refused to ask exemption, went to war, and as Corporal York of Company G, 328th Infantry, killed twenty Germans on October eighth, captured one hundred and thirty-two prisoners, including a major and three lieutenants, put thirty-five machine guns out of business, and thereby broke up an entire battalion which was about to counterattack against the Americans on Hill 223 in the Argonne sector near Chatel-Chehery [sic].[13]

On October 8, at 6:00 A.M., an American battalion that included Company G left its trenches between Hill 223 and Châtel-Chéhéry and attacked westward into a broad open valley; the valley was surrounded on three sides by wooded hills, and German machine-guns sited in these hills soon began to decimate the Americans. Three squads, including one led by York, were ordered to try to outflank the hill on the left and silence its guns. Making their way through the woods, the Americans surprised approximately 30 Germans, including a German major, having breakfast in a clearing and captured them. Machine guns on a hill behind the clearing opened up, killing or wounding nine of the 16 Americans. Using the prisoners as shields York began to pick off the machine gunners with his American-made Enfield rifle. The Germans attempted to rush York who, when his rifle was empty, used his American-made automatic pistol. He was deadly with both! Eventually the machine-gunners, including their lieutenant, surrendered. Seven Americans were now guarding several dozen German prisoners. The strange parade led by Corporal York began the trek through German held positions back to the American lines with the Germans carrying the American wounded. Along the way, the captured German officers ordered other German units to surrender and the prisoner contingent grew. When they finally reached American lines, York and the six Americans had apparently emptied the hill of its German defenders.[14] Although York's exploit was without doubt heroic and revealed his qualities both as a marksman and leader, it also said a lot about the decline of the German Army in the fall of 1918. German soldiers seemed to be surrendering in droves everywhere, becoming a POW was a ticket out, a way of surviving the pointless killing.

> There were never any such mutinies as wrecked the German Navy at the last; the army fought desperately down to the Armistice, and still had more fight left in it, but there was a difference. As one who is proud of what the American Army did, I wonder what we might have done against the German Army of 1914? Not so well.[15]

While York seemed to be capturing the entire Imperial German Army in the Argonne, General Pershing was trying to revive his stalled offensive against the tenacious and still deadly German Army. General Liggett, a deft hand with an apt phrase put it thus, "A cornered rat is a symbol of fury, but the odds are on the cat."[16] Pershing's men would suffer the rat's fury while the General tried to raise the cat's odds.

The American attack of September 26 ran out of steam on September 29.[17] Other than the fighting in the Argonne Forest relating to the Lost Battalion, the American offensive paused for five days to regroup; a kind of time-out for the coach to come up with a better game plan. Some divisions were replaced, e.g., the veteran 1st Division replaced the shattered 35th and the 32nd replaced the 37th. As the fresh divisions marched by the haggard, muddy and unshaven men they replaced, what they heard was not reassuring, "Better make your place with Jesus, fellows, before you go up there."[18]

Sergeant Alvin York, an American legend; York is credited with killing 25 Germans, capturing 132 prisoners and silencing 35 machine guns on the evening of October 8, 1918, during the Argonne offensive. He stayed in the line for the rest of October. York returned home in June 1919, his troopship docking in Hoboken, from where he ferried to New York City. Put up in a suite in the Waldorf-Astoria, York endured five days of receptions, dinners and honors. The Waldorf's bellboys are said to have fought for the privilege of carrying his blanket-roll, pack and trench helmet (*The Outlook*, Volume 122, 1919).

Troops repaired roads leading to the new front line and brought up supplies, munitions and artillery. At 5:00 A.M. on October 4, the Americans attacked again; this time in order not to forewarn the enemy, they omitted a preliminary artillery bombardment, an omission that was perhaps costly because the Germans were ready and waiting.[19] In addition to their artillery and machine guns, German trench mortars (*minenwerfer*) took a heavy toll.

> One who has never "picked his way through a barrage" can scarcely be expected even to imagine the sensations that throbbed through the heart and mind in such a time as that. One feels in the presence of those powerful and death-dealing instruments how infinitesimally small is man, how life and death are separated by a mere chance.[20]

In his original plan of attack in the Meuse-Argonne, Pershing committed the same error the Crown Prince did during the battle of Verdun in 1916; each restricted his initial attack to one side of the Meuse River. The Crown Prince attacked on the east side of the river, thus allowing French artillery sited on the hills west of the river to target German attackers; Pershing attacked only west of the river, thus allowing German artillery on the hills east of the river to ravage the Americans.

> Once more our artillery from beyond the Meuse[21] had been very effective, according to unanimous statements of prisoners, who spoke of very heavy losses on their side.[22]

The topography of the area required control of the heights both east and west of the river. Pershing later attempted to rectify this error by sending American and French divisions to cross the river and its parallel canal to attack the eastern heights. The attack soon bogged down as the Germans blasted the attackers with high explosives and suffocated them with poison gas.[23] German artillery on the heights east of the river continued to send its storm of steel on to Americans west of the river through most of October.

> Just outside my place I literally walked over the top of dead men and a hundred feet from the place at the edge of the woods where I turned to the right towards the ravine dead men were lying everywhere. I remember particularly a group of three that had been killed by the concussion of one shell. They were as calm and peaceful as if they had been asleep, but one brief glance gave me the ghastly picture. The Boche artillery had indeed wrought terrible execution upon American boys. I cannot describe my own feelings as I picked my way through that storm of shells.[24]

American artillery barrages were very effective against German positions behind the front, hindering the bringing up of reserves and the dispatch of orders.[25] However, there was generally a lack of coordination between the field artillery and the infantry.[26] Rather than taking out machine gun nests with French 75 mm field gun fire, the doughboys primarily relied upon their rifles as had Corporal York. What artillery fire there was often was inaccurate.

> American shells were falling on the hill above us just a kilometer too short to harm the enemy. German shells were Satanic enough but it seemed to me

that American shells had just a little more of the devil in them. Oh, yes, I know some of the officers have claimed that these were German shells from across the Meuse. It seems to me that it would have been impossible for Boche shells to have come from the southwest which was certainly the direction from which they hailed, so, they could only have been of American origin.[27]

General Max von Gallwitz, German commander for the Meuse-Argonne battle, remembered talking to numerous wounded German soldiers and finding "They were not greatly impressed with the effect of the American artillery."[28] Presumably, the soldiers were not wounded by artillery fire! Nor was the general overly impressed with American tactics.

Severe local attacks were directed by the Americans against Group Meuse-West. Some of these were executed in mass formation of greatest density, which accounted for the fact that many of them broke down as soon as they were covered by machine-gun and artillery fire.[29]

Notwithstanding its self-professed military prowess, the Imperial German Army continued to retreat before the American onslaught. What the American First Army lacked in military skills and finesse, it compensated for with enthusiasm, courage, valor and numbers — and one might say a near contempt for casualties by some of its senior officers.[30]

Field hospitals followed in the wake of the fighting, one in the village of Cheppy, not far from Varennes. Learning of the hospital from their Zone Major, Sallies of the Salvation Army began the trek to Cheppy. Traveling by night to avoid German shells, three Salvation Army women (Sallies) arrived in Cheppy bruised and sore from head to foot: one had come via a mule team, another rode a reel cart and the last came on a broken down wagon. They immediately began making coffee and sandwiches for the soldiers passing through the village, but then the fighting heated up and there were more pressing needs. They worked eighteen-hour shifts in the hospital, which was overwhelmed with wounded.

The wounded men continued to pour in, later to be evacuated to the base hospital; they kept coming and coming, a thousand men where two hundred had been expected. There was plenty to be done. The girls were put in charge of different wards. They were under shell fire continually, but they were too busy to think of that as they hurried about ministering to the brave soldiers, who gave never a groan from their white lips no matter what they suffered.[31]

The Salvation Army "hut" was in a cave, a huge warren of dark passageways, the Germans had excavated as their headquarters when they occupied

Cheppy. American army medical facilities were in tents scattered throughout the village. All this activity in the village soon drew the attention of German artillery. Since the canvas-tented field hospital gave no protection from high-explosive shells, it became necessary almost immediately to move one hundred wounded to the Salvation Army "hut." One day a large shell exploded just inside the cave's entrance and partly buried a Sally with rocks from the cave's roof. After she was dug out, she said nothing of her wounds, determined to stay. After five days of near continuous shelling, an American general, motivated by concern for the women's welfare, ordered them to leave because Cheppy was just too close to the fighting. The Sallies revolted, refusing to leave their men. The general relented. The Sallies stayed in Cheppy as long as the hospital needed them.[32]

> The Americans were quiet on the 13th, evidently because they, like ourselves, were in need of reorganization and rest. Engaged in continuous fighting for nine days, they gained but 6 or 7 kilometers along the Aire, and only 2 to 4 kilometers along the Meuse, and to the east of it. American prisoners stated unanimously that they paid for these results very dearly. In one single battalion subsector opposite Group Meuse-East we counted not less than 400 dead Americans.[33]

The most significant American achievement in those nine days was Liggett's offensive down the Aire River valley. As the American Army approached the gap where the Aire turned west crossing the hills, the Germans quickly abandoned the Argonne so as not to be cut off. They had occupied the Argonne Forest since the fall of 1914. During their four years of occupation, they constructed numerous defenses, anticipating nearly all eventualities of attack from within the forest, all of which they abandoned because Liggett did not enter the forest but flanked it.

On October 14, the Americans renewed their attacks on a broad front from the Argonne to the Meuse. Their tactics were that of a human battering ram, butting thousands of American heads against the defenses of the Kriemhilde Stellung. Despite the high casualties, they breached the Stellung. The front had moved one to two miles by October 17, when the attack paused. Writing post-war, General Ludendorff summarized Pershing's battering ram approach to war.

> I believe, however, that General Pershing did not aim so much at achieving important objectives, but rather at smashing the German front opposing him.[34]

By October 17, the American First Army had pushed back the German front in the Meuse-Argonne approximately 8 miles (13 km) since its offensive began on September 26. There were still 24 miles (38.6 km) to fight over before they would reach the railway at Sedan, the goal of the offensive. Of the total distance between the jump-off on September 26 to Sedan, around 32 miles (51.5 km), the Americans had taken only 25 percent. Although Pershing had optimistically predicted that his army would breach the Kriemhilde Stellung on the first day of the Meuse-Argonne Offensive, it had taken 3 weeks to do so.

> The main objective of our initial attack of September 26th had now been reached. Failing to capture it in our first attempt, the army had deliberately, systematically, and doggedly stuck to the task in the face of many difficulties and discouragements.[35]

At any other time on the Western Front, pushing the enemy back 8 miles (12.9 km) in 3 weeks would have been a considerable achievement, but not in the late summer and fall of 1918. For example, despite suffering high casualties, the British had pushed back the Germans 25 miles (40 km) on a forty-mile-front (64 km). They were poised to break the Hindenburg Line, which they did in late September.[36]

On October 12, Pershing split the American First Army into two armies: the original American First Army and the American Second Army, with Pershing as overall commander of both. The First Army would continue the battle in the Meuse-Argonne whereas the Second Army would form along the base of the old St. Mihiel Salient for a drive toward Metz, a drive that never materialized because the war ended too soon.[37] Major General Hunter Liggett commanded the First Army and Major General Robert L. Bullard, the Second. On October 16, Liggett took over a badly mauled, disorganized and wrecked army.[38] No one even knew where many of the men were; Liggett described them as "The Vanishing Doughboys."

> I found, on my inspection of the army, that, due to the hard and bitter fighting which had been continuous since September 26, day and night, some signs of discouragement were beginning to appear among both men and officers, the most conspicuous evidence of which was the great number of stragglers, estimated as high as 100,000.[39]

Since approximately 25,000 men made up an American division, 100,000 stragglers equated to roughly 4 divisions worth of men who had opted out of the war.[40] They hid in abandoned German bunkers, old trenches and in out-of-the-way campsites in the woods. When discovered, they always claimed to be looking for their units. American stragglers actually outnumbered the German army in the Meuse-Argonne! In mid October, General von Gallwitz had only 7 depleted divisions facing the Americans,[41] probably less than 90,000 men since German divisions were half the size of American divisions.

Liggett needed two weeks to revitalize the American First Army before it was ready for his planned offensive. In spite of Pershing nagging him to attack, Liggett remained immovable. Military Police brought in the stragglers, artillery was assembled, munitions and supplies were brought up, targets for artillery fire were identified — the attack would be very much like the St. Mihiel closure, well thought out and surgical. However, it would be more effective because the Americans were veterans and they had a better general. During this period, Liggett cleaned out a German strong point on the western part of his planned jump-off line.

> The left wing of the Third Army lost Grandpré on October 18th. There was very heavy traffic in the enemy's rear that day, indicating that the opponent intended to offer battle once more. Units of our combat flyers attacked ten tanks advancing on the Fléville–St. Juvin road and dropping bombs upon infantry units in the Aire valley.[42]

During the last week of October, Pershing and his staff at GHQ issued the plan of attack for the American First Army. Liggett thought the plan a colossal mistake and essentially rejected it out of hand! Pershing wanted to attack the Germans where they were the strongest — and where they anticipated an attack. It was the "human battering ram" approach all over again. Pershing assigned the honor of leading the "power thrust" to the First Corps. Led by General Dickman, three divisions (78th, 77th, and 80th) made up the First Corps. On the left, they faced the wooded hills of the Bois de Bourgogne behind Grandpré; the Bois de Bourgogne is essentially a geological extension of the Argonne Forest beyond the Aire River gap. Attacking into the Bourgogne Forest had all the military problems that the Argonne Forest had. The front then crossed a valley to a wooded hill on the right, the Bois des Loges. German artillery batteries on both these heights would make life hell for attackers.

> To those of us at First Army headquarters who knew from observation the excessive strength of these positions, how the German was waiting for us just here and had weakened his lines elsewhere in the assurance that he had guessed our minds, such an attack seemed doubtful of success, certain to entail frightful losses, and dubious strategy generally. One of the least of the difficulties was that an advance here would expose us to converging artillery fire.[43]

Liggett and his staff drew up an alternate plan and submitted it to Pershing at GHQ. They proposed Dickman's First Corps sit out the first day's attack on November 1, and instead the "power thrust" be made by the Fifth and Third Corps against the center of the German line where it was most weakened, thereby flanking and pinching off the Bois de Bourgogne and Bois des Loges without the necessity of attacking them at all. The French army would attack west of the Bois de Bourgogne and then converge on the Americans, crossing the Bois de Bourgogne at the village of Boult aux Bois, pinching off the forest. While Pershing accepted the plan, Dickman was not happy — glory had vanished. But maybe not!

On November 1, after a short "but finely systematized artillery bombardment,"[44] the attack hit the Germans where they least expected it, punching through their entire defensive system to a depth of seven miles (11.2 km). Dickman's First Corps on the left was to "threaten furiously, but not to fight the first day."[45] Disregarding orders, Dickman attacked the village of Champigneulle at the base of the Bois des Loges. The Germans were waiting. Liggett lamented the folly.

> It was magnificent but it was not war, for it played into the enemy's hands and led to deplorable waste of life. Having expected an attack just here, the German was more than prepared to stop any such spontaneous combustion as this.[46]

The following day, November 2, Dickman's First Corps attacked as part of the general offensive; he found that the enemy had abandoned its lines fronting him in the Bois de Bourgogne and Bois des Loges — Liggett's plan had worked. The Imperial German Army was on the run, trying to slow the American avalanche with rear-guard machine gun detachments. The final phase of the Battle of the Meuse-Argonne had begun.

> After the attack of November 3d the operation was no longer a battle. It was a pursuit and the rapidity of the American advance depended only on the speed with which bodies of troops could be pushed forward.[47]

On the night of November 8, the American 42nd Division, a National Guard division, cut the great Metz-Sedan railroad corridor south of Sedan. The American First Army had achieved its mission. Artillery blasted apart the four parallel track beds, catching long trains loaded with supplies that now would never make it back to Germany.[48] The Imperial German Army retreated from Sedan on foot, crossing the Ardennes Mountains into Belgium. In addition to wagons and trucks, goats, calves, pigs, sheep, and dogs joined the parade, which now resembled an animal circus rather than an army. Parallel to the road, droves of cattle were driven through the fields in order to keep the road clear. Horses that had fallen from exhaustion were killed, butchered and their meat loaded into the wagons, which were now pulled and pushed by men. Butchered bodies of horses dotted the roadside. American prisoners of war were pushed along with the exodus.[49] The retreat had been going on for almost two weeks, beginning just after the November 1 attack. General Max von Gallwitz, the German Army Group Commander, sensed it was over after the first day of Liggett's offensive.

> The picture that presented itself at 5 P.M. was not rosy.... Undoubtedly, we had suffered a defeat![50]

At the front, there was a sense that the war would soon draw to a close. On November 8, an A.E.F. switchboard operator based in the village of Bras on the eastern edge of the Meuse-Argonne battlefield overheard a strange message from the German government.[51] Its content became grist for the doughboy rumor mill.

"Bras — Meuse-Argonne Front. Nov. 8, 1918
Intercepted Message through
Switchboard By
Merritt F. Garland, U.S. 26th Division

German Wireless from Knaun, Ger.

   The German government desires the president of the U.S. to initiate the bringing about of peace. To notify all warring powers of this desire and to invite them to send envoys for the purpose of discussion. The German government assumes that the program outlined by the president in his messages to Congress on Aug. 10th, 1918 and in later utterances particularly the speech of the 22nd of Sept. is the program for the foundation of peace in order to avoid the future shedding of blood. The German government is ready to bring about immediately general cecession [sic] of hostilities on land, water and in the air.

   (Signed by) German Councillor"

The German high command also realized the war was ending and from its viewpoint, it was ending badly. The Bolshevik infection had spread from Russia to Germany, first to the sailors in the Imperial Navy who mutinied when ordered to engage the British fleet in a final suicidal battle, then to the workers in the cities, and finally to the soldiers at the front where it undermined military discipline. It was only a matter of time before there would be no credible army. The relentless Allied attacks added to the demoralization. The Western Front was collapsing. On October 29, Kaiser Wilhelm II traveled from Berlin to the Belgian resort city of Spa, which at the time was headquarters of the German High Command (*Oberste Heeresleitung, OHL*). There he spent ten days in rosy delusion before events in Berlin forced a *de facto* abdication on November 9.[52] Revolution was in the air and on the streets, the German Republic had been proclaimed on November 8. Advised by Field Marshall Hindenburg that revolutionaries might hunt down the Imperial War Lord in Spa, Kaiser Wilhelm left in a hurry.

14. Attack, Attrition, Pursuit

When the Armistice terms arrived at Spa, the Emperor had gone. All through the night of 9 November he was in a motor car, traveling steadily toward Holland. He arrived at Eysden, the Dutch-Belgian frontier, at 8 A.M. on November 10; seeing a Dutch soldier loitering about, he walked up to him, saying, *"I am the German Emperor,"* and handed the amazed fellow his sword! Tableau! For the moment, no one knew what to do.[53]

Almost as a fitting end to the tragedy and stupidity of the war, a Dutch border official pondered whether to admit the most notorious war criminal in Europe into Holland — after all, he had no passport! The Kaiser impatiently waited, puffing cigarettes. Eventually the Queen of the Netherlands agreed to give a fellow royal asylum. Escorted to the railroad station, the Kaiser and his party waited for his imperial train to steam in. As soon as they boarded, the train rolled into Holland.[54] Supposedly, the first thing the Kaiser asked for upon reaching the sanctuary of Holland was a cup of good English tea! He was half–English after all.[55]

On November 8, the curtain came up on another, and near final, act in the folly that became known as "the war to end all wars." Representatives of what was left of the German government were ushered into a railway car in the forest of Compiègne, France; they had come to negotiate an end to the war. The French response to the Germans was rude and arrogant at best; they had been waiting for this moment since their defeat in the Franco-Prussian War (1871). After days of wrangling while men died, the final armistice session began at 2:15 A.M. on November 11, the last signature affixed to the document at 5:10 A.M.; the Armistice would come into effect at 11:00 A.M. French time.[56] At 5:45 A.M., a radio transmitter on the Eiffel Tower transmitted a message from Marshal Ferdinand Foch confirming the signing. Radiomen in different American units picked up the broadcast, translated it, and relayed the news via telephone. The news spread like wildfire.[57] At 6:25 A.M., American GHQ informed field commanders that the war would end at eleven o'clock.[58]

The French Army stood down on November 10 and 11, waiting to see what would come of the talks at Compiègne; there was no sense in squandering lives if peace might be imminent. The Kaiser had abdicated after all and Germany was now a republic just like France. The French figured they could easily switch from defense to offense if the talks failed. In contrast, the American high command ordered the continuation of vigorous attacks against German positions during the last days of the war. Squandering lives seemed less important than the grand tally of real estate captured. In fact, the number of casualties and ground gained were metrics of success, both should be high; they were how American divisions and their commanders were rated.[59]

But those men were so wrapped up in their professional studies that they entirely forgot the human side.... I think in those last days of the war it was much like a child who had been given a toy that he is very much interested in and that he knows within a day or two is going to be taken from him and he wants to use that toy up to the handle while he has it.[60]

Now came what to many Americans seemed unconscionable. In the waning hours of the morning of November 11, Pershing failed to halt a series of costly and essentially meaningless attacks against German positions, attacks that continued until the last minutes of the war.[61] Men died or received serious wounds for pieces of real estate that in a couple of hours, or even minutes, would be had without a shot being fired. The insanity of these pointless attacks mystified the German troops. The war was over for God's sake! After the war, the army high command generally covered up the story. It only surfaced because of a letter that Captain Livermore, an officer with the African-American 92nd Division, sent to Representative Alvan T. Fuller of Massachusetts, describing an attack by the 92nd in the last hours of the war.[62] Representative Fuller made it his mission to get the A.E.F. attacks on the morning of November 11, 1918, included in the agenda of the upcoming congressional hearings on the war.[63] Because of the agenda item, the committee compiled statistics on just how extensive the November 11 attacks had been. Thirteen American divisions had companies that fought that morning: there were 306 killed in action, 2,700 wounded severely in action and 177 gassed severely.[64] The 89th and 90th divisions took Stenay that morning. The town, which had been the Crown Prince's headquarters during the battle of Verdun in 1916 and long since abandoned as German headquarters, was without military significance.[65] The 26th Division attacked a well defended part of the old Verdun battlefield east of the Meuse River, and the 92nd contested an obscure woodland northeast of Pont-à-Mousson.[66] All these attacks and others on November 11 were essentially pointless; they should have been called off on November 10.

Much has been written about the last day of the war, but perhaps a doughboy from the state of Mississippi said it best.[67]

> And there with the Germans only three hundred yards away, with the four American boys killed on the road the day before lying as they were slain, with the battalion by peaceful campfires for the first time in weeks, I lay and thought of all that had passed and was present and might come in the future.
> And with the sodden earth beneath me and sodden clouds above me, with skies weeping as it were over the useless slaughter, I slept by the blazing bonfire and dreamed of the Long, Long Trail that wound westward and ever westward and finally ended at the best of all places HOME!

15

Armistice, Peace, War

> The Argonne has not been cleaned up yet and is full of things that will be of greatest interest to tourists. Deep trenches and thick wire entanglements are everywhere — I don't doubt that searchers can find skeletons without much trouble, if they want to. — "Outlook for Touring in Europe next Autumn," *The New York Times*, May 18, 1919

Immediately following the Armistice, the battlefields became places to visit even before they had been totally cleared of their dead. Travel agencies, sensing the macabre attraction of the Western Front, promoted tours to the districts where the fighting had been the fiercest, with the tour tailored to fit the nationality of the visitors whether they were German, French, British, or American. The more independent travelers motored from Paris by automobile to reach places of interest.

> Tourists must bear in mind that prices in Europe are very high. Much of the traveling must be done in automobile, the charge for which is somewhat more than $1 per mile. Gasoline, when I was in Europe, cost $5 per gallon. Food prices are up everywhere. In Paris a good dinner, not including wine, comes to about $15 per person.[1]

The Michelin Tire Company especially catered to such adventurous and well-heeled visitors; Michelin embarked upon a campaign to facilitate and encourage battlefield tourism by publishing detailed guides and maps. Not to appear as profiting from the war's aftermath, Michelin donated profits from the guides to an association that encouraged French families to have more babies, *Alliance Nationale pour l'Accroissment de la Population Francaise*.[2] Many French believed that the single long-term cause of the war had been the higher birthrate of the Germans.[3]

André Michelin began planning the guides in 1916, two years before the war's end, when its outcome was uncertain.[4] He believed that battlefields in France would be of keen interest to the post-war tourist. Michelin hoped the guides would bring visitors and cash to the war-devastated areas and perhaps sell some tires to motorists who dared the battlefield roads. *Michelin Illustrated Guides to the Battlefields (1914–1918)*, which covered the entire Western Front, grew into a collection of twenty-nine books aimed at the battlefield tourist. There were even German translations. For the American market, there was *The Americans in the Great War* series in three volumes, two of which covered the American campaigns in Lorraine.[5] The guidebooks were available from the company's factory in Milltown, New Jersey.

For the less adventurous, there was the organized tour for only $1,375, advertised as "A Pilgrimage of Homage." The pilgrim sailed from New York, spent thirty-three days visiting battlefields, taking photographs, and collecting souvenirs (German helmets were very popular as were artistically etched brass artillery shell cartridge cases).

> Europe and the Battlefields
> Spring 1920
> We are deeply impressed with the conviction that the great need of both France and America is that every American who can possibly visit France during the Spring and early Summer of 1920 — before the aspect of the ruined regions is changed by nature and reconstruction — should do so — the need of France being material, the need of America spiritual.
> Incidentally you will find the hundreds of ruined cities and towns and the vast spaces of the devastated regions profoundly impressive as is nothing else in the world, while some of the ruins are sublimely beautiful.
> It is an undeniable fact that after-the-war-traveling in Europe is quite a different thing from before-the-war travel.
> Raymond Whitcomb Tours

Of course, prowling around the battlefields did have some associated risks; the tourist had to be careful what he or she picked up or kicked.

> Southwest of Verdun the surface soil is loaded with "duds," both Allied and Boche, so thickly that plowing is not only dangerous but suicidal. Each "dud" is a shell that for some reason has failed to explode upon impact. It may be perfectly harmless — or it may just be waiting for that touch of a plowshare in order to complete its mission of destruction.[6]

However, there was more in the ground than "duds." Millions of dead were interred one way or another in the torn-up earth of the Western Front. Some were buried in shallow war-time graves by comrades, others in forgotten mass graves, still others buried by shell fire in collapsed trenches or filled-in craters, others blown to bits and scattered as so much human mulch. The following statistics illustrate the scale of what was, and still may be, under the ground of the Western Front: the British Empire had 1,000,000 dead, the remains of 500,000 were never found, or if found, not identified; the French had 1,700,000 war dead, with presumably a similar proportion of "never found."[7] In the years following the war, the search for the dead resulted in hundreds of thousands of exhumations. Officials identified the remains when possible and reburied them in military cemeteries. The British, French and Germans established military cemeteries usually near where their men perished; these cemeteries, large and small, delineate the Western Front from the North Sea to Switzerland.

America established eight World War One military cemeteries overseas: one in England, one in Belgium and six in France. War dead could be either shipped to America for reburial if the family wished, at the government's expense, or reburied in a military cemetery in Europe. In Lorraine two cemeteries were established, one in the St. Mihiel Salient and the other in the Meuse-Argonne battlefield.[8] The St. Mihiel American Cemetery grew to contain 4,153 graves, each marked with a marble headstone, either Latin Crosses or Stars of David. The 117 Unknowns have the epitaph:

> Here Rests in Honored Glory an
> American Soldier Known Only to God

Listed in the cemetery chapel are the names of 284 soldiers whose remains were either not identified or not found. Thus the remains of possibly as many as 167 American soldiers are still lost somewhere on the St. Mihiel battlefield, (284 – 117 = 167). The Meuse-Argonne American Cemetery contains 14,246 graves of which 486 are Unknowns and the cemetery chapel records the names of 954 Missing, thus the remains of 468 American soldiers may be still somewhere in the Meuse-Argonne battlefield. Unusually the Meuse-Argonne Cemetery includes graves of a few civilian volunteers: ambulance drivers, Red Cross nurses and a member of the Lafayette Escadrille, Victor Chapman.

> And hear your step and fly to your call —
> Every one of you won the war.
> But you, you Dead, most of all![9]

While the gruesome task of dealing with American dead was going on, American volunteers arrived to help the living. Vassar College of Poughkeepsie, New York, sent the Vassar Relief Unit to Verdun; twenty women[10] arrived in the shell-wrecked city in March 1919. Vassar's instruction detailing the unit's mission in France was concise, consisting of only two short sentences: "Use your own judgment. We are behind all you do."[11]

The unit focused on the needs of the refugees returning to the city, nearly all of whom were women and children. They organized a school and library, including classes for young mothers, and established a *Cantine Populaire* near the Verdun train station to help people returning to the city and as a social retreat for those already there. The canteen opened daily from nine in the morning until eight at night and was quite crowded when the trains arrived.

> A large bowl of chocolate can be bought for three cents, café noir is also three with a cent added for milk, sandwiches of corned beef, ham or jam are six cents and a cake of chocolate is sixteen.[12]

Probably the most important and remembered Vassar enterprise was the *Goutte de Lait*.[13] The unit purchased a small truck, collected milk from local farms, pasteurized and bottled it, and then distributed the milk free of charge to local children. The French government so appreciated the Vassar milk distribution program for children it donated a special war trophy to the Vassar campus — a forty-ton war camouflaged French tank! Admittedly, a strange gift, but impossible to refuse. The tank remained on the campus for two decades before the rusty hulk was taken to a scrap yard.

Not far from Verdun, in the St. Mihiel Salient, a Vassar alumna took on the rebuilding of an entire village.[14] Miss Belle Skinner, the daughter of a wealthy mill owner from Holyoke, Massachusetts, had made a European tour before the war. While motoring through France, she happened to visit the village of Hattonchâtel. The village crowns a hill, overlooking a broad flat plain (the Woëvre), a picturesque site with a view that is said to have reminded her of the Connecticut River valley near Holyoke, Massachusetts. Miss Skinner never forgot the place even though war came.

> Hattonchâtel on the Côtes-de-Meuse, in all its quaint beauty, has been unknown to tourists. Before the war the only way of visiting the village was on foot.[15]

During the war, Germans occupied Hattonchâtel and, because of the fine view it afforded of French lines, used the village for artillery spotting. Consequently, after four years of heavy bombardment by the French, Hattonchâtel was mostly in ruins. Supposedly, Miss Skinner was in France during the war[16] and seeing the ruins through field glasses from the French lines, she vowed to rebuild Hattonchâtel at her own expense when the French finally drove the Germans out.[17] Remarkably, the Yankee Division,[18] a division made up of National Guard companies from the six New England states, including a National Guard company from Miss Skinner's hometown of Holyoke, liberated Hattonchâtel.

Miss Skinner oversaw the reconstruction of Hattonchâtel's town hall, library, school and bishop's palace as well as the installation of a modern water system. When questioned by a reporter[19] about how she carried out her project, Miss Skinner declared,

It wasn't as hard as it sounds to spend that million. Rebuilding the town didn't seem the least bit more difficult than putting additions on my house in Holyoke. I do not think it any more unusual for a woman to have a head for business than for a man. I simply opened my headquarters in Paris and then waited for bids of the French contractors. There were plenty of them.

Miss Skinner intended to live in the bishop's palace, a château that had once belonged to Bishop Hatton of Verdun, from whom the village took its name. The building suffered severe damage during the war, but Miss Skinner funded its reconstruction. She died in 1929, before restoration was completed. A plaque in French and English on the nearby town hall tells of the villagers' deep regard for its American patron.

> To the Lamented
> Miss Belle Skinner
> Their Sweet Godmother
> Their Munificent Benefactress
> The Inhabitants of Hattonchâtel
> Vow Unending Gratitude

In the 1920s, monuments sprouted like mushrooms on the Western Front. All the belligerents, excepting of course Germany, were busy planning and erecting edifices to honor their dead and show case their war efforts in a heroic light. History was being written, and sometimes rewritten, in marble and bronze.

Congress created the American Battle Monuments Commission in 1923. The seven-member commission elected General Pershing as its chair. Thus, the commander of the A.E.F. became the guiding hand in determining how to memorialize American participation in the Great War in Europe. The commission decided the largest and therefore most significant monuments should be erected in the Aisne-Marne, the St. Mihiel Salient and the Meuse-Argonne "to help preserve the glorious record of America's achievement in the World War."[20] The main site selection criterion for each was that it be "of such prominence that the monument will be visible across the country."[21] From the monument, visitors should have a commanding view of where the fighting took place. Consequently, the three major American monuments were built upon hilltops. The most prominent American architects of the time were assigned to develop several designs for each monument, final selections being made by the commission, i.e., General Pershing. The overall design theme for the monuments was Greco-Roman with an overlay of Art-Deco, the Classical Style of the nineteen twenties. Pershing felt strongly the size of a given monument should reflect the importance of the American contribution: the Aisne-Marne being lowest on the scale and, of course, the Meuse-Argonne being highest. There should be a hierarchy of imposing monuments.

The Aisne-Marne Monument, constructed on a hilltop, Hill 204, overlooks the city of Château-Thierry at what had been the apex of the Marne Salient in the spring of 1918. The site easily fit the American Battle Monuments Commission criteria: it was a dominant landmark with a panoramic view of the Marne battlefield. Approaching the monument from the Château-Thierry side, the structure, except for the addition of the large Art-Deco eagle,[22] is reminiscent of the Lincoln Memorial in Washington, D.C.[23]

The Butte de Montsec, the most prominent hill in the St. Mihiel Salient, was selected for the St. Mihiel monument. During the war, Montsec developed as the main German artillery observation post in the salient; because of its fortifications, it was an ersatz German Gibraltar. After the Armistice Montsec became a tourist attraction. One tourist penetrated the Gibraltar and left a description. On December 12, 1918, Katharine Morse, a YMCA volunteer, traveled across the salient on a "speeder," a small gasoline-engine powered car made for narrow-gauge German military railroad lines. One of the stops she made was at Montsec.

> At the foot of Mont Sec we stopped. There in the woods were the remains of a German camp; it had been a jolly little place fixed up like a beer garden underneath the trees, with fancy "rustic" work and chairs and tables. We left the speeder there, and tramping across the fields, climbed Mont Sec. Near the top we found the entrances to the dugouts. The hill was tunneled through from side to side, all the corridors and rooms walled, roofed and floored with the heaviest oak lumber. Everywhere through the passage-ways ran a perfect network of electric wires. Long stairs led to the different levels. No furnishings were left except the bunks and some rough tables. We ate our luncheon ... in what had evidently been the officers' quarters; the room was nicely finished with cement, there was a fancy moulded pattern in bas relief over the doorway, a pipe-hole showed where a stove had been. After lunch we inspected the concrete machine-gun pill-boxes which dotted the hill top.[24]

The pill-boxes were flattened and the dugout entrances filled-in to make a space on the summit for the American monument. The resulting monument is a circular Doric colonnade that crowns the summit of Montsec. Although described as an oversized Temple of Vesta,[25] most Americans approaching the monument think of the Jefferson Memorial in Washington, D.C. The setting is so dramatic that the St. Mihiel Monument is very probably the most beautiful commemorative monument on the Western Front. Montsec is also the only American monument damaged during the Second World War. On September 2, 1944, American artillery shelled the monument while attempting to drive out a German machine gun nest. The damage was considerable. Restoration was completed in 1948.

A robust shell-proof pillbox constructed from the ruins of the Montfaucon village church; it is said that Crown Prince Wilhelm observed the attacks on Mort Homme and Côte 304 during the battle of Verdun from this pillbox. The French government decided that the village ruins should be preserved as *un vestige de la guerre* and thus prevented Pershing from clearing the site for his victory column (© Collection Mémorial deVerdun).

The most imposing monument was to be the one commemorating the Meuse-Argonne campaign. The site selected was the Butte de Montfaucon; a hill heavily fortified by the Germans and captured by American forces in the early days of the battle. A monument on the highest point, Montfaucon, would dominate the battlefield and be visible for a long distance across country. Unfortunately, the top of Montfaucon was unavailable! There had been a village atop the hill, and the French government declared that village ruins were to be preserved as *un vestige de la guerre*. The ruins included a small observation tower supposedly used by the Crown Prince during the battle of Verdun. No amount of pressure by the American Battle Monuments Commission could change French minds.[26] However, a nearby lower hill was available so that was where they built the monument. However, since the site was less imposing, the monument would have to be more so.

Pershing and the commission studied various designs proposed by the architect before deciding that a victory column was the most appropriate. A tall column would be more visible given the available site. Pershing had considerable angst about how to make the Montsec monument less imposing and Montfaucon more; consequently, the Montsec monument shrank and the

The American monument at Montfaucon commemorating the victory in the Meuse-Argonne was dedicated in 1937, barely two years before the start of World War II (© Collection Mémorial deVerdun).

Montfaucon column grew.[27] Eventually a 175-foot Doric column surmounted by a statue of liberty was erected, following the assumption that bigger is better. In late summer and fall of 1937, two years before the start of the Second World War, the American monuments at Montfaucon, St. Mihiel and Château-Thierry were dedicated with great ceremony.[28]

The American Battle Monuments Commission also had charge of the designs for the military cemeteries. Each cemetery had a nonsectarian chapel, restrained in size so as not to distract the visitor from the sea of white marble gravestones. The war dead should be the focus, not the chapel. Pershing closely supervised all aspects of cemetery design and ornamentation, including restraining the architects. To beautify the cemeteries, he employed the best American sculptors; probably the most notable was Paul Manship, the sculptor who later (1933–34) created the much-photographed statue of Prometheus for Rockefeller Center in New York City. Pershing visited the Manship studio in Paris in the mid twenties, probably 1925, to view an urn Manship was making for the St. Mihiel American Cemetery near Thiaucourt. In the studio was another war sculpture, a life-size figure of a young American officer. Inquiring about the statue, Pershing learned a mother commissioned it in memory of her son who was killed in France during the war. She had purchased a plot of land in the village where her son had died and gotten permission from the village council to erect the statue. Pershing informed Manship that the American Battle Monuments Commission absolutely banned private monuments to war dead. The monuments were to commemorate the United States and the A.E.F. rather than the fallen.[29] A tense impasse ensued until Pershing learned that the mother was Mrs. Harriet Beale, daughter of the Republican senator from Maine. Permission was given to erect the statue, but not in the village. The statue, known as the Soldiers Monument, stands in the St. Mihiel American Cemetery.[30] Evidently, private war monuments were more likely to be permitted if they somehow benefited the place where they were erected. Consequently, many French villages gained fountains, watering troughs for livestock and wash houses for laundry, all adorned with American commemorative plaques.

Americans also contributed funds to build French war monuments. A banker from Buffalo probably financed one of the strangest. While touring the Verdun battlefield in 1919, George F. Rand heard a macabre story. A filled-in trench had been found marked by a row of French rifles with their bayonets attached; dirt covered the rifles so only the bayonets protruded from the ground. According to the tale, on June 11, 1916, soldiers had propped their rifles against the parapet in preparation to attack with hand grenades; shellfire collapsed the trench, burying the men alive, leaving the bayonets to mark

The Tranchée des Baïonettes (trench of bayonets) monument at Verdun is the strangest and very probably least attractive war monument on the Western Front. The columned arcade with its massive concrete roof protects a line of rusty French bayonets protruding from the ground. The American banker George F. Rand funded its construction after seeing the trench in 1919 ((c) Collection Mémorial deVerdun).

their mass grave.[31] So moved by the row of sharp spike-like bayonets, Rand pledged 500,000 francs for a monument to commemorate and protect what became known as the Tranchée des Baïonettes. Soon after visiting Verdun, Rand was the sole passenger on a flight from Paris to London when the plane crashed while attempting to land. He became the first fatality of the newly inaugurated London-Paris Air Service.[32] Rand's estate honored his pledge and construction of the monument proceeded. The best that one can say of the somber cement structure is that it is long and massive and does protect the trench.[33]

In 1920, another story surfaced about the bayonet trench's origin, this version from a priest who had been the lieutenant commanding the French soldiers in the trench. After 48 hours of continuous fighting and suffering 57 dead the trench was taken and the lieutenant captured. The Germans filled in the trench, leaving the dead in place with their rifles upright so that the bayonets marked the grave.[34] If the priest's story is true, then Rand's monument is a tribute to this act of remembrance more than anything else.

The Verdun battlefield, especially the area near Fort Douaumont, was

A battlefield at the war's end; in many places the Western Front resembled an open-air charnel house. Rats, some the size of cats, had reduced the dead to a deposit of fleshless bones (Sue Alward, Captain Arthur R. Phillips personal collection).

literally awash with human skeletal remains after the war. On a high ridge near Fort Douaumont, the French constructed a large ossuary in which to inter these remains. In the nineteen twenties, students, often led by priests, combed the woods and fields searching for human bones to deposit in the ossuary. These pilgrimages were not without danger, and in one instance led to the death of the searchers. A priest and his students had made a bone collection, but before taking it to the ossuary, they honored the dead by singing hymns around a fire they had made in an old shell hole. The heat penetrated the steel casing of a buried artillery shell, a dud, which then exploded, killing the priest and a student and badly injuring eight others.[35]

The ossuary grew to contain the bones of 130,000 unidentified French and German soldiers. Funds from American sources financed the building of the central tower of the Douaumont Memorial Monument and Ossuary. Another American, Miss Thorburn Van Buren, gave the twenty-five ton bell for the tower.[36] The ossuary became the focal point for numerous events honoring the dead and promoting an end to war, the bell tolling as part of the ceremonies.

On July 12, 1936, German, French, American, British and Italian war veterans held a peace rally on the Verdun battlefield, standing in vigil at the ossuary from 9:00 P.M. to midnight.[37]

Douaumont Memorial Monument and Ossuary contains the bones of 130,000 unidentified French and German dead collected from Verdun battlefields. The bones are in crypts beneath the structure. Begun in 1920, the monument honors the dead whose bones literally carpeted the nearby landscape — the monument is sited where the worst of the right bank fighting took place. American donations built the 150 foot high bell tower; the 25 ton bell, a gift of Miss Thorburn Van Buren, an American, memorialized the French and American soldiers who perished in the war (© Collection Mémorial deVerdun).

However, peace was not to be; the Armistice had been just a pause to rearm and reorganize. In 1939, when Germany attacked Poland, the fighting in Europe started again. The German Army took Verdun and its surrounding forts on June 17, 1940; the second battle of Verdun took less than twenty-four hours with practically no French resistance. The German Army celebrated its easy victory with a military parade through the city.[38] Germans occupied Verdun for four years and during that time generally respected monuments and cemeteries from the previous war. Many German senior officers had begun their careers in The Great War of 1914–1918, and they did not dishonor their old enemies.

On September 1, 1944, American tanks roared into Verdun to the cheers of thousands who lined the streets. General George S. Patton's Third American Army had already taken the old Meuse-Argonne battlefield and was on its way to the former St. Mihiel Salient.[39] The Yanks were "over there." Again!

Chapter Notes

Introduction

1. The war lasted nearly 52 months, America only got into the fighting for the final 10; the Yanks were hardly "over there" before they were back "over here." A couple of decades later when the Second World War erupted and American soldiers were back fighting nearly the same enemies, in many of the same places, memories of events and battles morphed into one *Weltkrieg*—the Americans seemed to be always fighting the Germans. Sometimes the Japanese and Italians were on the U.S. side, and sometimes not.

2. Brand Whitlock, Belgium, *A Personal Narrative* Volume 1 (New York: D. Appleton, 1919), 28.

3. The emperor's son, Crown Prince Rudolf, committed suicide at Mayerling. The emperor's brother, Maximilian, was shot by Mexican revolutionaries. Archduke Franz Ferdinand was Maximilian's son.

4. James W. Gerard, *My Four Years in Germany* (New York: Grosset and Dunlap, 1917), 78.

Chapter 1

1. Florence Finch Kelley, "Eye Witness of the War," *Bookman*, December 1915, 462, review of Edith Wharton, *Fighting France: From Dunkerque to Belfort* (New York: Charles Scribner's Sons, 1915), price $1 in 1915.

2. Also included in the party were Mildred Bliss and Victor Bérard according to Hermione Lee, *Edith Wharton* (New York: Alfred A. Knopf, 2007), 487.

3. Edith Wharton, *A Backward Glance* (New York: D. Appleton-Century, 1934), 353. A French translation of "The House of Mirth."

4. Anonymous, translated by J. Koettgen, *A German Deserter's War Experience* (New York: B. W. Huebsch, 1917), originally published as columns in the *New Yorker Volkszeitung*, a newspaper for German-speaking socialists in the United States. The author's identity was concealed for fear of reprisal against his relatives living in Germany. A die-hard socialist, he ended his essay, "But to-day I have recovered sufficiently to take up again in the ranks of the American Socialists the fight against capitalism the extirpation of which must be the aim of every class-conscious worker." One cannot but wonder how he fared in his adopted country.

5. Anonymous, 170.

6. Anonymous, 173.

7. Jean Des Vignes Rouges, *Bourru, Soldier of France* (New York: E.P. Dutton, 1929), 245.

8. Rouges, 361.

9. Rouges, 234–235.

10. Rouges, 380.

11. Original letter in Bienecke Rare Book and Manuscript Library, Yale University. Reprinted by permission of the estate of Edith Wharton and the Watkins/Loomis Agency. For the entire letter, see *Henry James and Edith Wharton, Letters: 1900–1915*, edited by Lyall H. Powers (New York: Charles Scribner's Sons, 1990).

12. Percy Lubbock, *The Letters of Henry James* (New York: Charles Scribner's Sons, 1920), 452.

13. Original letter in Bienecke Rare Book and Manuscript Library, Yale University. Reprinted by permission of the estate of Edith Wharton and the Watkins/Loomis Agency. For the entire letter see *Henry James and Edith Wharton, Letters: 1900–1915*, edited by Lyall H. Powers (New York: Charles Scribner's Sons, 1990).

14. In 1984, he joined German Chancellor Kohl and President François Mitterrand at the Franco-German reconciliation ceremony at Verdun. David Binder, "Ernst Jünger, Contradictory German Author Who Wrote About War, is Dead at 102," *New York Times*, February 18, 1998.

15. The Kingdom of Hanover was annexed by Prussia in 1866 after Hanover had chosen the wrong side in the Austro-Prussian War of that year.

16. Ernst Jünger, *Storm of Steel*, Michael

Hofmann translation (New York and London: Penguin, 2003), 25.

17. *Letters from André Chéronnet-Champollion, 1914–1915* (New York: privately printed, 1915), 117.

18. Mrs. Wharton's war-time contributions were not limited to junkets along the Western Front. In Paris she established orphanages for Belgian and French children displaced by the war. She also organized workshops where refugee women could earn money to support their families. Mrs. Wharton used her connections with wealthy Americans to raise money for her charities. For her war work she was made a Chevalier of the French Legion of Honor, France's highest civilian award. Allan Price, *The End of the Age of Innocence: Edith Wharton and the First World War* (New York: St. Martin's, 1996).

19. Edith Wharton, *Fighting France: From Dunkerque to Belfort* (New York: Charles Scribner's Sons, 1917), 108–109.

20. Wharton, *Fighting France: From Dunkerque to Belfort*, 112–113.

21. "Rupprecht Dies; Bavarian Prince," *New York Times*, August 3, 1955.

22. *Letters from André Chéronnet-Champollion, 1914–1915*.

23. *Letters from André Chéronnet-Champollion, 1914–1915*.

24. A *Chicago Tribune* reporter with the German army observed firsthand the consequences of the new trench war. "None of these men are ever wounded. Most of those who are struck by bullets are struck in the head and death is instantaneous." Edwin F. Weigle, *On Four Battle Fronts with the German Army* (Chicago, IL: Chicago Tribune, 1915), 20.

25. Mrs. W. K. Vanderbilt, "My Trip to the Front," *Harper's Monthly Magazine*, January, 1917, 134:177.

Chapter 2

1. James R. McConnell, "With the American Ambulance in France," *The Outlook*, 1915, 111:125–132.

2. "Attacks his Chief, Asst Sec Andrew Resigns from The Treasury Dept, Declares MacVeagh by Temperament Unfit for his Position," *Boston Daily Globe*, July 4, 1912; "Andrew Inefficient, Retorts MacVeagh," *New York Times*, July 5, 1912; "Andrew Efficient, In Lodge's Opinion," *New York Times*, July 6, 1912.

3. Andrew Gray, "The American Field Service," *American Heritage*, 1974, 26:58–63.

4. A. Piatt Andrew, *Letters Written Home from France in the First Half of 1915* (Cambridge, MA: Riverside, 1916), 18–19.

5. A. Piatt Andrew, "For Love of France," *The Outlook*, 1916, 114: 923–931.

6. A section usually consisted of 20 to 22 Model T ambulances, a staff car and 24 men.

7. Andrew, *Letters Written Home from France in the First Half of 1915*, 97–98.

8. Leslie Buswell, *With the American Ambulance Field Service in France* (New York: Houghton Mifflin, 1915). 9.

9. Leslie Buswell, *Ambulance No. 10, Personal Letters from the Front* (New York: A. L. Burt, 1916), 57.

10. Henry Sheahan, *A Volunteer Poilu* (New York: Houghton Mifflin, 1916), 105.

11. Philip Van Doren Stern, *Tin Lizzie* (New York: Simon and Schuster, 1955), 78.

12. A. Piatt Andrew, "Some of the Early Problems," in *History of the American Field Service in France: "Friends of France" 1914–1917, Told by its Members* (Boston, MA: Houghton Mifflin, 1920), 1:32.

13. The American Ambulance Field Service went by a variety of names in American newspapers. They seldom got it right.

14. "Won Cross for Bravery," *New York Times*, February 18, 1916.

15. Trench mortar.

16. James R. McConnell, "With the American Ambulance in France," *The Outlook* (1915), 111:125–132.

17. Perhaps this is the origin of the name for the surrounding forest, Bois-le-Prêtre, Priest Wood.

18. Buswell, *With the American Ambulance Field Service in France*, 22–30.

19. Emory Pottle, "Christmas at Pont-à-Mousson," *The Century Magazine* 95 (1917): 181–191.

20. Pottle, 181–191.

21. It is interesting to contrast the visits of Mrs. Wharton and Mrs. Vanderbilt to Pont-à-Mousson. Although Wharton came in 1915 and Vanderbilt in 1916, in both instances heavy fighting was going on in the Bois-le-Prêtre. Mrs. Wharton, because she was only on the east side of the Moselle, witnessed the fighting from a distance, whereas Mrs. Vanderbilt was much closer to the action. After Pont-à-Mousson she visited Verdun, where she actually came under fire. "Mrs. W. K. Vanderbilt Under Fire at the Front," *New York Times*, August 25, 1916.

22. Mrs. W. K Vanderbilt, "My Trip to the Front," *Harper's Monthly Magazine*, 134 (1917): 175–186.

23. Buswell, *Ambulance No. 10, Personal Letters from the Front*, 15.

24. Vanderbilt, "My Trip to the Front," 175–186.

25. Pottle, 181–191.

26. Robert Matter, a driver in the Section.

27. Waldo Pierce, "Christmas Eve, 1915," In *Friends of France: Field Service of the American Ambulance Described by its Members* (Boston,

MA, and New York: Houghton Mifflin, 1916), 143.
28. "Attractions at the Theaters," *Boston Globe*, November 8, 1914.
29. Buswell, *With the American Ambulance Field Service in France*.
30. Buswell, *Ambulance No. 10, Personal Letters from the Front*.
31. *Friends of France: The Field Service of the American Ambulance Described by its Members*.
32. "Ambulance Corps in France Filmed," *New York Times*, July 6, 1916.
33. "Newport Men in Film," *New York Times*, Aug. 7, 1916.
34. Gray, 58–63.
35. Henry D. Sleeper, "The Effort in America," in *History of the American Field Service in France: "Friends of France" 1914–1917, Told by its Members* (Boston, MA: Houghton Mifflin, 1920), Volume 1, 45–46.
36. Presumably registration for the draft.
37. L. D. Geller, "Friends of France: The American Field Service with the French Armies 1914–1917, 1939–1945," Exhibit Catalogue A.F.S.—Blerancourt Exhibition, 1989.
38. William Martin, *Verdun 1916* (Oxford, UK: Osprey, 2001); Malcolm Brown, *Verdun 1916* (Stroud, Gloucestershire, UK; Charleston, SC: Tempus, 2000); Alistair Horne, *The Price of Glory, Verdun, 1916* (New York: St. Martin's, 1963).

Chapter 3

1. Clara E. Laughlin, *The Martyred Towns of France* (New York: G. P. Putnam's Sons, 1919), 106.
2. Winston Spenser Churchill, "The Meaning of Verdun," *Collier's*, November 18, 1916, 5–7.
3. Erich von Falkenhayn, *The German General Staff and its Decisions, 1914–1916* (New York: Dodd, Mead, 1920), 249.
4. William Martin, *Verdun 1916* (Oxford, UK: Osprey, 2001), 84.
5. Asa Don Dickinson, *The Kaiser* (Garden City, NY: Doubleday, Page, 1914), 172.
6. "Prince Wilhelm, 69, is Dead in Germany," *New York Times*, July 21, 1951.
7. T. W. H. Crosland, *The Soul of a Crown Prince* (London: Wyman and Sons, 1916), 59.
8. *The Kaiser's Heir: A Pen-Portrait* (London: Mills and Bonn, 1914), 246.
9. "A Crown Prince Being Trained for an Empire," *New York Times*, January 27, 1904.
10. "Did Not Refer to Miss Farrar—Berlin Publisher Agrees to Say So in Tomorrow's Welt am Montag," *Boston Globe*, January 10, 1904.
11. "Geraldine Farrar's Own Story," *Boston Globe*, March 26, 1916; "Geraldine Farrar, Met Soprano, Dies," *New York Times*, March 12, 1967.
12. *The Kaiser's Heir: A Pen-Portrait*, 86
13. "Kaiser at Odds with Sons?" *New York Times*, January 26, 1915.
14. Winston S. Churchill, *The Great War* (London: George Newnes, 1933), 13: 816.
15. William, Crown Prince of Germany, *My War Experiences* (New York: Robert M. McBride, 1923), 68.
16. Philippe Voluer, *La Guerre De 14 Au Pays De Stenay* (Beaufort-En-Argonne: Les Amis de Montserrat, 2006), 9–60. Translation by Ulrich von Koppenfels.
17. Voluer, 63–64.
18. Sven Hedin, *With the German Armies in the West* (London and New York: John Lane, 1915), 64.
19. *Memoirs of the Crown Prince of Germany* (New York: Charles Scribner's Sons, 1922), 63.
20. Churchill, *The Great War*, 816.
21. *Memoirs of the Crown Prince of Germany*, 212.
22. Anonymous, *The Diary of a German Soldier* (New York: Alfred A Knopf, 1919), 243–244. The author deserted to Denmark before the end of the war.
23. William, Crown Prince of Germany, 182.
24. Jacques-Henri Lefebvre, *Verdun* (Paris: G. Durassié, 1966), 120. "The stupid abandonment of Douaumont, terrible in its consequences, remains the colossal error of the military history of the war of 1914–1918." The French certainly do not mince words.
25. Christina Holstein, *Verdun—Fort Douaumont* (South Yorkshire, UK: Pen and Sword, 2002), 45–56; Malcolm Brown, *Verdun 1916* (Stroud, Gloucestershire, UK, Charleston, SC: Tempus, 2000), 53–57.
26. Alistair Horne, *The Price of Glory, Verdun, 1916* (New York: St. Martin's, 1963), 105–124
27. Richard Griffiths, *Marshal Pétain* (London: Constable, 1970), 22.
28. *Memoirs of the Crown Prince of Germany*, 213–214.
29. Charles F. Horne, *Source Records of the Great War* (New York: National Alumni, 1923), 5: 232.

Chapter 4

1. Kathleen Burke, *The White Road to Verdun* (New York: George H. Doran, 1916), 95.
2. Frank Hoyt Gailor, "An American Ambulance in the Verdun Attack," *Living Age*, 1916, Volume 3, 413–420.
3. General Pétain's headquarters in Souilly, left unchanged and unguarded for ninety years, was one of the sacred places of the French war

effort at Verdun, respected as a special place even during the German occupation of Souilly during the Second World War. Then it was violated. The German newspaper *Die Zeit* reported on the sacrilege: "Telefon — Frevel" (Telephone Sacrilege), *Die Zeit*, 2006, 36 (translated by Ulrich von Koppenfels). "Almost ninety years after the end of World War I, Philippe Pétain, the hero of Verdun and later Hitler's marionette despot, had his field telephone stolen. In 1916 the set was installed in the first floor of the town hall of Souilly in Lorraine, which served as headquarters of the French forces…. The telephone had been sitting there ever since, but last week it disappeared during an ordinary flea market in the town hall."

4. William Hermanns, *The Holocaust, From a Survivor of Verdun* (New York: Harper and Row, 1972), 129. Hermanns survived forty months captivity rebuilding La Route and the war devastated areas around Verdun. He immigrated to the United States where he taught at San José State College in California. In the spring of 1968, during the Vietnam War, a student delegation asked him to speak at an antiwar rally. He read to the young audience parts of his then-unpublished memoir describing his own experiences in a war fifty years earlier. The students were so moved that they encouraged him to publish the work. He dedicated the book to his sister, who sent food parcels to soldiers in the First World War and perished in a Nazi concentration camp in the Second.

5. William, Crown Prince of Germany, *My War Experience* (New York: Robert M. McBride, 1923), p. 223.

6. William Yorke Stevenson, *At the Front in a Flivver* (Boston, MA: Houghton Mifflin, 1917), 174–175 abbreviated.

7. Philip Dana Orcutt, *The White Road of Mystery: The Note-Book of an American Ambulancier* (New York: John Lane, 1918), 61–62.

8. Anonymous, *Diary of Section VIII: American Ambulance Field Service* (privately printed, 1917), 40–41 abbreviated.

9. Anonymous, *Diary of Section VIII: American Ambulance Field Service*, 45.

10. Anonymous, *Diary of Section VIII: American Ambulance Field Service*, 45–46.

11. William Yorke Stevenson, 114–115.

12. Jack Edward McCallum, "Les Sections Sanitaires: American Volunteers in the Great War," Ph.D. dissertation (Fort Worth: Texas Christian University, 2001), 218.

13. "Split in American Ambulance Corps," *Boston Daily Globe*, July 17, 1916, 8. This was not the first controversy at the American Hospital; see Ellen N. La Motte, "An American Nurse in Paris," *The Survey*, July 10, 1915, 333–336 and rebuttals, 563.

14. After World War I, the American Field Service funded scholarships for Americans to study in French universities. During World War II, it served again as an ambulance corps at the front. In the post-war years, it became an international exchange program for students and teachers and is still very active.

15. Edith Wharton, *Fighting France, From Dunkerque to Belfort* (New York: Charles Scribner's Sons, 1917), 73.

16. *History of the American Field Service in France: "Friends of France" 1914–1917, Told by its Members* (Boston, MA: Houghton Mifflin, 1920), 1:327

17. Letter published in its entirety in Anonymous, "Ten Days at Verdun The Story of an American Ambulance Driver," *The American Red Cross Magazine*, October 1916, 335–338.

18. Edwin W. Morse, *The Vanguard of American Volunteers* (New York: Charles Scribner's Sons, 1919), 152–156.

19. W. Kerr Rainsford, "An American Ambulancier at Verdun," *World's Work*, December 1916, 33: 83–194, quotation on 185–186.

20. Pejorative name for Germans used during World War I.

21. Edward R. Coyle, *Ambulancing at the French Front* (New York: Britton, 1918), 92–93.

22. E. Alexander Powell, *Vive La France!* (New York: Charles Scribner's Sons, 1915), 41.

23. Robert Whitney Imbrie, *Behind the Wheel of a War Ambulance* (New York: Robert M. McBride, 1918), 101.

24. Rainsford, 185.

Chapter 5

1. William, Crown Prince of Germany, *My War Experiences* (New York: Robert M. McBride, 1923), 185–186.

2. D. Thomas Curtin, *The Land of Deepening Shadow: Germany-at-War* (New York: George H. Doran, 1917), 269.

3. Curtin, 267.

4. Curtin, 271.

5. *History of the American Field Service in France: "Friends of France" 1914–1917, Told by its Members* (Boston, MA: Houghton Mifflin, 1920), 1:424.

6. *History of the American Field Service in France*, 3:158–159.

7. *History of the American Field Service in France*, 1:422.

8. Edith Wharton, *Fighting France, from Belfort to Dunkerque* (New York: Charles Scribner's Sons, 1917), 66–67.

9. Wharton, 69.

10. Wharton, 70.

11. William Yorke Stevenson, *At the Front in a Flivver* (Boston, MA, Houghton Mifflin, 1917), 233–234 abbreviated. Very probably the distant battle Stevenson saw was the continuing battle

for the Butte de Vauquois, the same battle Mrs. Wharton saw in 1915.

12. Fifteen years later, in 1931, the German director Paul Heinze made a film about the German capture and loss of the fort, *Douaumont—Die Holle von Verdun*, with a cast that included surviving soldiers. Heinze edited in clips of 1916 French newsreel footage showing the firing of the 400 mm railway guns used to destroy Fort Douaumont that October. The one-ton projectiles from these monster weapons penetrated the roof of the fort, exploding inside, and were the principal cause of the German surrender.

13. Henry Bordeaux, *The Deliverance of the Captives: Douaumont-Vaux* (London: Thomas Nelson and Sons, 1919), 171, 175 abbreviated.

14. Bordeaux, 295 abbreviated.

15. Woodrow Wilson was first elected president of the United States in 1912 and narrowly reelected in 1916, running on the campaign slogan, "He kept us out of war." The slogan was correctly framed in the past tense. On April 2, 1917, Wilson asked Congress for a declaration of war against Imperial Germany. In his War Message to Congress, he stated the following goal: "The world must be made safe for democracy." What resulted was not as he intended. Allied arrogance, perhaps bolstered by a huge American Army in Europe, resulted in the draconian Versailles Treaty; a treaty that did not make the world safe for democracy but rather made Europe safe for fascism.

16. Philip Sidney Rice, *An American Crusader at Verdun* (published by the author at Princeton, 1918), 4.

17. They did not survive the war.

18. Rice, 6.

19. Information kindly supplied by Casey Babcock, special collections assistant, Seeley G. Mudd Manuscript Library, Princeton University.

20. Rice, 9.

21. Rice, 17.

22. Rice, 37.

23. Rice, 38.

24. William Yorke Stevenson, *From Poilu to Yank* (Boston, MA: Houghton Mifflin, 1918), 122.

25. Robert Whitney Imbrie, *Behind the Wheel of a War Ambulance* (New York: Robert M. McBride, 1918), 121.

26. Rice, 51.

27. Rice, 36.

28. Stevenson, *From Poilu to Yank*, 124.

29. An English ambulance section composed of big cars (Rolls-Royces Napiers and Panhards) also operated in the sector, limited in their use because of their poor off-road capabilities compared to the Model T's.

30. Rice, 77–78.

31. See Jack Edward McCallum, "Les Sections Sanitaires: American Volunteers in the Great War," Ph.D. dissertation (Fort Worth: Texas Christian University, 2001), 298–309, for a discussion of the militarization of the A.F.S.

32. L. D. Geller cited in McCallum, 299.

Chapter 6

1. A. Piatt Andrew, "For the Love of France," *The Outlook*, December 27, 1916, 114:926.

2. William Fenwick Harris, "Richard Norton, 1878–1918," *The Harvard Graduates' Magazine*, December 1918, 37:182.

3. "Charles Eliot Norton, Aged 80, The Scholar of Shady Hill," *Boston Daily Globe*, November 17, 1907.

4. Francis W. Kelsey, "Richard Norton," *Art and Archaeology*, November–December 1919, 8:329–335.

5. Arlen J. Hansen, *Gentlemen Volunteers* (New York: Arcade, 1996), 31 for examples.

6. Francis W. Kelsey, "1911, Tragedy at Cyrene," *The Nation*, June 1, 1911, 553–554.

7. Richard Goodchild, "Death of an Epigrapher: The Killing of Herbert De Cou," *The Michigan Quarterly Review*, 1968, 153.

8. Goodchild, 149–154.

9. Harris, 37: 81–182.

10. Hansen, 174.

11. M. A. DeWolfe Howe, *Memoirs of the Harvard Dead in the War Against Germany* (Cambridge, MA: Harvard University Press, 1922), 3:644, from notes contributed by Sara Norton.

12. Sara Norton was a staunch financial contributor to Edith Wharton's war charities.

13. An interesting career choice considering his previous lack of interest in writing for publication, see Harris, 182.

14. Howe, 3:645.

15. Edward R. Coyle, *Ambulancing on the French Front* (New York: Britton, 1918), 28–29.

16. Percy Lubbock, *The Letters of Henry James* (New York: Charles Scribner's Sons, 1920), 2:431.

17. Issued as a pamphlet in 1914, republished in Henry James, *Within the Rim and Other Essays 1914–15* (London: W. Collins Sons, 1918).

18. Lubbock, 2:441.

19. Preston Lockwood, "Henry James's First Interview," *New York Times*, March 21, 1915.

20. Hansen, 36.

21. Coyle, 37

22. The more interesting of the letters Eliot Norton had published in newspapers as part of fund-raising appeals.

23. Wheels?

24. Howe, 3:657.

25. That was not the case earlier.

26. Howe, 3:653.

27. Gasoline.

28. Howe, 3:664.

29. Richard S. Meryman, *With the American Volunteer Motor Ambulance Corps* (unpublished diary, 1916), with permission of family, 8.
30. *Springfield Republican*, July 8, 1916, reprinted in Edwin W. Morse, *The Vanguard of American Volunteers* (New York: Charles Scribner's Sons, 1919), 126.
31. Star shells.
32. Stretcher bearers.
33. Ambulances.
34. Lead shrapnel balls.
35. Soldier Letters, Coleman Tileston Clark, Slater Storrs Clark, Jr., Their Stories (privately printed, L. Middleditch, 1919), 26, abbreviated.
36. *Boston Daily Globe*, August 6, 1916, "How Americans Bring in Wounded at Verdun"; October 8, 1916, "American Ambulance Corps is Cited for Bravery"; James F. Muirhead, "American Volunteer Ambulance Corps," *The Nation*, January 18, 1917, 104:72–73; *New York Times*, August 5, 1916, Richard Norton, "The American Ambulance Corps at Verdun."
37. Coyle, 81–83 abbreviated.
38. Meryman, 32.
39. *History of the American Field Service: "Friends of France" 1914–1917, Told by its Members* (Boston, MA: Houghton Mifflin, 1920), 1:221.
40. *History of the American Field Service*, 1:239.
41. "Verdun Americans in Baseball Game," *New York Times*, October 22, 1916.
42. Charles F. Horne, *The Great Events of the Great War* (New York: National Alumni, 1920), 4: 265.
43. The *Chicago* doggedly sailed throughout the war on its monthly run from New York to France, successfully avoiding German submarines for nearly one hundred war-time Atlantic crossings. She could carry 1,500 passengers each "no-frills" trip, three times what a luxury liner her size carried. The ship was scrapped in 1936.
44. Townsend Ludington, *John Dos Passos: A Twentieth Century Odyssey* (New York: E. P. Dutton, 1980), 122–123.
45. Later in life Dos Passos' politics swung to the right; he became ardently anti-communist and in the 1960s supported Goldwater and Nixon and backed the draft and the Vietnam War.
46. General Nivelle's disastrous campaign on the Aisne.
47. Townsend Ludington, *The Fourteenth Chronicle, Letters and Diaries of John Dos Passos* (Boston, MA: Gambit, 1973); for the full text of this letter see 91–92.
48. Richard S. Kennedy, *Dreams in the Mirror: A Biography of E. E. Cummings* (New York: Liveright, 1980).
49. *Selected Letters of E. E. Cummings*, edited by F. W. Dupee and George Stade (New York: Harcourt, Brace World, 1969), 36; English translation: Richard S. Kennedy, 499.
50. See Hansen, Chapter 9; McCallum, 267–277 for details of the final days of the Norton-Harjes Formation.
51. Harris, 37:181–182.

Chapter 7

1. T. Bentley Mott, *Myron T. Herrick, Friend of France* (Garden City, NY: Doubleday, Doran, 1929), 145 abbreviated.
2. When war began, Bacon returned to France to become an administrator at the American Ambulance Hospital where he was instrumental in founding the American Ambulance Field Service. James Brown Scott, *Robert Bacon, Life and Letters* (New York: Doubleday, Page, 1923), 211–215.
3. Mott, 144.
4. Before the war, the Foreign Legion consisted of two regiments, Premier Régiment étranger (First Foreign Regiment) and Deuxième Régiment étranger (Second Foreign Regiment), both based in Algeria. When the war began, because of the large number of volunteers, each of these regiments divided into four regiments designated as Régiments de Marche, or marching regiments, each with about 4,400 men. Thus, the Premier Régiment étranger consisted of the First Marching Regiment, the Second Marching Regiment, the Third Marching Regiment and the Fourth Marching Regiment. The same designations applied to the marching regiments in the Deuxième Régiment étranger. See Russell A. Kelly, *Kelly of the Foreign Legion* (New York: Mitchell Kennerley, 1917), 137.
5. Mott, 144.
6. *War Letters of Edmond Genet*, edited by Grace Ellery Channing (New York: Charles Scribner's Sons, 1918), 148.
7. *Victor Chapman's Letters from France* (New York: Macmillan, 1917), 47.
8. Haversack or knapsack.
9. *Victor Chapman's Letters from France*, 52.
10. *War Letters of Edmond Genet*, edited by Grace Ellery Channing, 54.
11. *Letters and Diary of Alan Seeger* (New York: Charles Scribner's Sons, 1917), 5.
12. Alan Seeger's brother Charles was the father of the American folk singer Pete Seeger.
13. Paul Ayres Rockwell, "Writings of American Volunteers in the French Foreign Legion during the World War," *Ex Libris*, October 1923, 1:99–110.
14. Frederic Martyn, *Life in the Legion* (New York: Charles Scribner's Sons, 1911), 286.
15. Metal canteen, holds two liters.
16. David King, *Ten Thousand Shall Fall* (New York: Duffield, 1927), 60–61.
17. Irving Werstein, *Sound No Trumpet: The Life and Death of Alan Seeger* (New York: Thomas Crowell, 1967), 109.

18. King, 62–63.
19. Kenneth Weeks, *A Soldier of the Legion, France, 1914–1915* (London: George Allen and Unwin, 1916), 31.
20. Edward Morlae, *A Soldier of the Legion* (Boston, MA: Houghton Mifflin, 1916), 117–119.
21. Morlae, "A Soldier of the Legion," *Atlantic Monthly*, March 1916, 117:383–396.
22. *War Letters of Edmond Genet*, edited by Grace Ellery Channing, 125.
23. "With the Foreign Legion," *The Literary Digest*, May 15, 1915, 50:1168–1170, abbreviated. See also *Victor Chapman's Letters from France*, 74 for a less flamboyant description of the same Christmas truce; in it the Legionnaire killed the morning of December 26 is Portuguese, not American.
24. Paul Ayres Rockwell, *American Fighters in the Foreign Legion 1914–1918* (Boston, MA: Houghton Mifflin, 1930), 93–95.
25. *War Letters of Edmond Genet*, edited by Grace Ellery Channing, 85–86.
26. Morlae, *A Soldier of the Legion*, 40–41.
27. *War Letters of Edmond Genet*, edited by Grace Ellery Channing, 77–78.
28. "With the Foreign Legion," *The Literary Digest*, May 15, 1915, 50:1168–1170.
29. Weeks, 20.
30. John Mosier, *The Myth of the Great War* (New York: Harper Collins, 2001), 153.
31. Legion losses were exacerbated by the transfer of nationals, e.g. Russians, into their own national armies.
32. Mosier, 39–51.
33. John Bowe, *Soldiers of the Legion* (Chicago, IL: Press of Peterson Linotyping, 1918), 114.
34. Rockwell, 59.
35. Bowe, 159–161.
36. Morlae, *A Soldier of the Legion*, 16.
37. "Many Americans Killed," *New York Times*, October 5, 1915. Five days later a retraction was published. "Edmond Genet Escaped," *New York Times*, October 10, 1915.
38. *War Letters of Edmond Genet*, edited by Grace Ellery Channing, 129–143. Genet's letters are probably the most graphic and well written descriptions of World War I combat by an American.
39. Bowe, 147.
40. Bowe, 162.

Chapter 8

1. Paul Ayres Rockwell, "Writings of the American Volunteers in the French Foreign Legion during the World War," *Ex Libris*, October 1923, 1:99.
2. Irving Werstein, *Sound No Trumpet: The Life and Death of Alan Seeger* (New York: Thomas Crowell, 1967), 122–125.
3. Alan Seeger, "I Have a Rendezvous with Death," *The North American Review*, October 1916, 204: 594. Seeger was killed in action July 4, 1916.
4. "A Poet's Death in Battle," *The Literary Digest for November 4, 1916*, 53:1190.
5. "A Poet's Death in Battle," 53:1190.
6. John Bowe, *Soldiers of the Legion* (Chicago, IL: Press of Peterson Linotyping, 1918), 55.
7. Paul Ayres Rockwell, *American Fighters in the Foreign Legion 1914–1918* (Boston, MA: Houghton Mifflin, 1930), 161–165.
8. Alice S. Weeks, *Greater Love Hath No Man* (Boston, MA: Bruce Humphries, 1939), 114.
9. Weeks, 118.
10. Weeks, 137.
11. David Wooster King, *L. M. 8046* (New York: Duffield, 1927), 106.
12. King, 114.
13. King, 115.
14. Lord Northcliffe quoted in Charles F. Horne, *Source Records of the Great War* (New York: National Alumni, 1923), 5:52.
15. Bordeaux, Henry, *The Last Days of Fort Vaux, March 9 – June 7, 1916*, translated by Paul V. Cohn (New York: Thomas Nelson and Sons, 1917), 104–116.
16. Herbert Jäger, *German Artillery of World War One* (Marlborough, UK: Crowood, 2001), 34–66.
17. King, 118.
18. King, 118.
19. Francis Whiting Halsey, *The Literary Digest History of the World War* (New York: Funk and Wagnalls, 1920), 3: 97.
20. Karl H. von Wiegand cited in Halsey, 3: 98.
21. Bordeaux, 109.
22. Pierre Teilhard de Chardin, *The Making of the Mind*, translation by René Hague (New York: Harper and Row, 1965), 118–119.
23. Teilhard de Chardin, 134. Teilhard died April 10, 1955, in New York City; he was in residence at the Jesuit Church of St. Ignatius of Loyola, Park Avenue.
24. King, 122–125.
25. Cited in Halsey, 3:93.
26. P. J. Carisella and James W. Ryan, *The Black Swallow of Death* (Boston, MA: Marlborough House, 1972), 70. For a recent biography, see Craig Lloyd, *Eugene Bullard* (Athens: University of Georgia Press, 2000).
27. Carisella and Ryan, 128.
28. Frank Hoyt Gailor, "An American Ambulance in the Verdun Attack," *Living Age*, 1916, 290: 414.
29. Gailor, 290: 415.
30. Will Irwin, "Flashes From the Front," *The Saturday Evening Post*, July 15, 1916, 13.
31. Carisella and Ryan, 139.

Chapter 9

1. James R. McConnell, "Flying for France," *World's Work*, 1916, 33: 44.
2. Joseph A. Phelan, *Heroes and Airplanes of the Great War 1914–1918* (New York: Grosett and Dunlap, 1966), 12; John R. McMahon, *The Wright Brothers* (Boston, MA: Little, Brown, 1930), 256.
3. McMahon, 146.
4. McMahon, 215.
5. McMahon, 238–241.
6. Marvin W. McFarland, *The Papers of Wilbur and Orville Wright* (NY: McGraw Hill, 1933), 2: 965.
7. McMahon, 241.
8. Sherwin Hawley, "Types of Airplanes," *Country Life in America*, September 15, 1911, 54.
9. "The Fatal Aeroplane Accident in Boston," *Scientific American*, 1912, 107; for further information about Harriet Quimby, see Harriet Quimby, "American Bird Women," *Good Housekeeping*, 1912, 55:315–316; Elizabeth Anna Semple, "Harriet Quimby, America's First Woman Aviator," *The Overland Monthly*, 1911, 58: 525–532; "The Fatal Aeroplane Accident at Boston," *Scientific American*, 1912, 107: 27.
10. Phelan, 1966, 31.
11. In 1911, Colonel Issac Newton Lewis of the U.S. Army invented the Lewis machine gun. The U.S. Army rejected the weapon, probably for being too unconventional. Colonel Lewis retired from the army in 1913, formed an arms company in Belgium, Armes Automatiques Lewis, and went into production in the eventful year of 1914. He licensed the patent to the British arms manufacturer Birmingham Small Arms. The cheap and simple Lewis gun was the most widely used and effective light machine gun of the war. Because of its light weight, 28 pounds, and that it was air-cooled, the Lewis gun was adapted for use aboard aircraft early in the war.
12. Arch Whitehouse, *Legion of the Lafayette* (Garden City, NY: Doubleday, 1967), 1–13 for James Bach's story.
13. American POW's Club.
14. Dennis Gordon, *The Lafayette Flying Corps* (Atglen, PA: Schiffer Publishing, 2000), 435–447.
15. James J. Davilla and Arthur M. Soltan, *French Aircraft in the First World War* (Stratford, CT: Flying Machine, 1997), 185.
16. Edwin W. Morse, *The Vanguard of American Volunteers* (New York: Charles Scribner's Sons, 1919), 271 abbreviated.
17. Davilla and Soltan, 357.
18. As noted earlier, the Wright brothers gave flying lessons at Pau in 1909.
19. Davilla and Soltan, 544–545.
20. George F. Babbitt, *Norman Prince, Letter Dated May 20, 1915* (Boston, MA: Houghton Mifflin, 1917), 27.
21. Morse, 234–235.
22. Gordon, 117–118.
23. "Norman Prince Home, Wearing War Cross," *Boston Globe*, December 24, 1915; "American Hero First had to Bluff French," *Boston Globe*, October 7, 1915; "Boston Aviator in 10 Bombardments," *Boston Globe*, October 16, 1915; "Corps of American Fliers," *New York Times*, January 22, 1916. A number of Americans were instrumental in founding the Escadrille Américaine: Frazier Curtis, an advocate with Norman Prince, suffered two serious accidents during flight training and was discharged; Dr. Edmund Gros of the American Hospital was an important spokesman with links to both French authorities and American expats; Mr. W. K. Vanderbilt assumed most of the financial responsibilities of the organization. See Whitehouse, 13–25.
24. *Victor Chapman's Letters from France* (New York: Macmillan, 1917), 177.
25. Herbert Molloy Mason, Jr., *The Lafayette Escadrille* (New York: Konecky and Konecky, 1964), 58.
26. James R. McConnell, *Flying for France* (Garden City, NY: Doubleday, Page, 1917), 33.
27. William Morse, *Rotary Engines of World War One* (Buckinghamshire, England: Nelson and Saunders Aviation, 1987), 9. For early aviation, the rotary engine "had the same impact on flying as anesthetics had on surgery."
28. Davilla and Soltan, 360–361.
29. Davilla and Soltan, 379.
30. Bert Hall, *En l'Air!* (New York: New Library, 1918), 721.
31. Stephen Morehouse Avery, "Balm of Bar-le-Duc," *Collier's*, July 10, 1926. In this short story, Avery, who had been a fighter pilot during the war, captured some of the color of war-time Bar-le-Duc. He later wrote screen plays for motion pictures; see obituary, *Los Angeles Times* February 12, 1948.
32. An "ace" had at least five enemy planes downed; Lufberry had 17 before he was killed.
33. Bert Hall and William Thaw.
34. McConnell, *Flying for France*, 37.
35. McConnell, *Flying for France*, 53–55.
36. McConnell, *Flying for France*, 38–39.
37. Hall, 71.
38. *Victor Chapman's Letters from France*.
39. *Victor Chapman's Letters from France*, 15.
40. See Edmund Wilson, *The Triple Thinkers and the Wound and the Bow* (Boston, MA: Northeastern University Press, 1984), 133–163 for a biography of the strange John Jay Chapman.
41. See Mason, Jr., 70–71 and 128, for a contemporary account of the antics of the Americans.
42. Mason, Jr., 69–70.
43. Whitehouse, 167. One month after McConnell's fatal flight, Edmond Genet perished

on April 16, 1917, when his Nieuport plunged to the ground at full speed. The plane may have been hit by a shell splinter. Edwin C. Parsons, *The Great Adventure* (Garden City, NY: Doubleday, Doran, 1937), 258. The photograph of Genet in his Nieuport was originally published by Georges Thénault, *The Story of the Lafayette Escadrille* (Boston, MA: Small, Maynard, 1921), opposite 53, where the pilot is identified as Dudley Hill. Parsons republished the photo and identified the pilot as Edmond Genet, in Parsons, opposite 216.

44. Mason, Jr., 298–299.
45. Carl P. Dennett, *Prisoners of the Great War* (Boston, MA: Houghton Mifflin, 1919), 96.
46. Dennett, 1919, 97–98.
47. Dennett, 105–134.
48. Mason, Jr., 280–281. See also Charles J. Biddle, *The Way of the Eagle* (New York: Charles Scribner's Sons, 1919), for a memoir of Lafayette Flying Corps volunteer who later flew in the 103d Aero Squadron.

Chapter 10

1. Edward Lyell Fox, *Behind the Scenes in Warring Germany* (New York: McBride, Nast, 1915), 98–99.
2. Fox, 147.
3. Fox, 150.
4. Fox, 60–61.
5. Fox, 71–72.
6. Charles Belmont Davis, *Adventures and Letters of Richard Harding Davis* (New York: Charles Scribner's Sons, 1918), 367.
7. Richard Harding Davis, *With the Allies* (New York: Charles Scribner's Sons, 1917), 121.
8. Davis, *With the Allies*, 123.
9. Davis, *With the Allies*, 135.
10. Davis, *With the Allies*, 136.
11. Richard Harding Davis, "In the Trenches of Champagne," *The Boston Globe*, December 26, 1915; Richard Harding Davis, "Rheims during Bombardment," *Scribner's Magazine*, January, 1915, 57: 70–76; Richard Harding Davis, *With the Allies*, Chapter 6, "The Bombardment of Rheims." However, there is a story behind the story. Davis and three colleagues set off for Reims in a rented chauffeur-driven auto, traveling from Paris and covering the nearly one hundred miles to Reims without the necessary military passes to be in the war zone. The trip was well lubricated with wine and champagne. The foursome somehow talked their way through military check points. It was on the return trip that their luck ran out; they tried to go beyond Reims to see the active battlefield. There they were arrested, sent to Paris under guard and jailed. For the full story, see E. Ashmead-Bartlett, *Some of My Experiences in the Great War* (London: George Newnes, 1918), 32–58; Arthur Lubow, *The Reporter Who Would Be King* (New York: Charles Scribner's Sons, 1992), 306–312.
12. Edith Wharton, *Fighting France, From Dunkerque to Belfort* (New York: Charles Scribner's Sons, 1917), 185.
13. Percy Lubbock, *The Letters of Henry James* (New York: Charles Scribner's Sons, 1920), 2, 405.
14. Irwin S. Cobb, *Paths of Glory* (New York: George H. Doran, 1915), 233.
15. Cobb, 240–241.
16. Cobb, 227.
17. Cobb, 259.
18. Edwin F. Weigle, *On Four Battle Fronts with the German Army* (Chicago, IL: Chicago Tribune, 1915). Weigle filmed the initial invasion of Belgium in 1914; the *Tribune* donated more than $25,000 to Belgian relief organizations from the profits of showing these films.
19. Villa Perin near German headquarters, Charleville, France.
20. Weigle, 17–18.
21. Léon van der Essen, *The Invasion and the War in Belgium from Liège to the Yser* (London: T. F. Unwin, 1917), 50.
22. Walter Hale, "Notes of an Artist at the Front," *The Century Magazine*, June 28, 1915, 91:258.
23. Mabel Potter Daggett, *Women Wanted* (New York: George H. Doran, 1918), 46.
24. Daggett, 59–60.
25. Karl von Wiegand, "Crown Prince of Germany Interviewed," reprinted in "Current Misconceptions about the War," a booklet published by The Fatherland Corporation, New York, 1915).
26. Klaus W. Jonas, *The Life of the Crown Prince*, English translation (Pittsburgh, PA: University of Pittsburgh Press, 1961), 96 for Wiegand letter.
27. Philippe Voluer, *La Guerre De 14 Au Pays De Stenay* (Beaufort-En-Argonne: Les Amis de Montserrat, 2006), 83. Translation by Ulrich von Koppenfels.
28. Charles Belmont Davis, 411.
29. Francis Whiting Halsey, *The Literary Digest History of the World War* (New York: Funk and Wagnalls, 1920), 3:91–92.
30. Halsey, 98.
31. Karl Friedrich Wiegand, "No Race Like Us Can Die," *The Literary Digest*, February 27, 1915.
32. Walter Hale, "My Two Visits to Verdun," *Harper's Magazine*, February, 1917, 307.
33. Hale, "My Two Visits to Verdun," 308.
34. Hale, "My Two Visits to Verdun," 309.
35. Hale, "My Two Visits to Verdun," 306.
36. Hale, "My Two Visits to Verdun," 318.
37. "Walter Hale, Writer, Artist, and Actor,

Dead," *Chicago Daily Tribune*, December 5, 1917. Walter Hale visited the Western Front in 1915 and wrote two magazine articles describing his experiences: Walter Hale, "Back of the Front in a Motor," *Collier's*, January 8, 1916, 56: 82, 84, 86, 88, 90; Walter Hale, 1915, "Notes of an Artist at the Front," *The Century Magazine*, June 28, 1915, 91: 250–261. This article includes a vivid description of the gutted cathedral at Reims.

38. "*The Fatherland* and the Passaic Library," *The Fatherland*, October 6, 1915, 3(9): 158; "Is *The Fatherland* in Your Library?" *The Fatherland*, October 13, 1915, 3 (10): 173.

39. Max Stein, "Why Germany Sends Beer to the Front," *The Fatherland*, April 12, 1916, 4(10): 149–150.

40. *The Fatherland*, May 24, 1916, 4 (16): 251.

41. "Thrashes Gambler on German Liner," *New York Times*, November 3, 1909; the ship was named after the Crown Princess Cecilie, wife of Crown Prince Wilhelm.

42. Granville Fortescue, *Front Line Dead Line* (New York: G. P. Putnam's Sons, 1937).

43. Granville Fortescue, "The Burden France has Borne," *National Geographic* 31: 322–344.

44. Fortescue, "The Burden France has Borne," 324.

45. G. J. Meyer, *A World Undone* (New York: Delacorte, 2006), 463.

46. John J. Pershing, *My Experiences in the World War* (New York: Frederick A. Stokes, 1931), 1: 139.

Chapter 11

1. Heywood Broun, *The A.E.F.* (New York: D. Appleton, 1918), 13.

2. Cimetière de Picpus.

3. Emmet Crozier, *American Reporters on the Western Front* (New York: Oxford University Press, 1959), 138.

4. John J. Pershing, *My Experiences in the World War* (New York: Frederick A. Stokes, 1931), 1: 93.

5. Pershing, 1: 1.

6. John S. D. Eisenhower, *Yanks* (New York: Simon and Schuster, 2001), 46, 295.

7. Pershing, 1: 37.

8. Frederick Palmer, *America in France* (New York: Dodd, Mead, 1918), 6–7.

9. Pershing, 1: 16.

10. Floyd Gibbons, *And They Thought We Wouldn't Fight* (New York: George H. Doran, 1918), 24.

11. Gibbons, 26–27.

12. Gibbons, 28.

13. Gibbons, 33.

14. Gibbons, 41; Mrs. Hoy and her daughter Elizabeth, graduate of Smith College, were returning to England after spending the holidays with relatives and friends in Chicago. Mrs. Hoy had twice delayed sailing because of a fear of submarines. The wooden boards of No. 8 life boat ripped open as it hit the side of the ship so that the boat flooded with seawater at the center. Mrs. Hoy and Elizabeth stood up to their hips in the cold Atlantic water. Mrs. Hoy died around 2:00 A.M. and Elizabeth about 2:30 A.M. At 5:15 A.M., their bodies were put overboard and at 6:45 A.M., H.M.S. *Crocus* picked up the surviving passengers of lifeboat No. 8. Special to *New York Times*, February 27, 1917.

15. David M. Kennedy, *Over Here* (New York: Oxford University Press, 1980, 2004), 45–92.

16. Walter Millis, *Road to War, America, 1914–1917* (Boston, MA: Houghton Mifflin, 1935), 407.

17. Pershing, 1: 79.

18. Robert B. Bruce, *A Fraternity of Arms* (Lawrence: University Press of Kansas, 2003), 32–59.

19. Bruce, 105.

20. Three American ordinance firms (Winchester Repeating Arms Company, Remington Arms Company and Midvale Ordinance Company) manufactured the American Enfield rifle for the British Army. Over a million American Enfields were supplied to the British Army in 1916 and early 1917. This was just another instance of America's biased neutrality, a policy that irked the Germans and helped provoke their submarine campaign. The American Enfield was chambered for the British .303 cal. cartridge. After the United States entered the war, the rifle was chambered for the standard U.S. .30 cal. (.30-'06) cartridge and was known as the U.S. Model of 1917 rifle, the principal doughboy rifle. The American Enfield was considered superior to the Springfield for combat purposes. Bruce N. Canfield, "The Doughboy Rifle," *American Rifleman*, July 1996, 31–33, 67.

21. Pershing, 1: 26.

22. Pershing, 1: 81.

23. James G. Harbord, *Leaves from a War Diary* (New York: Dodd, Mead, 1931), 119.

24. Eisenhower, 56–57.

25. "U.S. Headquarters at Chaumont," *The Hartford Courant*, December 27, 1918.

26. Pershing, 1: 175; the American telephone operators were known as "Hello Girls." Lettie Gavin, *American Women in World War I* (Niwot: University Press of Colorado, 1997), 77–100.

27. Pershing, 1: 317–318.

28. Virginia Vassallo, *Unsung Patriot: Guy T. Viskniskki* (Danville, KY: Krazy Duck, 2007), 83–84.

29. Pershing, 1: 282.

30. Anonymous, *Wine, Women and War* (New York: J. H. Sears, 1926). A candid look at the

war, in diary form that was never meant for publication. Reading it, one realizes why the author remained anonymous, especially since he was apparently married. An iconoclastic memoir published in a decade of many self-congratulatory war memoirs, it went through four editions in 1926.

31. Anonymous, 18 abbreviated.
32. Anonymous, 25 abbreviated.
33. Anonymous, 121 abbreviated.
34. Craig S. Herbert, *Eyes of the Army* (Self-published, 1986), 219. Mr. Herbert remembered *La Vie Parisienne* and *Le Sourie* as the *Playboy* magazines of his day.
35. Evangeline Booth and Grace Livingstone Hill, *The War Romance of the Salvation Army* (Philadelphia, PA: J. B. Lippincott, 1919), 51.
36. Katharine Morse, *The Uncensored Letters of a Canteen Girl* (New York: Henry Holt, 1920), 83. Katherine Morse, a Smith College graduate, served with the YMCA in France from November 1917 until April 1919. She wrote letters to her family in Amherst, Massachusetts, that she never mailed because she did not want her letters read by a censor who might, she said, sit across the mess-table from her. She was 29 when she sailed for France.
37. Morse, 74–75. Pershing's censors would *never* have passed this letter.
38. Morse, 101.
39. Emerson Gifford Taylor, *New England in France 1917–19* (New York: Houghton Mifflin, 1920), 114.
40. Augustin F. Maher and Clarence Ransom Edwards, *When Connecticut Stopped the Hun* (New Haven, CT: S. Z. Field, 1919), 2.
41. An American trench system near the village.
42. Maher and Edwards, 2.
43. Crozier, 206–207.
44. For the experiences of these American POWs see: "American Captives Tell of Brutality," *New York Times*, November 30, 1918. The 26th was not the only American division to have prisoners taken by the Germans in the Salient in 1917 and early 1918. The 1st lost 11 men during its tenure there in November 1917; the 2nd had 26 captured in March and May 1918. The difference was that the 26th was hit the hardest.
45. Otto von Ledebur, "Rushing the St. Mihiel Salient," in *As They Saw Us*, ed. George Sylvester Viereck (Garden City, NY: Doran, 1929), 179. The founder and publisher of *The Fatherland*, the stridently pro–German weekly magazine that ceased publication after America entered the war, edited this volume of post-war essays by German and French military leaders. Presumably, Viereck's German contacts enabled him successfully to solicit contributions from prominent Prussian generals such as Major General Baron Otto von Ledebur, Chief of Staff for German Army Unit C that defended the St. Mihiel salient in 1918.
46. Max von Gallwitz, "The Retreat to the Rhine," in *As They Saw Us*, ed. George Sylvester Viereck (Garden City, NY: Doran, 1929), 235. General Max von Gallwitz served as commander of *Heeresgruppe Gallwitz*, the German army group that opposed the American army in the Meuse-Argonne in 1918.
47. Joël Huret, *Les Américains sur le front de Lorraine 1917–1918* (Metz, France: Éditions Serpenoise, 1998), 75.
48. "American Girls Under Fire," *The Hartford Courant*, April 25, 1918; "Gas Shell Hits Salvation Army Hut," *The Hartford Courant*, June 2, 1918.
49. "Met Manchester Girl in Trenches," *The Hartford Courant*, April 27, 1918.
50. Herbert, 107.
51. "Salvation Army Women are Armed with Revolvers," *The Hartford Courant*, June 11, 1918.
52. Herbert, 108.
53. Booth and Hill, 141.
54. Booth and Hill, 141.
55. Herbert, 108.
56. Herbert, 107.
57. Elsie Janis, *The Big Show* (New York: Cosmopolitan, 1919), 75.
58. Probably a YMCA hut.
59. Janis, 76.

Chapter 12

1. "God is with us," a statement of hope embossed upon German army belt buckles and other equipment.
2. Elsie Janis, *The Big Show* (New York: Cosmopolitan Book, 1919), 78, "*Ich weiss nicht*" translates as "I don't know."
3. Edward Lyell Fox, *Wilhelm Hohenzollern & Co.* (New York: Robert M. McBride, 1917), 18.
4. *Gott mit uns*.
5. Fox, 7.
6. Louise Townsend Nicholl, "The 18 Girls From Smith College," *The Ladies' Home Journal*, April, 1918, 19, 60; Ruth Gaines, "Yankee Peddlers in the Somme," *The Survey*, March 2, 1918. The Smith College Relief Unit was founded in memory of Elizabeth Hoy, class of 1898, who perished on the *Laconia* when Germans torpedoed that ship. The unit arrived in France in September of 1917 and was based in Grécourt in the Somme area. Its mission was to help restore agriculture and bring food, medical aid, shelter and schooling to 16 war-ravaged villages. See also "War's Terrors Can Not Keep Smith Girls From the Front," *The Literary Digest*, June 15, 1918; Marie L. Wolfs, "The Last to Leave," *The Independent*, June 22, 1918.

7. Red Cross testimonial in Ruth Gaines, *Ladies of Grécourt* (New York: E. P. Dutton, 1920), 112–113; Major Perkins, American Red Cross (ARC) commissioner to France, had an association with the National City Bank, an organization affiliated with J. P. Morgan and Company. Most of upper administration of the ARC had ties to J. P. Morgan. It appeared a Wall Street financial house tightly controlled the primary American welfare organization. Carter H. Harrison, *With the American Red Cross in France 1918–1919* (Chicago, IL: Ralph Fletcher Seymour, 1947), 25.

8. G. J. Meyer, *A World Undone* (New York: Delacorte, 2006), 555.

9. The planned Flanders offensive never occurred.

10. Winston S. Churchill, *The World Crisis* (New York: Charles Scribner's Sons, 1927), 2:171.

11. A.E.F. offices

12. John J. Pershing, *My Experiences in the World War* (New York: Frederick A. Stokes, 1931), 2: 89.

13. Floyd Gibbons, *And They Thought We Wouldn't Fight* (New York: George H. Doran, 1918), 297.

14. Gibbons, 298.

15. Erich Ludendorff, "The American Soldier in the World War as Seen by a Foe," in *As They Saw Us*, ed. George Sylvester Viereck (Garden City, NY: Doubleday, Doran, 1929), 36. General Ludendorff, First Quartermaster General, was the *de facto* chief manager of the German war machine from August 1916 until almost the war's end.

16. During the First Battle of the Marne in 1914, the victorious Foch supposedly said, "Hard pressed on my right. My center is yielding. Impossible to maneuver. Situation excellent. I attack!"

17. Paul von Hindenburg, *Out of My Life* (New York: Cassell, 1920), 385.

18. Pershing, 2: 225. Pershing often seemed more interested in how he was viewed by others, especially the French, than in the strategic imperative.

19. Joël Huret, *Le saillant de Saint-Mihiel 1914–1918* (Metz, France: Éditions Serpenoise, 1998), 100.

20. Pershing, 2: 227.

21. Pershing, 2: 227.

22. Pershing, 2: 243.

23. Pershing, 2: 243–254.

24. John S. D. Eisenhower, *Yanks* (New York: Simon & Schuster, 2001), 188.

25. Pershing, 254–255.

26. Erich Ludendorff, *My War Memories* (London: Hutchinson, 1919), 2, 708.

27. Frederick Palmer, *America in France* (New York: Dodd, Mead, 1918), 436.

28. Hunter Liggett, A.E.F. (New York: Dodd, Mead, 1928), 155.

29. Thomas M. Johnson, *Without Censor* (Indianapolis, IN: Bobbs-Merrill, 1928), see chapter IV, "The Battle That Might Have Been," 90–108, for a summary of the arguments for attacking Metz.

30. Clayton Donnell, *The German Fortress of Metz, 1870–1944* (Oxford, UK: Osprey, 2008).

31. Anthony Kemp, *The Unknown Battle: Metz, 1944* (New York: Stein and Day, 1981), 233–238.

32. Max von Gallwitz, "The Retreat to the Rhine," in *As They Saw Us*, ed. George Sylvester Viereck (Garden City, NY: Doran, 1929), 232. General Max von Gallwitz served as commander of Heeresgruppe Gallwitz, the German army group that opposed the American army in the Meuse-Argonne in 1918.

33. Kemp, 236.

34. Liggett, 160.

35. Harrison, 41.

36. Alice M. Hills, *Red Cross and YMCA Report* (Amherst, MA: Special Collections, Jones Library, 1919). Mrs. Hills traveled to France in 1917, on the French liner *Espagne*. Attacked by a German submarine, the liner escaped although the ship following her was sunk with a loss of three hundred. "Wild Scenes During Battle with U-Boat," *Boston Daily Globe*, July 8, 1917.

37. Georges Clemenceau, *Grandeur and Misery of Victory* (New York: Harcourt, Brace, 1930), 76.

38. Dale Van Every, *The A.E.F. in Battle* (New York: D. Appleton, 1928), 314.

39. Frank H. Simonds, *History of the World War* (New York: Doubleday, Page, 1919), Volume 3, 330.

40. Simonds, 332.

41. "How Pershing Lived Behind the Front," *New York Times*, January 11, 1931, 35. Perhaps as part of his studied image as the Spartan commander sharing the hardships of his men, Pershing does not mention this train in his memoirs. The train emerged from the shadows only when the train's skipper, Earl L. Thornton, described the rolling headquarters to the press more than a decade after the war's end. In 1919, the French considered sending the train to America as a war memorial. "French May Present Pershing's Train to Us," *New York Times*, September 7, 1919, 21.

42. Donald Smythe, *Pershing, General of the Armies* (Bloomington: Indiana University Press, 1986), 296–301.

43. Pershing, 2: 286–287.

Chapter 13

1. Ashby Williams, *Experiences of the Great War* (Roanoke, VA: Stone, 1919), 77.

2. Max von Gallwitz, "The Retreat to the

Rhine," in *As They Saw Us*, ed. George Sylvester Viereck (Garden City, NY: Doran, 1929), 241–242. General Max von Gallwitz served as commander of *Heeresgruppe Gallwitz*, the German army group that opposed the American army in the Meuse-Argonne in 1918.

3. Vincent J. Esposito, *The West Point Atlas of American Wars* (New York: Henry Holt, 1997), Volume 2 (1900–1918) Maps 69 and 70.
4. Esposito, 1997, text opposite map 69.
5. Williams, 81.
6. Dale Van Every, *The A.E.F. in Battle* (New York: D. Appleton, 1928), 321.
7. The line of advance was north.
8. Van Every, 322, 324.
9. Donald Smythe, *Pershing, General of the Armies* (Bloomington: Indiana University Press, 1986), 196.
10. Van Every, 325.
11. Van Every, 325–326.
12. Williams, 126.
13. Clair Kenamore, *From Vauquois Hill to Exermont* (St. Louis, MO: Guard, 1919), 254.
14. Robert H. Ferrell, *Collapse at the Meuse-Argonne* (Columbia: University of Missouri Press, 2004), 34.
15. The Bethlehem Steel Works of Bethlehem, Pennsylvania, was a major arms manufacturer for the Allies before, and after, America entered the war.
16. Kenamore, 123.
17. Varennes has one claim to historical fame, and that event occurred in 1791. While fleeing Paris during the French Revolution, King Louis XVI and his queen Marie-Antoinette were arrested in Varennes when their coach was stopped at the bridge crossing the Aire River. The royal couple was returned to Paris for their eventual execution.
18. Ferrell, *Collapse at the Meuse-Argonne* 39.
19. Ferrell, *Collapse at the Meuse-Argonne* 41–42.
20. Ferrell, *Collapse at the Meuse-Argonne* 85.
21. Kenamore, 137.
22. Kenamore, 139–140.
23. Ferrell, *Collapse at the Meuse-Argonne* 87.
24. Ferrell, *Collapse at the Meuse-Argonne* 83.
25. Ferrell, *Collapse at the Meuse-Argonne* Chapter 4.
26. Williams, 136.
27. Three integrated German defensive positions (*Stellungen*) defended the Meuse-Argonne. From south to north, they were the Giselher Stellung, Kriemhilde Stellung and Freya Stellung, names probably based upon characters in the *Nibelungenlied*. Of the three, the Kriemhilde Stellung was the most difficult to breach.
28. Hunter Liggett, *A.E.F. Ten Years Ago in France* (New York: Dodd, Mead, 1928), 167–168.
29. Liggett, 168.
30. "Through Six Days of Heroism with the 'Lost Battalion,'" *Literary Digest*, March 29, 1919, 60: 44–47. Excerpts from a letter originally published in *The American Hebrew*, March 7, 1919, by Private Robert Manson, who served as orderly to Major Whittlesey.
31. World War I foxholes
32. Robert H. Ferrell, *Five Days in October* (Columbia: University of Missouri Press, 2005), a day-by-day account of the Lost Battalion.
33. "Through Six Days of Heroism with the 'Lost Battalion,'" 60: 44–47.
34. Eric Ludendorff, "The American Soldier in the World War as Seen by a Foe," in *As They Saw Us*, ed. George Sylvester Viereck (Garden City, NY: Doubleday, Doran, 1929), 40.
35. Ferrell, *Five Days in October*, 44–45.
36. "Through Six Days of Heroism with the 'Lost Battalion,'" 60: 44–47.
37. Ferrell, *Five Days in October*, 33–34.
38. Ferrell, *Five Days in October*, 59.
39. L. C. McCollum, *History and Rhymes of the Lost Battalion* (Privately printed, 1919, 1929), 65–82. For a slightly different version of this story, see "Through Six Days of Heroism with the 'Lost Battalion,'" 60: 44–47.
40. McCollum, 1919, 63.
41. American newsmen needing a more dramatic response wrote that Whittlesey shouted, "Go to Hell!" at the German lines. "'Lost' Unit Scorned Surrender Request," *Boston Daily Globe*, October 11, 1918, 4; "Battalion Spurned Offer of Safety," *New York Times*, October 11, 1918, 5. This bit of imaginary profanity offended some pious Americans. "'Go to Hell' not Swearing; Just Good Advice—For Hun," *Boston Daily Globe*, October 12, 1918, 10.
42. Ferrell, *Five Days in October*, 80.
43. "Col. Whittlesey, of the 'Lost Battalion,' Vanishes From Ship," *New York Times*, November 29, 1921, 1; "Whittlesey Talked About War on Ship," *New York Times*, December 1, 1921, 16; "Lost Battalion Hero a Suicide," *Boston Daily Globe*, November 29, 1921, 1.
44. "Through Six Days of Heroism with the Lost Battalion," 60:44–47.

Chapter 14

1. Erich Ludendorff, *My War Memories* (London: Hutchinson, 1919), Volume 2, 719.
2. *The Americans in the Great War Volume III, Meuse-Argonne Battle* (Clermont-Ferrand, France: Michelin, 1919), 20–25.
3. John J. Pershing, *My Experiences in the World War* (New York: Frederick A. Stokes, 1931), 2:320.
4. Edward G. Lengel, *To Conquer Hell* (New York: Henry Holt, 2008), 233.
5. Hunter Liggett, *A.E.F., Ten Years Ago in France* (New York: Dodd, Mead, 1928), 186–187.

6. Not to be confused with the village of Apremont la Forêt in the St. Mihiel Salient.
7. H. G. Proctor, *The Iron Division* (Philadelphia, PA: John C. Winston, 1919), 278.
8. Proctor, 285.
9. Proctor, 291.
10. American Battle Monuments Commission, *82nd Division Summary of Operations in the World War* (Washington, D.C.: United States Government Printing Office, 1944), 22.
11. American Battle Monuments Commission, 25. The railway and road were reached and cut at 5:00 P.M., October 8.
12. David, D. Lee, *Sergeant York* (Lexington: University Press of Kentucky, 1985), 53–55.
13. George Pattullo, "The Second Elder Gives Battle," *The Saturday Evening Post*, April 26, 1919, 3.
14. York earned a host of medals for his exploit including the *Croix de Guerre*, the Distinguished Service Cross, and the Medal of Honor. After the war, he used his public image to bring better roads and schools to his part of Tennessee. Lee, 5.
15. Liggett, 137.
16. Liggett, 137.
17. Donald Smythe, *Pershing, General of the Armies* (Bloomington: Indiana University Press, 1986), 201.
18. Horace L. Baker, *Argonne Days* (Aberdeen, MS: The Aberdeen Weekly, 1927), 33.
19. Smythe, 205.
20. Ashby Williams, *Experiences of the Great War* (Roanoke, VA: Stone, 1919), 115.
21. East of the river.
22. Max von Gallwitz, "The Retreat to the Rhine," in *As They Saw Us*, ed. George Sylvester Viereck (Garden City, NY: Doran, 1929), 252. General Max von Gallwitz served as commander of *Heeresgruppe Gallwitz*, the German army group that opposed the American army in the Meuse-Argonne in 1918.
23. Smythe, 205.
24. Williams, 128.
25. von Gallwitz, 239, 241.
26. Liggett, 250.
27. Baker, 53.
28. von Gallwitz, 250.
29. von Gallwitz, 259.
30. U.S. House of Representatives, Sixty-Sixth Congress, Hearings Before Subcommittee No. 3, Select Committee on Expenditures in the War Department (Washington, D. C.: Government Printing Office, 1920), 1843, testimony of John H. Sherburne, formerly Brigadier General, A.E.F., "A great many Army officers were very fine in the way that they took care of their men. However, there were certain very glaring instances of the opposite condition, and especially among these theorists, these men who were looking upon this whole thing as, perhaps, one looks upon a game of chess, or a game of football, and who were removed from actual contact with the troops."
31. Evangeline Booth and Grace Livingstone Hill, *The War Romance of the Salvation Army* (Philadelphia, PA: J. B. Lippincott, 1919), 252.
32. Booth and Hill, 251–259.
33. von Gallwitz, 263.
34. Erich Ludendorff, "The American Soldier in the World War as Seen by a Foe," in *As They Saw Us*, ed. George Sylvester Viereck (Garden City, NY: Doubleday, Doran, 1929), 32.
35. Pershing, 2:341.
36. John Toland, *No Man's Land* (New York: Smithmark, 1980), 437–441.
37. The A.E.F. command train left its siding in Souilly for Liny-en-Barrois so Pershing could be closer to the proposed field of operations of the new American Second Army.
38. Smythe, 217.
39. Liggett, 206–207.
40. Pershing put a different spin on the state of his army, "The difficult and continuous attacks since September 26th had been very trying on our troops and had resulted in a certain loss of cohesion." Pershing, 2:351.
41. Smythe, 224.
42. von Gallwitz, 269.
43. Liggett, 216.
44. Liggett, 222.
45. Liggett, 222.
46. Liggett, 222.
47. Dale Van Every, *The A.E.F. in Battle* (New York: D. Appleton, 1928), 367.
48. Liggett, 227.
49. Leonard P. Kurtz, *Beyond No Man's Land* (Buffalo, NY: Foster and Stewart, 1937), 104–105.
50. von Gallwitz, 275.
51. Message discovered in the field diary of Merritt F. Garland, an enlisted man in the 51st Brigade Field Artillery, U.S. 26th Division. Courtesy of the Garland family.
52. The Kaiser did not actually abdicate. Prince Max of Baden, the Imperial Chancellor, had been pressuring the Kaiser to abdicate on November 8, but when he did not Prince Max took the situation in hand on November 9; he sent out an announcement to the Berlin press that the Kaiser had abdicated. As far as Berliners were concerned the Kaiser was finished, and so he was. Otto Friedrich, *Before the Deluge* (New York: Harper and Row, 1972), 23.
53. Nora Bentinck, *The Ex-Kaiser in Exile* (New York: George H. Doran, 1921), 17.
54. Toland, 571. Kaiser Wilhelm remained in Holland for the rest of his life. He purchased a villa, Huis Doorn, in 1919, died there on June 4, 1941, and is interred in a mausoleum on the grounds.
55. Bentinck, 23.

56. Toland, 573–574.
57. U.S. House of Representatives, Sixty-Sixth Congress, 1833, 1835.
58. Liggett, 236.
59. U.S. House of Representatives, Sixty-Sixth Congress, 1841.
60. U.S. House of Representatives, Sixty-Sixth Congress, 1841, testimony of John H. Sherburne, formerly Brigadier General, A.E.F.; Sherburne was one of the few National Guard officers promoted during the war. A Boston lawyer, he was not one of the West Point crowd and therefore seemed uninhibited about speaking his mind. As a colonel, he was an artillery officer assigned to the Afro-American 92nd Division, Captain Livermore was his chief of staff.
61. "Pershing Denies Waste of Lives," *Boston Daily Globe,* January 11, 1920.
62. Charles S. Groves, "Yankee Lives Sacrificed Needlessly, Says Fuller," *Boston Daily Globe,* February 1, 1919.
63. U.S. House of Representatives, Sixty-Sixth Congress, 1920; "Puts Armistice Day Losses up to Staff," *New York Times,* January 9, 1920, 23.
64. U.S. House of Representatives, Sixty-Sixth Congress, 2186.
65. Phillipe Voluer, *La Guerre De 14 Au Pays De Stenay* (Beaufort-En-Argonne: France, Les Amis de Montserrat, 2006), 87. The German Army essentially left Stenay on November 9, accompanying the departing troops were the members of five Stenay families whose daughters had been overly intimate with the Crown Prince.
66. Joseph E. Persico, *Eleventh Month, Eleventh Day, Eleventh Hour* (New York: Random House, 2004), Chapter 30.
67. Baker, 122. Private Baker was in the 32nd Division.

Chapter 15

1. "Outlook for Touring in Europe next Autumn," *New York Times,* May 18, 1919.
2. Stephen L. Harp, *Marketing Michelin* (Baltimore, MD: The Johns Hopkins University Press, 2001), 97–98.
3. Harp, 117.
4. Harp, 92.
5. *The Americans in the Great War, Volume II The Battle of Saint Mihiel* (Clermont-Ferrand, France: Michelin, 1920); *Volume III Meuse-Argonne Battle* (Clermont-Ferrand, France: Michelin, 1919).
6. "'Dud'-Finders to Clear Late Battlefields," *Illustrated World,* January 1919, 652.
7. John Keegan, *The First World War* (New York: Alfred A. Knopf, 1999), 421–422.
8. American military cemeteries were respected during the German occupation of France in the Second World War; the Latin crosses and Stars of David were unharmed. Margaret Lambie, *Verdun Experiences* (Washington, D.C.: Courant, 1945), 48.
9. Edith Wharton, "You and You; to the American Private in the Great War," *Scribner's Magazine,* February 1919, 65:152–153.
10. From a plaque in Verdun commemorating the unit; twenty women are named.
11. Lambie, 58.
12. Lambie, 31.
13. Roughly translated, "A Drop of Milk."
14. Frederick Palmer, "The Best Story in Europe Today," *Collier's,* Nov. 17, 1923, 18; "Thanks Americans for Hattonchatel," *New York Times,* September 16, 1923, 18.
15. Belle Skinner, "The Christening of the Bell," *The Atlantic Monthly,* July–December 1921, 63.
16. "Memorable Trip for Miss Skinner," *Springfield Republican,* Oct. 13, 1917.
17. "Adopting a Village," *The Outlook,* December 20, 1922, 694.
18. As part of the American St. Mihiel offensive.
19. "Tells How She Spent a Million," *Boston Post,* October 5, 1923.
20. Elizabeth G. Grossman, "Architecture for a Public Client: The Monuments and Chapels of the American Battle Monuments Commission," *The Journal of the Society of Architectural Historians* 43 (1984), 123.
21. Grossman, 126.
22. The eagle would have done Albert Speer proud.
23. Grossman, 129.
24. Katharine Morse, *The Uncensored Letters of a Canteen Girl* (New York: Henry Holt, 1920), 192–193.
25. Grossman, 129.
26. Grossman, 129.
27. Grossman, 131.
28. "U.S. Will Dedicate 13 War Memorials," *New York Times,* July 4, 1937, 6.
29. Even as late as 1931, Pershing was still dictating what should or should not be memorialized on American monuments in France. When he learned the 316th Infantry Veteran's Association (U.S. 79th Division) had erected a private monument in Sivry-sur-Meuse (Meuse-Argonne battlefield), Pershing objected bitterly. He first demanded the French destroy the monument. When the French resisted, he insisted that the inscription "Dedicated to the Men who Died in Action" be erased and replaced with "In Memory of the High Achievements of the American Troops who Fought in this Region During the World War." Evidently, monuments should glorify the A.E.F. (and, of course, Pershing's leadership) rather than the sacrifices of his men. "Gold Star Mothers Charge Desecration," *New*

York Times, December 14, 1931, 21. Ron Robin, *Enclaves of America: The Rhetoric of American Political Architecture Abroad 1900–1965* (Princeton, NJ: Princeton University Press, 1992), Chapter 2.

30. John Manship, *Paul Manship* (New York: Abbeville, 1989), 110–111.

31. "New Stories Told of the Bayonet Trench," *New York Times*, December 7, 1920, 15.

32. "American Is Killed in Paris-London Flight," *New York Times*, December 12, 1919, 19.

33. In the Second World War, the massive concrete monument served as part of a German battery site that shelled General Patton's American troops at the end of August 1944 as they liberated Verdun. Lambie, 75.

34. "New Stories Told of the Bayonet Trench," *New York Times*, December 7, 1920, 15.

35. "Buried Shell Kills Two," *New York Times*, April 28, 1929, 58.

36. "Verdun's Glory Tower," *New York Times*, July 31, 1927, 5; "American Gift Bell Going to Verdun," *New York Times*, June 1, 1927, 6.

37. "Former Foes Hold Peace Rally at Graves of Heroes of Verdun," *Baltimore Sun*, July 13, 1936, 1.

38. "Nazis Took Verdun in Brief Operation," *New York Times*, June 18, 1940, 6; "German Forces Reach Cherbourg," *New York Times*, June 19, 1940, 6 for a photograph of the Verdun parade.

39. The rapidity of the American advance was such that pockets of German soldiers were left behind. In Clermont-en-Argonne, the village that Mrs. Edith Wharton visited in 1915 and described in a letter to Henry James, four German tanks and one hundred infantry ambushed a small number of American soldiers sprawled out on the sidewalks napping after a long march. After the skirmish in the village, the Germans withdrew into the hills near the Butte de Vauquois. Gene Currivan, "Drive Resembles Parade," *New York Times*, September 3, 1944, 4; "This Time Verdun Escapes Damage," *New York Times*, September 2, 1944, 3.

Bibliography

Books

American Battle Monuments Commission. *82nd Division Summary of Operations in the World War*. Washington, D.C.: United States Government Printing Office, 1944.

The Americans in the Great War. Volume II, The Battle of Saint Mihiel. Clermont-Ferrand, France: Michelin, 1920.

The Americans in the Great War. Volume III, Meuse-Argonne Battle. Clermont-Ferrand, France: Michelin, 1919.

Andrew, A. Piatt. *Letters Written Home from France in the First Half of 1915*. Cambridge, MA: Riverside, 1916.

———. "Some of the Early Problems." In *History of the American Field Service in France, "Friends of France" 1914–1917, Told by its Members*. Volume 1. Boston, MA: Houghton Mifflin, 1920.

Ashmead-Bartlett, E. *Some of My Experiences in the Great War*. London: George Newnes, 1918.

Babbitt, George F. *Norman Prince, Letter Dated May 20, 1915*. Boston, MA: Houghton Mifflin, 1917.

Baker, Horace L. *Argonne Days*. Aberdeen, MS: The Aberdeen Weekly, 1927.

Bentinck, Nora. *The Ex-Kaiser in Exile*. New York: George H. Doran, 1921.

Biddle, Charles J. *The Way of the Eagle*. New York: Charles Scribner's Sons, 1919.

Booth, Evangeline, and Grace Livingstone Hill. *The War Romance of the Salvation Army*. Philadelphia, PA: J. B. Lippincott, 1919.

Bordeaux, Henry. *The Deliverance of the Captives: Douaumont-Vaux*. London: Thomas Nelson and Sons, 1919.

———. *The Last Days of Fort Vaux, March 9–June 7, 1916*. Translated by Paul V. Cohn. New York: Thomas Nelson and Sons, 1917.

Bowe, John. *Soldiers of the Legion*. Chicago, IL: Peterson Linotyping, 1918.

Broun, Heywood. *The A.E.F.* New York: D. Appleton, 1918.

Brown, Malcolm. *Verdun 1916*. Stroud, Gloucestershire, UK and Charleston, SC: Tempus, 2000.

Bruce, Robert B. *A Fraternity of Arms*. Lawrence: University Press of Kansas, 2003.

Burke, Kathleen. *The White Road to Verdun*. New York: George H. Doran, 1916.

Buswell, Leslie. *Ambulance No. 10, Personal Letters from the Front*. New York: A. L. Burt, 1916.

———. *With the American Ambulance Field Service in France*. New York: Houghton Mifflin, 1915.

Carisella, P. J., and James W. Ryan. *The Black Swallow of Death*. Boston, MA: Marlborough House, 1972.

Churchill, Winston S. *The Great War*. Part 13. London: George Newnes, 1933.

———. *The World Crisis*. Volume 2. New York: Charles Scribner's Sons, 1927.

Clemenceau, Georges. *Grandeur and Misery of Victory*. New York: Harcourt, Brace, 1930.

Cobb, Irwin S. *Paths of Glory*. New York: George H. Doran, 1915.

Coyle, Edward R. *Ambulancing at the French Front*. New York: Britton, 1918.

Crosland, T. W. H. *The Soul of a Crown Prince*. London: Wyman and Sons, 1916.

Crozier, Emmet. *American Reporters on the Western Front*. New York: Oxford University Press, 1959.

Curtin, D. Thomas. *The Land of Deepening Shadow: Germany-at-War*. New York: George H. Doran, 1917.

Daggett, Mabel Potter. *Women Wanted*. New York: George H. Doran, 1918.

Davila, James J., and Arthur M. Soltan. *French Aircraft in the First World War*. Stratford, CT: Flying Machine, 1997.

Davis, Charles Belmont. *Adventures and Letters of Richard Harding Davis*. New York: Charles Scribner's Sons, 1918.

Davis, Richard Harding. *With the Allies*. New York: Charles Scribner's Sons, 1917.

Dennett, Carl P. *Prisoners of the Great War*. Boston, MA: Houghton Mifflin, 1919.
Des Vignes Rouges, Jean. *Bourru, Soldier of France*. New York: E. P. Dutton, 1929.
The Diary of a German Soldier. New York: Alfred A. Knopf, 1919.
Diary of Section VIII: American Ambulance Field Service. Privately printed, 1917.
Dickinson, Asa Don. *The Kaiser*. Garden City, NY: Doubleday, Page, 1914.
Donnell, Clayton. *The German Fortress of Metz, 1870–1944*. Oxford, UK: Osprey, 2008.
Dupee, F. W., and George Stade, ed. *Selected Letters of E.E. Cummings*. New York: Harcourt, Brace World, 1969.
Eisenhower, John S. D. *Yanks*. New York: Simon and Schuster, 2001.
Esposito, Vincent J. *The West Point Atlas of American Wars*, Volume 2. New York: Henry Holt, 1997.
Ferrell, Robert H. *Collapse at the Meuse-Argonne*. Columbia: University of Missouri Press, 2004.
_____. *Five Days in October*. Columbia: University Of Missouri Press, 2005.
Fortescue, Granville. *Front Line Dead Line*. New York: G. P. Putnam's Sons, 1937.
Fox, Edward Lyell. *Behind the Scenes in Warring Germany*. New York: McBride, Nast, 1915.
_____. *William Hohenzollern & Co*. New York: Robert M. McBride, 1917.
Friedrich, Otto. *Before the Deluge*. New York: Harper and Row, 1972.
Friends of France: The Field Service of the American Ambulance Described by its Members. Boston, MA, and New York: Houghton Mifflin, 1916.
Gaines, Ruth. *Ladies of Grécourt*. New York: E. P. Dutton, 1920.
Gavin, Lettie. *American Women in World War I*. Niwot: University Press of Colorado, 1997.
Geller, L. D. *Friends of France; The American Field Service with the French Armies 1914–1917, 1939–1945*, Exhibit Catalogue A.F.S., Blerancourt Exhibition, 1989.
Genet, Edmond. *War Letters of Edmond Genet*. Grace Ellery Channing, ed. New York: Charles Scribner's Sons, 1918.
Gerard, James W. *My Four Years in Germany*. New York: Grosset and Dunlap, 1917.
A German Deserter's War Experience. Translated by J. Koettgen. New York: B. W. Huebsch, 1917.
Gibbons, Floyd. *And They Thought We Wouldn't Fight*. New York: George H. Doran, 1918.
Gordon, Dennis. *The Lafayette Flying Corp*. Atglen, PA: Schiffer, 2000.
Griffiths, Richard. *Marshal Pétain*. London: Constable, 1970.
Hall, Bert. *En l'Air!* New York: New Library, 1918.
Halsey, Francis Whiting. *The Literary Digest History of the World War*, Volume 3. New York: Funk and Wagnalls, 1920.
Hansen, Arlen J. *Gentlemen Volunteers*. New York: Arcade, 1996.
Harbord, James G. *Leaves From a War Diary*. New York: Dodd, Mead, 1931.
Harp, Stephen L. *Marketing Michelin*. Baltimore, MD: The Johns Hopkins University Press, 2001.
Harrison, Carter H. *With the American Red Cross in France 1918–1919*. Chicago, IL: Ralph Fletcher Seymour, 1947.
Hedin, Sven. *With the German Armies in the West*. London and New York: John Lane, 1915.
Herbert, Craig S. *Eyes of the Army*. Self-published, 1986.
Hermanns, William. *The Holocaust, from a Survivor of Verdun*. New York: Harper & Row, 1972.
Hills, Alice M. Red Cross and YMCA Report. Amherst, MA: Special Collections, Jones Library, 1919.
History of the American Field Service in France: "Friends of France" 1914–1917, Told by its Members. Three Volumes. Boston, MA: Houghton Mifflin, 1920.
Holstein, Christina. *Verdun—Fort Douaumont*. South Yorkshire, UK: Pen and Sword, 2002.
Horne, Alistair. *The Price of Glory, Verdun, 1916*. New York: St. Martin's, 1963.
Horne, Charles F. *The Great Events of the Great War*, Volume IV. New York: National Alumni, 1920.
_____. *Source Records of the Great War*, Volume V. New York: National Alumni, 1923.
Howe, M. A. DeWolfe. *Memoirs of the Harvard Dead in the War Against Germany*. Cambridge, MA: Harvard University Press, 1922.
Huret, Joël. *Le saillant de Saint-Mihiel 1914–1918*. Metz, France: Éditions Serpenoise, 1998.
_____. *Les Américains sur le front de Lorraine 1917–1918*. Metz, France: Éditions Serpenoise, 1998.
Imbrie, Robert Whitney. *Behind the Wheel of a War Ambulance*. New York: Robert M. McBride, 1918.
Jäger, Herbert. *German Artillery of World War One*. Marlborough, UK: Crowood, 2001.
James, Henry. *Within the Rim and Other Essays 1914–15*. London: W. Collins Sons, 1918.
James, Henry, and Edith Wharton. *Letters: 1900–1915*. Edited by Lyall H. Powers. New York: Charles Scribner's Sons, 1990.
Janis, Elsie. *The Big Show*. New York: Cosmopolitan, 1919.
Johnson, Thomas M. *Without Censor*. Indianapolis, IN: Bobbs-Merrill, 1928.
Jonas, Klaus. *The Life of the Crown Prince*. Pittsburgh, PA: University of Pittsburgh Press, 1961.
Jünger, Ernst. *Storm of Steel*. Trans. Michael

Hofmann. New York and London: Penguin, 2003.
The Kaiser's Heir: A Pen-Portrait. London: Mills and Bonn, 1914.
Keegan, John. *The First World War*. New York: Alfred A. Knopf, 1999.
Kelly, Russell A. *Kelly of the Foreign Legion*. New York: Mitchell Kennerley, 1917.
Kemp, Anthony. *The Unknown Battle: Metz, 1944*. New York: Stein and Day, 1981.
Kenamore, Clair. *From Vauquois Hill to Exermont*. St. Louis, MO: Guard, 1919.
Kennedy, David M. *Over Here*. New York: Oxford University Press, 1980.
Kennedy, Richard S. *Dreams in the Mirror: A Biography of E. E. Cummings*. New York: Liveright, 1980.
King, David. *Ten Thousand Shall Fall*. New York: Duffield, 1927.
King, David Wooster. *L. M. 8046*. New York: Duffield, 1927.
Kurtz, Leonard P. *Beyond No Man's Land*. Buffalo, NY: Foster and Stewart, 1937.
Lambie, Margaret. *Verdun Experiences*. Washington, D. C.: Courant, 1945.
Laughlin, Clara E. *The Martyred Towns of France*. New York: G. P. Putnam's Sons, 1919.
Lee, David D. *Sergeant York*. Lexington: University Press of Kentucky, 1985.
Lee, Hermione. *Edith Wharton*. New York: Alfred A. Knopf, 2007.
Lefebvre, Jacques-Henri. *Verdun*. Paris: G. Durassie, 1966.
Lengel, Edward G. *To Conquer Hell*. New York: Henry Holt, 2008.
Letters and Diary of Alan Seeger. New York: Charles Scribner's Sons, 1917.
Letters from André Chéronnet-Champollion, 1914-1915. New York: Privately printed, 1915.
Liggett, Hunter. *A.E.F. Ten Years Ago in France*. New York: Dodd, Mead, 1928.
Lloyd, Craig. *Eugene Bullard*. Athens, GA: University of Georgia Press, 2000.
Lubbock, Percy. *The Letters of Henry James*. New York: Charles Scribner's Sons, 1920.
Lubow, Arthur. *The Reporter Who Would Be King*. New York: Charles Scribner's Sons, 1992.
Ludendorff, Erich. *My War Memories*. Volume 2. London, England: Hutchinson, 1919.
———. "The American Soldier in the World War as Seen by a Foe," In *As They Saw Us*, edited by George Sylvester Viereck. Garden City, NY: Doubleday, Doran, 1929.
Ludington, Townsend. *The Fourteenth Chronicle, Letters and Diaries of John Dos Passos*. Boston, MA: Gambit, 1973.
———. *John Dos Passos: A Twentieth Century Odyssey*. New York: E. P. Dutton, 1980.
Maher, Augustin F., and Clarence Ransom Edwards. *When Connecticut Stopped the Hun*. New Haven, CT: S. Z. Field, 1919.
Manship, John. *Paul Manship*. New York: Abbeville, 1989.
Martin, William. *Verdun 1916*. Oxford, UK: Osprey, 2001.
Martyn, Frederic. *Life in the Legion*. New York: Charles Scribner's Sons, 1911.
Mason, Herbert Molloy, Jr. *The Lafayette Escadrille*. New York: Konecky and Konecky, 1964.
McCallum, Jack Edward. *Les Sections Sanitaires: American Volunteers in the Great War*. Ph.D. dissertation. Fort Worth, TX: Texas Christian University, 2001.
McCollum, L. C. *History and Rhymes of the Lost Battalion*. Privately printed, 1919, 1929.
McConnell, James R. *Flying for France*. Garden City, NY: Doubleday, Page, 1917.
McFarland, Marvin W. *The Papers of Wilbur and Orville Wright*. McGraw Hill, 1933.
McMahon, John R. *The Wright Brothers*. Boston, MA: Little, Brown, 1930.
Memoirs of the Crown Prince of Germany. New York: Charles Scribner's Sons, 1922.
Meryman, Richard S. *With the American Volunteer Motor Ambulance Corps*. Unpublished diary, 1916.
Meyer, G. J. *A World Undone*. New York: Delacorte, 2006.
Millis, Walter. *Road to War, America, 1914-1917*. Boston, MA: Houghton Mifflin, 1935.
Morlae, Edward. *A Soldier of the Legion*. Boston, MA: Houghton Mifflin, 1916.
Morse, Edwin W. *The Vanguard of American Volunteers*. New York: Charles Scribner's Sons, 1919.
Morse, Katharine. *The Uncensored Letters of a Canteen Girl*. New York: Henry Holt, 1920.
Morse, William. *Rotary Engines of World War One*. Buckinghamshire, England: Nelson and Saunders Aviation, 1987.
Mosier, John. *The Myth of the Great War*. New York: HarperCollins, 2001.
Mott, T. Bentley. *Myron T. Herrick, Friend of France*. Garden City, NY: Doubleday, Doran, 1929.
Orcutt, Philip Dana. *The White Road of Mystery: The Note-Book of an American Ambulancier*. New York: John Lane, 1918.
Palmer, Frederick. *America in France*. New York: Dodd, Mead, 1918.
Parsons, Edwin C. *The Great Adventure*. Garden City, NY: Doubleday, Doran, 1937.
Pershing, John J. *My Experiences in the World War*. Volumes 1 and 2. New York: Frederick A. Stokes, 1931.
Persico, Joseph E. *Eleventh Month, Eleventh Day, Eleventh Hour*. New York: Random House, 2004.
Phelan, Joseph A. *Heroes and Airplanes of the*

Great War, 1914–1918. New York: Grosett and Dunlop, 1966.
Pierce, Waldo. "Christmas Eve, 1915." In *Friends of France*. Boston, MA, and New York: Houghton Mifflin, 1916.
Powell, E. Alexander. *Vive La France!* New York: Charles Scribner's Sons, 1915.
Price, Allan. *The End of the Age of Innocence: Edith Wharton and the First World War*. New York: St. Martin's, 1996.
Proctor, H. G. *The Iron Division*. Philadelphia, PA: John C. Winston, 1919.
Rice, Philip Sidney. *An American Crusader at Verdun*. Published by the author at Princeton, 1918.
Robin, Ron. *Enclaves of America: The Rhetoric of American Political Architecture Abroad 1900–1965*. Princeton, NJ: Princeton University Press, 1992.
Rockwell, Paul Ayres. *American Fighters in the Foreign Legion, 1914–1918*. Boston, MA: Houghton Mifflin, 1930.
Scott, James Brown. *Robert Bacon, Life and Letters*. New York: Doubleday, Page, 1923.
Sheahan, Henry. *A Volunteer Poilu*. New York: Houghton Mifflin, 1916.
Simonds, Frank H. *History of the World War*, Volume 3. New York: Doubleday, Page, 1919.
Sleeper, Henry D. "The Effort in America." In *History of the American Field Service in France, "Friends of France" 1914–1917, Told by its Members*. Three Volumes. Boston, MA: Houghton Mifflin, 1920.
Smythe, Donald. *Pershing, General of the Armies*. Bloomington: Indiana University Press, 1986.
Soldier Letters, Coleman Tileston Clark, and Salter Storrs Clark, Jr., Their Stories. Privately printed, L. Middleditch, 1919.
Stern, Philip Van Doren. *Tin Lizzie*. New York: Simon and Schuster, 1955.
Stevenson, William Yorke. *At the Front in a Flivver*. Boston, MA: Houghton Mifflin, 1917.
———. *From Poilu to Yank*. Boston, MA: Houghton Mifflin, 1918.
Taylor, Emerson Gifford. *New England in France, 1917–19*. New York: Houghton Mifflin, 1920.
Teilhard de Chardin, Pierre. *The Making of the Mind*. Trans. René Hague. New York: Harper and Row, 1965.
Thénault, Georges. *The Story of the Lafayette Escadrille*. Boston, MA: Small, Maynard, 1921.
Toland, John. *No Man's Land*. New York: Smithmark, 1980.
U.S. House of Representatives, Sixty-Sixth Congress, Hearings Before Subcommittee No. 3, Select Committee on Expenditures in the War Department, Washington, D.C.: Government Printing Office, 1920.
Van der Essen, Léon. *The Invasion and the War in Belgium from Liège to the Yser*. London: T. F. Unwin, 1917.
Van Every, Dale. *The A.E.F. in Battle*. New York: D. Appleton, 1928.
Vassallo, Virginia. *Unsung Patriot: Guy T. Viskniskki*. Danville, KY: Krazy Duck, 2007.
Victor Chapman's Letters from France. New York: Macmillan, 1917.
Voluer, Philippe. *La Guerre De 14 Au Pays De Stenay*. Beaufort-En-Argonne, France: Les Amis de Montserrat, 2006.
Von Falkenhayn, Erich. *The German General Staff and its Decisions, 1914–1916*. New York: Dodd, Mead, 1920.
Von Gallwitz, Max. "The Retreat to the Rhine." In *As They Saw Us*, edited by George Sylvester Viereck. Garden City, NY: Doran, 1929.
Von Hindenburg, Paul. *Out of My Life*. New York: Cassell, 1920.
Von Ledebur, Otto. "Rushing the St. Mihiel Salient." In *As They Saw Us*, edited by George Sylvester Viereck. Garden City, NY: Doran, 1929.
Von Wiegand, Karl. "Crown Prince of Germany Interviewed." In *Current Misconceptions About the War*. New York: Fatherland, 1915.
Weeks, Alice S. *Greater Love Hath No Man*. Boston, MA: Bruce Humphries, 1939.
Weeks, Kenneth. *A Soldier of the Legion France, 1914–1915*. London: George Allen and Unwin, 1916.
Weigle, Edwin F. *On Four Battle Fronts with the German Army*. Chicago, IL: Chicago Tribune, 1915.
Werstein, Irving. *Sound No Trumpet: The Life and Death of Alan Seeger*. New York: Thomas Crowell, 1967.
Wharton, Edith. *A Backward Glance*. New York: D. Appleton-Century, 1934.
———. *Fighting France, from Dunkerque to Belfort*. New York: Charles Scribner's Sons, 1915, 1917.
Whitehouse, Arch. *Legion of the Lafayette*. Garden City, NY: Doubleday, 1967.
Whitlock, Brand. *Belgium, A Personal Narrative*, Volume l. New York: D. Appleton, 1919.
William, Crown Prince of Germany. *My War Experiences*. New York: Robert M. McBride, 1923.
Williams, Ashby. *Experiences of the Great War*. Roanoke, VA: Stone, 1919.
Wilson, Edmund. *The Triple Thinkers and the Wound and the Bow*. Boston, MA: Northeastern University Press, 1984.
Wine, Women and War. New York: J. H. Sears, 1926.

Periodicals

Newspapers

Baltimore Sun
Boston Daily Globe

Boston Post
Chicago Daily Tribune
Die Zeit
The Hartford Courant
New York Times
Springfield Republican
Wall Street Journal

Magazines

The American Hebrew
American Heritage
The American Red Cross Magazine
Art and Archaeology
Atlantic Monthly
Bookman
The Century Magazine
Collier's
Ex Libris
The Fatherland
Harper's Magazine
Harper's Monthly Magazine
The Harvard Graduates' Magazine
Illustrated World
The Independent
The Ladies' Home Journal
The Literary Digest
Living Age
The Nation
National Geographic
The North American Review
The Outlook
The Saturday Evening Post
The Survey
World's Work

Index

Numbers in ***bold italics*** indicate pages with photographs.

Aire River 193, 195
airplane markings 122, 123
Aisne-Marne Monument 220
Aisne River 195
American Ambulance Field Service 20, 26–40, 87, 119; recruitment 36–40; at Verdun 56, 58–63
American Ambulance Service 127
American Battle Monuments Commission 219
American cemeteries 217
American Enfield rifle 160
American Expeditionary Forces (A.E.F.) 160–164, 203, 212, 214
American Field Service 63, 65, 71, 81, 88; recruitment 75, ***76***
American First Army 176, 208, 209
American neutrality 6
American POWs 167, ***168***
American Red Cross 183
American Relief Clearing House 149
American Second Army 209
American Volunteer Motor Ambulance Corps 82, 85; cars ***87***; scanty record 84
Andover Academy 81
Andrew, A. Piatt 26–28, ***37***, 62, 81, 82, 87, 88
Anheuser-Busch 152
Apremont 201
Apremont-la-Forêt 165, 166
Archaeological Institute of America expedition 83, 84
Argonne Forest 9, 46, 73, 190, 195
Armistice 213, 226
Armour, Allison 84
Auberge St. Pierre 34
Aviation missions 123, 124; over Verdun 129–136

Bach, James 124, 125
Bacon, Robert 27, 95

Baltic (ship) 156
Bar-le-Duc 55, 93, 129, 130, 149
Barbed wire 102
Barber, William M. 65
Battlefield tourism 215, 216
Beale, Harriet 223
Bear, Rif 111
Behonne 129
Belleau Wood 174
Berry, Walter 9
Bethlehem Steel Works 193
Big Bertha mortar 61
Blériot, Louis 122
Bois Brulé 166
Bois de Bourgogne 210, 211
Bois des Caures 52
Bois le Comte 52
Bois-le-Prêtre 20–25, 28, ***29***, 30, 34, 35
Boston Museum of Fine Arts expedition 83, 84
Boston Red Sox 33
Bowe, John 107
Bras 63–66, 89, 90, 212
British Red Cross 87
British Royal Flying Corps 104
Brown, William Slater 94
Buckley, Everett, 135; POW 135, 136
Bullard, Eugene 118–120
Bullard, Robert L. 209
Buswell, Leslie 37–39
Butte, Montana 39

Cabaret Rouge 61, 63
Café de la Paix 77
Caserne Marceau 78, 79
casque Adrian (Adrian helmet) 103
Caudron bomber ***135***
Cercle Militaire 58
Champigneulle 211
Champollion, Andrè Chèronnet 20–24, 28
Chapman, Victor 98, ***99***, ***129***, 130–132

249

Charlevaux Brook 196
Charleville-Mézières 189
Château des Monthairons 91, 92; baseball game 92
Château des Tilleuls 47, *147*, 148
Château Thierry 174
Châtel-Chéhéry 201, 203, 204
Chaumont 160, 161
Chemin des Dames 133, 173
Chêne Tondue 201
Cheppy 193; Salvation Army hut 207, 208
Chicago (ship) 75, 77, 93
Christmas truce 103, 104
Churchill, Winston Spencer 41, 46
Clemenceau, Georges 184
Clermont-en-Argonne 10, 46, 52, 56, 73, 74, 93, 190
Cleveland, Ohio 39
Clois Bois 34
Cobb, Irwin S. 143
Combres 16–17
Combs, William F. 95
Conflans 189
Connecticut National Guard 166, 168, 180
Cook, Charles 9
Coq Hardi (hotel) 13, *14*, 58
Cornell 39, 81
Côte 304 70, 71, 93, 190
Cowdin, Elliot 127
Crown Prince Rupprecht 20
Crown Prince Wilhelm 43, *44*–51, 117, 122, 147, 173, 202; abri *197*; Montfaucon *221*
Crown Princess Cecilie 48
Cummings, e.e. 94
Cyrene 83

Daggett, Mabel Potter 146
Dartmouth 39, 81
Davis, Richard Harding 139–142, 148, 153
de Callone, Charles Alexandre 179
Decauville railway 202, *203*
De Cou, Herbert 83
De Valles, John 166
Dickman, Joseph Theodore 210; pointless attack 211
Dos Passos, John 93, 94
Douaumont Memorial Monument and Ossuary 225, *226*
Douaumont village 118
Drachen (observation balloon) 48, *49*, *50*, 143, 144
Driant, Émile 52
duds 216
Dunkerque 27
Dun-sur Meuse 134–136
du Vernier 47

Eastern Front 171
éclats 51, 67, 71
Les Eparges 15–18
Epernay 77
Erize-la-Petite 93
Escadrille Américaine 127–133; original members 127, 129; Squadron N 124 127, 130
Esnes 71
Exermont 194

Farrar, Geraldine 46
Farrell, William 167
Fatherland (magazine) 150, *151*–153, 158; Verdun reporting 152
Faubourg Pavé 59
Fey-en-Hay 35
finned dart *124*
Fleury 117–119
Foch, Ferdinand 175, 178, 189, 213
Fokker interrupter gear 128
Ford, Henry 32
Foreign Legion 95–120; equipment 98; organization 100
Fort Douaumont 43; aerial combat 130, 131; capture by French 74, 78; capture by Germans 52, *53*–55, 60, 113; post-war 224, 225
Fort Tavannes 60, 61, 63, 119; aerial combat above 130, 132
Fort Vaux 60, 78, 112–*114*, 115–117; aerial combat above 130, 131
Fortescue, Granville 153
Fox, Edward Lyell 137–139
Franco-Prussian War 42, 181
Franz Joseph (Emperor) 5
French 75mm field gun 66, 106
Friends of France (Book) 38
Fuller, Alvin T. 214

Gailor, Frank Hoyt 119
Genet, Edmond 97, *99*, 107, 108, 133, *134*
Gerard, James W. 6
German 77mm field gun 66, 107
German war loan 116, 117
Gibbons, Floyd 157, 158, 174
Gibson, Charles Dana *140*
Giselher Stellung 195, 196
Gloucester, Massachusetts 26, 37
Goutte de Lait 218
Grandpré 195, 196, 210

Hale, Walter 148–150
Hall, Richard N. 36
Harbord, James G. 160
Hardon, Eugénie 54
Harjes Formation 87

Hartmannsweilerkopf 36
Harvard 21, 26, 28, 39, 82, 95, 98, 126, 127, 196
Hattonchâtel 218, 219
Hawley, Hudson 162
Heights of the Meuse 59, 63
Hello Girls 161
Herrick, Myron T. 95–97, 100
high explosive shell 67
Hilarion House 33–34
Hindenburg Line 187, 209
Hollingshead, Lowell R. 198, 199

Irwin, Will 120

James, Henry 13–15, 18, 86, 143, 190
Janis, Elsie 169–*170*, 171
Joffre, Joseph 52, 54, 159
Jünger, Ernst 16–17

Kaiser Wilhelm II *see* Wilhelm II, Kaiser
Kean, Jefferson R. 81
Kelley, Edward *72*, 73
Kriemhilde Stellung 200, 208, 209
Kultur 146

Laconia (ship) 157, 158, 174
Lafayette 155
Lafayette Escadrille 33, 38, 97, 98, 121–136; insignia 133; SPA 124 squadron 134
Lafayette Flying Corps 133–136
Lansing, Robert 133
Lewis gun 126, *134*
Liggett, Hunter 182, 183, 201, 205, 208, 209, 210
Lilenthal, Otto 121
Lille 189
Lions Whiskey and Soda 132, 133, 136
Loop, George Washington 62
Lorraine 18
Lost Battalion 196–202
Ludendorff, Erich 55, 200
Lufberry, Raul 130
Lusitania (ship) 141
Luxeuil-les-Bains 127

MacArthur, Douglas 179
MacVeagh, Franklin 26
Mandres 169
Mannschafts-Eisenbeton-Unterstände 16, *177*
Manship, Paul 223
Manson, Robert 199
Marchéville 187
Marine Corps 174
Marne battle (1914) 10, 96
Marne battle (1918) 174, 175
Marne Salient 174

Marre 71, 72
Massachusetts Institute of Technology 102
Massachusetts State House 166
McConnell, James R. 26, 33, 37, 38, 121, *129*, 130, 133
McIntyre, Gladys 169
McIntyre, Irene 169
McMurtry, George 196
Metz 180–182, 187
Metz feint 187, 188
Metz-Sedan Railway 211
Meuse-Argonne offensive 7, 178, 183, 186, 187–214; first day 189–191; German retreat 211, 212; Liggett takes charge 209; mission achieved 211; pointless attacks 213, 214; after three weeks 209; topography 206
Meuse River 46, 56, 58, 63, 68, 89, 92, 206
Michel Stellung 187
Michelin guides 215, 216
Microphone Hotel 135, 136
Mill on the Meuse 58
Minenwerfer 107, 205
Mitchell, William 179
Model T Ford 30, *31*, 32, *59*, *63*, *72*
Montauville 34
Montfaucon 195, 221; American monument 221, *222*
Montmédy 135, 189
Montsec 220
Morlae, Edward 102, 103
Morse, Edwin W. 65
Morse, Katharine 164, 220
Mort Homme 68, *69*–71, 93, 190
Moselle River 18
Musgrave, Frank 112, 113

Nancy, France 126
Neuilly-sur-Seine (American hospital) 26, 62, 73
Nieuport 10 126
Nieuport 11 (Bébé) 128, *129*
Nieuport 17 129, 132, *134*
Nivelle Offensive 153
Norton, Eliot 85, 86
Norton, Fredrick 77
Norton, Grace 86
Norton, Richard 82–94; letters 88, 89; meets Kaiser 84
Norton, Sara 85
Norton-Harjes Formation 92–94

Ochs, Adolph S. 152
Operation Georgette 173
Operation Michael 172, 173
Our Boys in the European War (film) 38–39

Paris 96; Chatham Bar 132; Harry's Bar 132; women 162–163
Patton, George 193, 226
Pattullo, George 203
Pau 122
Pershing, John J. 81, 82, 94, 154–162, 176, 178, 180, 182, 184, 187, 196, 200, 203, 205, 210; American Battle Monuments Commission 219; creates two armies 209; headquarters train 185; Meuse-Argonne error 206
Pétain, Henri-Philippe 54, 55, 57, 154, 180, 184; Verdun headquarters 185
Phélizot, René 101
Pont-á-Mousson 18–26, 28, 30, 33–35, 37, 214
Porte Chausée 59
Poste de secours X 34–35
Premonstratensian Monastery *19*
Prince, Norman 126, *129*
Princeton 39, 75
Prinz, Heinrich 198

Queen Victoria 45
Quimby, Harriet 122, *123*

Rader, Phil 103, 104
Rand, George F. 223, 224
Reims *23*, 77, 106; cathedral destruction 141–144, *145*, 146
Remarque, Erich Maria 16
Rendezvous with Death (poem) 110
Resco, Micheline 185, 186
Réserve Mallet 81
Riaville 187
Rice, Philip 75–80
Rockwell, Kiffen *129*, 132
Roosevelt, Theodore 153
Ross, Harold W. 162
rotary engine 128
Rough Riders 153

St. Mihiel American Cemetery 223
St. Mihiel Monument 220
St. Mihiel Salient 20, 25, 29, 165, 176, *177*–180, 187; post-war 218
Sainte Menehould 9
Salvation Army 163, 169
Sanders, Roswell 71
Scanlon, Bob 101
Schmidt von Knobelsdorf, Konstantin 46
screened road *24*
Sedan 189, 209
Seeger, Alan 100, 101, 108, 109, 110, *111*, 112
Seicheprey 166–168, 170
Selective Draft Act 156
Senard 134

Sharp, William G. 95, 99
shrapnel 66, 67, 114
Skinner, Belle 218, 219
Sleeper, Henry Davis 36–40, 81
Smith College 164; Relief Unit 172, 173
Somme 111, 132, 133
Souilly 55, 57, 184
Springfield rifle 160
Stanton, Charles E. 155
Stars and Stripes (newspaper) 161, 162
Stenay 47, 48, 147, 214
Stevenson, William 80
Stollen 48, 51
Street, John 104
Swallows of Death (170th Infantry Regiment) 109, 112, 113, 114, 117, 118
Système D 194, 195

Taft, William Howard 26, 84, 95
Taylor, J.B. 32
Teilhard de Chardin, Pierre 117, 118
Thaw, William 125, 126, 132, 133, 136
Thénault, Georges *129*, 131
Thiaucourt 184
Thorburn Van Buren, Anne 225
Toul 183
Tranchée de Calonne 179
Treaty of Brest-Litovsk 171
Trench of Bayonets Monument *224*
Triangle Film Corporation 38
Tripod (newspaper) 162
Truman, Harry S. 192
Turkington, Myrtle 169

U-boat *173*
Ullard, George 104
U.S. 1st Division 163, 165, 175, 179, 180, 186, 205
U.S. 2nd Division 163, 174, 175, 179, 186
U.S. 3rd Division 175
U.S. 4th Division 175, 179
U.S. 5th Division 179, 195
U.S. 26th Division (Yankee Division) 163, 165, 171, 175, 179, 186, 187, 214
U.S. 28th Division 175, 201
U.S. 32nd Division 175, 205
U.S. 35th Division 192–195, 205
U.S. 37th Division 205
U.S. 42nd Division 163, 175, 186, 211
U.S. 77th Division 175, 196, *197*, 201, 210
U.S. 78th Division 210
U.S. 80th Division 187, 210
U.S. 82nd Division 179, 202
U.S. 89th Division 179, 214
U.S. 90th Division 179, 214
U.S. 92nd Division 214
U.S. 103d Aero Squadron 136

United States Army Ambulance Service 81, 94
University of California 81

Vanderbilt, Mrs. W.K. *23*, 24, 26, 34, 35
vanishing doughboys 209
Varennes 193, 201
Vassar Relief Unit 217, 218
vaudeville 169
Vauquois 11–13, 46, 56, 59, 190, 192, 193
Vaux village 115, 116
Verdun (city) 13, 40, 41–55, 56–67, 148–150; railroads 56, 57; Verdun (1944) 226
Verdun attack (1917) 78, 134, 154
Verdun Battle (1916) 68, 69, 88–94, 129–136, 148, 184; casualties 40; east (right) bank 50–52, 113, 115–119; German wounded, 69, 70; Pétain headquarters 185; west (left) bank 68–71
Very pistol 194
Vickers machine gun 132
Viereck, George Sylvester 150, 158
Vigneulles 179, 180
Villa Glycine 35–36
Viskniskki, G.T. 161, 162
voie de rocade 188, 189
Voie Sacrée (La Route) 57, 58, 93, 149
Voisin bomber 126
von Falkenhayn, Eric 41, 43, 46, 55
von Gallwitz, Max 207, 212
von Hindenburg, Paul 175, 212
von Wiegand, Karl 147, 148

Warren, F.E. 155
Weeks, Alice 112
Weeks, Kenneth 102, 106
Weigle, Edwin F. 144
Wharton, Edith 9–15, 18–20, 28, 58, 64, 73, 143, 176, 190
Wheeler, Walter H. 65
Whitlock, Brand 5
Whittlesey, Charles 196, 199
Wilhelm II, Kaiser 5, 41, 43, *44*, 46, 48, 122, 172; escape to Holland 212, 213; monogram *85*; at Spa 212; yacht Hohenzollern 84
Williams College 196
Willis, Harold 136
Wilson, Woodrow 81, 95, 156, 159
Witwenwald **29**, 30
Woëvre Plain 16
Woolcott, Alexander 162
World War I: origins 5, 6; United States enters 157, 159; war dead 217
World War II 226
Wright, Orville 45, 121, 122
Wright, Wilbur 121, 122

Yale 39, 125, 162
YMCA 163–165, 169, 220
York, Alvin C. 203–***205***, 206
Young, Stella 169

Zimmermann, Arthur 159
Zimmermann telegram 159

www.ingramcontent.com/pod-product-compliance
Ingram Content Group UK Ltd.
Pitfield, Milton Keynes, MK11 3LW, UK
UKHW040610160426
5217IPUK00034B/497